FLIGHT AROUND THE WORLD

ISBN 978-0-9845431-0-6

Published by Ingenuity International
Seattle, Washington

www.flightaroundtheworld.net

Printed in the United States of America

FLIGHT
AROUND THE
WORLD

A perspective of the world as seen from the
flight deck during the formative years of
Trans World Airlines

**AUTOBIOGRAPHY
CAPTAIN
LYLE D. BOBZIN**

Ingenuity **I** *International*
Seattle, Washington

Acknowledgments

Technical support: Sarah C Buck, Wayne Ciesielski and Melodye Yamada. Critique: Ruth M Moorer

Organizations contributing to the enduring legacy and the esprit de corps of Trans World Airlines and the aviation industry:

TWA Active Retired Pilots Association-TARPA
Website: www.tarpa.com

TWA Seniors Club and "TWA Seniors SKYLINER" Official publication of the TWA Seniors Club
Website: http://www.twaseniorsclub.org

TWA Clipped Wings International Inc. for former TWA hostesses and cabin attendants
Website: http://www.twaclippedwings.org

TWA Silver Wings International, Inc.
Website: http//www.twasilverwings.com

Museum of Flight, Seattle, WA
Website: http://museumofflight.org

OX-5 Aviation Pioneers
Website: http://www.ox5news.com

This book is dedicated to Mother and Father.

The economic down turn of the century began in the United States in1929 with the collapse of the New York stock market on Wall Street and spread world-wide to encompass all nations of the world for over a decade. For most of the people these difficult conditions were to continue until the depression was interrupted by the most tragic conflict of all time, World War II.

The Great Depression of 1929 did not end. World War II began. The philosophy of Plato; War is a result of economic chaos. Tyrants of the 1920s, 1930s and 1940s would not have come to power were it not for the worldwide economic failure. In their desperation the people became victims of the economic promises of socialism. However, in retrospect socialism always fails.

Growing up during these years words of failure or loss of courage were not heard in our household. The family struggled to stay in business during which time their bank failed resulting in the loss of all their savings. Even then there was never a suggestion the world owed them a living, or the government should provide financial assistance. Their dedicated will to succeed was the most appropriate principle to follow and that will shaped the character of my life.

Legion of Merit Award

AWARDED TO

Lyle D. Bobzin

THE LEGION OF MERIT AWARD IS PRESENTED TO AN OX5 AVIATION
PIONEERS WHO HAS CONTINUOUSLY PARTICIPATED IN AVIATION OVER
A PERIOD OF FORTY (40) YEARS, WHILE DEMONSTRATING UNUSUAL
TECHNICAL AND SAFE FLYING ABILITY, AND THE USE OF AIRCRAFT
FOR THE BETTERMENT OF MANKIND.

By the

OX5 AVIATION PIONEERS
AND ITS MEMBERS

I, THEREFORE, AFFIX MY HAND AND SEAL,
AND DIRECT THE SECRETARY
TO AFFIX THE CLUB SEAL THIS 23 DAY OF SEPTEMBER, 2006

Robert Taylor
NATIONAL PRESIDENT

Robert Taylor
NATIONAL SECRETARY

Contents

x

BOOK THREE

THE FORMATIVE FORTIES

THE DIFFICULT TODAY—

THE IMPOSSIBLE TOMORROW

BOOK FOUR

THE FIFTIES

INTERNATIONAL DIVISION—

THE EXPANSION CONTINUES

BOOK FIVE

THE SIXTIES

BOOK SIX

THE SEVENTIES-THE CAREER ENDS

Addendum

AIR MASS MOVEMENT

AND THE LAWS OF MOTION -

Preface

In the late 1950s, TWA inaugurated flight operation of what was to be the last of the Constellation aircraft series, 1649A. An advertising program was developed around this aircraft; trademarked, the JetStream®, it became an industry standard. The basic Super Constellation fuselage profile remained the same. However, the complete passenger cabin area was totally redesigned. The cabin was made much more luxurious, which included the most recent "sleeper seat" configuration. The seat allowed the extension of the lower part of the seat to accommodate the passenger in a totally prone position. This innovation allowed the passenger to sleep in comfort and became the forerunner of today's 'Business Class' in the airline industry.

A phone call from the chief pilot's office requested my presence in full uniform at a photo shoot for publicity purposes to promote this new innovation. A mockup of the entire JetStream® cabin area had been constructed in the early design stages, and was to be used for the photographic shoot. Arriving at the location, Carlyle Blackwell, a most prominent Hollywood photographer, made the introductions to the other participants. Cary Grant was the principal figure. In addition, a large group of 'starlets' was provided, courtesy of RKO Motion Picture Studios, owned by Howard Hughes, who was also the majority stockholder of TWA. The group would portray passengers enjoying a flight featuring this revolutionary new 'sleeper seat'. My presence was to represent a TWA captain in command of the flight. No script was provided as the photographs were to be still shots, rather than motion pictures. After a brief period of photographing by Carlyle Blackwell, it became evident things were not going well. For some unknown reason, the major star had become aloof and uncooperative. Mr. Blackwell attempted to complete the shoot, but was unable to obtain the desired results when, due to the angst on the set, two of the 'starlets' broke into tears. These young actresses had accepted the assignment with good intentions, but were unable to withstand the strain. Under these difficult circumstances, Mr. Blackwell had no choice other than to cancel the shoot and dismiss all parties. The major character appeared indifferent to the failure of the desired program. Following the departure of Cary Grant and the group of starlets, Mr. Blackwell apologized to me for the loss of time and his failure to complete the desired TWA promotional shots. He also extended an invitation to visit his studio at a time of mutual convenience for a complimentary portrait session in appreciation of my participation. The visit was made prior to my next flight assignment while dressed in full TWA uniform. It is this photograph that appears on the cover of this book.

Later that day, while driving home from the failed TWA publicity assignment, in retrospect, thoughts of a life begun in obscurity turned now to one which had entered the world of challenging international personalities. How ironic to find out years later, my wife, Rita was one among the legions of Cary Grant fans!

BOOK ONE

FIRST FLIGHT

investment was minimal and the family spent most of the time involved with the business. By living in the adjoining building, time was saved going to and from work.

The home-factory location shared the same heating and energy system. Upon arrival at sundown, the challenge of getting heat in the house was confronted by a frozen and broken steam boiler in the basement of the factory. A long cold night followed, which was just the beginning of a difficult time for all.

The business of manufacturing soft drinks was a labor intensive existence. A small business required the participation of the whole family. The manufacturing operation required many steps from the washing of the returned glass bottles to the finished, cased beverages of twenty four bottles to the case.

The first step was to wash the returned glass bottles. This was long before a 'no-return' policy came into existence. The bottle washer was a large steel and cast iron monster. The bottles were placed into individual square steel 'pockets' in rows in the soaker portion at the rear of the machine. The many rows of pockets formed a continuous wheel which rotated downward through the lower tank. The lower tank was filled with a solution of caustic soda and water which was heated by a steam coil in the tank. As the pockets rotated downward, the entire unit became immersed in the caustic solution filling the bottles. In this manner the bottles were soaked and washed of their impurities. As the pockets rotated to the front, they were tilted just slightly downward. This opened the flap. The bottles slid out and down into a large flat tank filled with clear water, circulated by a pump. From this rinsing action in the clear water, bottles were removed by hand, and placed neck down in wood cases holding twenty four bottles. Above the water level was a double brush unit. A motor in the center powered a brush at the end of each shaft. The purpose of this unit was to remove any stubborn residue from the bottle not removed in the caustic bath. Bottles were placed on the constantly spinning brushes, and then rinsed in the water before being placed with the others in cases.

It was an encounter with this spinning brush that put my youthful efforts to their first test. At about the age of five, standing on a large box to reach the tank and spinning brush, my first corrective cleaning effort was attempted. My grip was not strong enough to hold the wet bottle on the brush for cleaning. As my grip failed, the bottle was thrown through the air by the centrifugal force created by the brush. It crashed against the wall with a loud noise, fell to the concrete floor below, shattering into a pile of rubble. Dad, who was working at the filler nearby, came to check on my well being. Without any negative comment, my new job assignment was to remove the clean bottles only. The touch up effort was left to those with more strength. The cases with clean bottles were stacked next to the filler. Dad was in charge of that operation. Filling required constant thought and coordination. The filler was called a "foot power." The motion was foot orientated. An empty bottle was placed on a half-circle platform. A crown or bottle cap was taken from the container located on the right of the machine. The crown was inserted top up into the filler head directly above the bottle. The serrated edges of the crown held it in place. The next step was to apply pressure with the foot to elevate the bottle into the head assembly above it. After the bottle had been elevated, a lever was actuated to add flavored syrup to the bottle. This unit measured a set amount of syrup into the bottle. Next, the other lever was actuated to fill the bottle with carbonated water. This operation was performed until the fill reached the desired level. The lever was moved to the closed position. The final step was to apply more foot pressure, which forced the neck of the bottle further up into the head. This action crimped the crown on the bottle. Removing pressure from the foot allowed the small platform to come down. The filled bottle was removed and placed in the case below. This procedure was repeated throughout the day until the required number of cases was reached. The business was pursued with diligence by the family. Sales were made after Dad had loaded the company truck with product and personally called on all his accounts.

All of the buildings which made up the complex were located at the same location on the edge of town. The residence was the first building at the front of the property. The factory and all associated buildings were located behind the residence. The entire site of five buildings made for what was then a sizeable complex. A wide stream flowed through the entire length of the property. A bridge then led to open fields.

On my fifth birthday Mother and Dad presented me with a Beagle puppy who we named Rex. A few days passed and late in the day, Rex was trying to sleep as the sun had set, and Rex had spent the day running and chasing rabbits. Rex had collapsed on the living room floor and was sound asleep. In an effort to awaken Rex, he was teased and disturbed. After several other efforts to get his attention, Rex awakened to my torments, and promptly snapped at me catching my lower lip with his puppy teeth. Mother immediately exclaimed, "That dog bit Lyle."

Dad had witnessed the entire proceedings and said nothing. Mother repeated the same horrified exclamation. Dad ignored her. After the third or fourth outburst, Dad could stand it no longer. In disgust, he replied, "Lyle teased and tormented the puppy. He did what he did. As a result, it is not the pup's fault. That is the end of it!"

As the antics continued Dad became disgusted, got up and left the room. That ended of the conversation and closed the incident. Dad was entirely correct; the puppy had been tormented while asleep, and when awakened, reacted accordingly. It is now frightening to think about how many pets have been put down for perhaps the same teasing and torment. Unfortunately, not all parents would have reacted prudently as mine did.

Dad had purchased a Beagle hound as our family pet and the setting was a Beagle's dream. In wide open fields just across the bridge, 'Rex the Beagle' had unlimited hunting ground. Every morning at sunrise Rex could be heard with his low howl, hunting rabbits in the large fields. His caroling was a daily sound to be heard. Dad often remarked that Rex had to be slower than the rabbits he hunted since Rex had not brought any of his quarries home.

One morning, as Rex was on his daily hunt, Dad departed with the company truck on one of the routes to sell and deliver beverages. Later, Mother departed on foot for a shopping trip to the business district. A neighborhood boy had come for a visit to play. We were about six years of age and got together often, as there were not many children in the immediate area.

Late morning Rex ceased caroling. We remarked that meant Rex would return home shortly. When Rex did arrive we received the shock of our lives. Rex was staggering and having great difficulty moving. We quickly ran to help Rex and were horrified at what we saw. Rex had come in contact with a raccoon. The infamous trait of the raccoon was to appear to be playing with the other animal and would roll over on his back to allow his quarry to be on top of him. The raccoon in this manner would disembowel the other animal with the long and sharp claws they possessed. Poor Rex had encountered a raccoon and had fallen victim to the raccoon's near fatal tactic. Rex, in terrible pain managed to return home with his entire under side shredded by a raccoon. The intestines and other organs were still attached to him though hanging out below his underside. Horrified, we both broke into tears and were left with the dilemma. Alone, what could we do?

Quickly, we retrieved my coaster wagon. The two of us, lifting and holding Rex and his entrails, placed him gently in the coaster wagon. We then headed to town. Fortunately, remembering where the veterinarian was located, we arrived at his location which was on the second floor of the building. We carried Rex up the stairs to the veterinarian's office trying not to do further damage to his organs. Tears rolling down our cheeks did not make our task any easier. Fortunately, the veterinarian was in his office when we arrived. Amid tears and wailing, we pleaded, "Please help our Rex."

Forever engrained in my memory is the look that crossed the veterinarian's face, for even he was shocked to see the condition of Rex. Shaking his head in the negative, he gently placed Rex on his treating table. After rearranging the intestines and other organs in the appropriate place, while at the same time cleaning off the blades of grass and other debris so as not to be placed back inside of Rex, he then began to stitch the skin back together. Horrified, we watched the surgical operation with tears still flowing on our dirt covered faces. The veterinarian had the tolerance of a saint as he understood our grief and continued his operation, ignoring our outbursts. In what seemed like an eternity, the veterinarian completed the surgery. He had stitched the entire underside of Rex back together. The skin had been split into many different strips which had hung down. His talents had been tested, as the raccoon had done unmerciful damage to the complete underside of my dog.

When the veterinarian had completed this operation, still shaking his head in the negative, he helped us carry Rex down stairs to place him in the coaster wagon. It was then the first time he had spoken, "I do not know if your dog will live. Take him home and hope for the best."

In what was the most amazing and gratifying occurrence of a childhood life a few days later Rex was back on his feet, wagging his tail. This happy Beagle lived.

Perhaps a week or so later, late in the afternoon the veterinarian appeared to talk to Dad about Rex. Even he was surprised to see Rex on his feet with the wagging tail. Dad asked the veterinarian how much he owed him. Smiling and shaking his head he replied, "I guess two dollars." Laughing both men walked out to his car. It then occurred to me, my dog had cost Dad two dollars. Rex returned to hunt in the meadow, his caroling continued until his last energy was spent.

At the age of six an important lesson had been learned; the comical deceiving face Mother Nature had given the raccoon was not to be trusted. The raccoon took full advantage of the trust his appearance gave to other beings only to inflict deadly injury to the unsuspecting. The raccoon has become the number one carrier of rabies in the United States, partly due to the tolerance of his presence which has allowed the raccoon to increase to great numbers.

Pictured with Rex sitting next to the child's version of a REO SPEEDWAGON, the car had been given to Lyle as a gift. The rear axle was broken so you could not pedal the car, nor did not move very well. Mostly, it was just to sit in and make believe. The initials REO stood for R. E. Olds. Later, the REO automobile became the Oldsmobile.

The author is sitting in a child version of a REO SPEEDWAGON.

Rex, the Beagle, next to the author in the REO.

Early Interest in Aviation

It was necessary for Dad to make trips to the distant major city from time to time to obtain materials for the manufacturing operation. After one of these journeys, Dad was observed climbing the oak tree from which he would string a wire to the house to serve as an antenna for his purchase. It perhaps would not have attracted attention except for the fact the sun had set. It was unusual to see someone with a ladder leaning against a tree after dark. The urgency was provoked by the fact that on the journey to the city Dad had purchased our first radio. He was naturally motivated to hear the first sounds from his new medium. Dad's efforts were rewarded. Before bedtime we heard the first reception of the radio. The popularity of the radio, as a part of most households, grew at an astounding pace. The conversation of the day would be how distant a station had been received the previous night. Great pride was taken by each radio buff to claim the reception of the station of a greater distance than others in the group. The year was 1923.

Time passed with the evenings devoted to the radio. News broadcasts were naturally of great interest. Aviation, news of aircraft and pilots who flew them, was part of the appeal of the radio news. A $25,000 prize offered by Raymond Orteig, a New York hotel owner, for the first non-stop flight between New York and France in either direction, was broadcast on the radio. Mr. Orteig was born in France, which increased his interest in the prize proposal. Mr. Orteig made his offer in 1924, and while publicized from time to time, the distance of 3,315 miles from New York to France was formidable.

In 1926, as aircraft with longer range capabilities became a reality, more pilots were to propose making this flight possible. The attempts to make the flight from Paris to New York met with fatal results, and the attempts for the New York to Paris flight were equally unsuccessful. The news was to focus on the proposed flight in a tri-motor aircraft by an Admiral Richard E. Byrd. Admiral Byrd was a well-known aviator, having made several discovery flights. Charles A. Lindbergh, a former Army pilot, later an air mail pilot, was mentioned to be preparing for the flight from New York to Paris.

The news reported Charles A. Lindbergh had flown a new Ryan airplane from San Diego, California, to St. Louis, Missouri and on to New York. That flight was in preparation for the flight New York to Paris. There was much speculation about who would make first flight, as there were three aircraft poised to make the flight, including one to be piloted by Byrd. The constant negative press predominantly mentioned those who had lost their lives or were injured in the attempt. Missing on an attempted flight from Paris to New York, French pilots Coli and Nungesser were subjects of an unsuccessful search by the U.S. Navy. There was a great deal of negative press opinion expressed about anyone who would make the attempt while the French pilots were still missing. The context being, it was disrespectful to attempt the flight while Nunguesser and Coli were perhaps not to be found.

On May 20, 1927, at 7:52 a.m. EST, Charles A. Lindbergh had taken off from New York bound for Paris, France. The "Lone Eagle," as he was now called, was on his way. In the next thirty-six hours, the Lone Eagle was to change the destiny of all those connected with aviation.

There was a need for more materials for the company. On May 21, 1927, Dad made the usual driving trip to the major city. This trip was to include taking me along to see the big city. The distance to be covered required starting early in the morning to arrive in the city by noon. After lunch in Dad's favorite restaurant, we began a round of suppliers to obtain his business requirements. The afternoon passed quickly. We arrived at the last business location late in the afternoon. As we entered the door there was great excitement and laughter. Everyone was talking at the same time. Greeting my Dad excitingly the business owner exclaimed, "Lindbergh has landed in Paris." The Lone Eagle had flown from Roosevelt Field, New York, to Le Bourget Field, Paris, over 3,800 miles, in 33 hours 30 minutes. Beaming with enthusiasm, Dad proudly exclaimed, "We knew it would take an American to do it!"

This great accomplishment in aviation was to change the lives of thousands, perhaps millions of people. It was to make Charles A. Lindbergh an International hero, and most important of all, it was to create a great role model, which would profoundly influence my life.

LINDBERGH DOES IT! TO PARIS IN 33½ HOURS;
FLIES 1,000 MILES THROUGH SNOW AND SLEET;
CHEERING FRENCH CARRY HIM OFF FIELD

Reprint from the Charles A. Lindberg Memorial Fund Catalogue 1977 reprinted by permission, ©The New York Times Company.

The Lone Eagle was perhaps the role model of the 20th century.

The Great Depression

It would be just over two years until the Great Depression would engulf the world; and a little over three years until the full impact of the financial crisis would set in. During this time frame, which lasted for over a decade, man and youth, in particular, would benefit from the idol image, or role model Charles A. Lindbergh would become.

Upon Lindbergh's return to the United States, many welcoming ceremonies in his honor were held at various major East coast cities. There were many demands for him to write a book about his life and the flight from New York to Paris. This was accomplished in a very short time period. Published in July 1927, the book was titled, "WE." Dad ordered a copy of "WE", to be obtained as soon as the book was available. The book was read by the family and is treasured by me to this day.

After completing the book, Charles Lindbergh was to fly a nationwide tour of the U.S. with the Spirit of Saint Louis. This trip was to make the aircraft and him available for all of his admirers to see. We waited with enthusiasm for the flight of the Spirit of Saint Louis to be made to the closest major city to us. On that day, the family joined the many thousands who wished to see Lindbergh and his airplane. The crowds were astronomical for the time, but very orderly. We were able to see him in person, and also see his aircraft without difficulty. At nine years of age these images of the occasion became an indelible memory for me, and the role he played became the sole influence in my desire to fly.

In 1929 the stock market crashed and the Great Depression began. A short time later accompanying Dad, we made a visit to the local bank to withdraw funds Dad needed for his business, and to visit my small account. We arrived at the entrance to the bank only to observe a large sign in the glass door, "CLOSED." This meant all of Dad's cash to operate the business was gone; my piggy bank money no longer existed. In retrospect it is difficult to understand how Dad was able to continue. Everyone was in the same predicament. There presently was not any money. Our business, manufacturing soft drinks, was not really a necessity. Soft drinks were one of the first items people could do without. Dad refused to submit to the failing market, perhaps because there was not any other avenue to pursue.

The ensuing decade was to present the greatest challenge of the century. The Great Depression was to require all of the human resources the populace could muster to survive. The period was one of desperation for all. Youth were not spared the anguish. As the elders struggled, the children tried to contribute to the support of the family. The fact capital or money was not available our youthful efforts could not be rewarded. Children wished they were older as childhood proved too limiting. They were often heard to say, "if only we were not too young to help...." This difficult time exacerbated the need for a role model; to have someone to look up to, to keep hope alive. The role model Charles A. Lindbergh was to portray would benefit society greatly.

As a family, we continued to survive due to the inexhaustible efforts of my Mother and Father. Throughout the country business failures predominated. It was difficult to do business because, at times, money was non-existent. Individuals and companies restarted, only to fail again, as the much needed capital to survive was not available to them.

The interest in flying prevailed throughout this period. With his wife Anne, Charles Lindbergh continued to be in the world news. The flights they made were of interest to the aviation world. While notable, their exploits were made for their love of flying. Commercial aviation, or airlines had been established throughout the U.S. Charles Lindbergh had given assistance to any and all who had desired his knowledge. He had become associated with one airline in particular, Trans-continental and Western Airlines.

My desire or intent to fly remained strong. However, the economics of the time were not in my favor. The money required to learn to fly, and all subsequent phases of that pursuit just, was not available. Unknown to me at the time, there would be an unusual association which would occur in our small town, ultimately affording me the opportunity to fly.

First Airplane

In the '30s, the Waters Dodge Garage stood across the street from Dad's office. It was a two-story building with a loft above, reached by an elevator. In the '20s, the famous old reliable Dodge four-cylinder truck had been a favorite of all who would come up with an extra hundred or two over the best selling Ford Model T. The low compression Dodge Four was extremely reliable and had a self starter (electric starter), while the "T" was still a hand cranked starter. It also featured a gear shift handle with three speeds forward, one reverse. Dad had a pickup truck version, which was borrowed at a very young age to teach myself to drive. While backing the Dodge out of the factory driveway, a glance in the rear view mirror revealed Dad driving in with his Buick. Caught in the act Dad said, "I guess if you are going to drive I had better be with you in the Buick."

At the Waters Dodge Garage, the Waters son, nicknamed "Cap," also had an interest in flying. Cap put the loft to use to store aircraft in various stages of destruction. Prohibition, the infamous Volstead Act, was still in force. The geographical location of our small town was close to both Milwaukee and Chicago. Those flying spirits of Canadian origin used some of the remote areas in our vicinity to land by the headlights of the pickup vehicles. Many of these landings came to grief, as the aircraft was damaged beyond possible use in any further flight. Of course, the pick-up car would depart quickly with the cargo, leaving the wreckage behind.

It was a well-known fact the Waters boy was a flying nut, recognized by all the farmers in the area. When a farmer found the wreckage of an airplane on his property at light of dawn, he would phone Cap Waters to get rid of the junk on his farm. It was in this manner the loft became the storage area for a conglomeration of different aircraft parts. When enough parts from different wrecks matched, Cap would attempt to make one 'good one' out of some bent ones. Many were Wacos, Eaglerocks, Travelires, etc. The popular engine was the Curtiss Wright OX-5. The advantage of the OX-5 was there were parts available from military surplus. In 1955 aviation enthusiasts formed an organization called OX-5 Aviation Pioneers, which is still active today. Membership was open to pilots who had flown airplanes powered by the OX-5 engine, and mechanics who had worked on them. Later, the organization expanded the membership to include a historian category.

With many lakes in the area, it was only natural the 'flying spirits' group would take advantage of the water for operation. A night operation with a Savoia Marchetti Flying Boat came to ruin with the usual results. Cap picked up the remains of the Savoia, but it stayed forever in the loft, as not enough parts were forthcoming to complete the restoration. Often on the loft floor, we would sit in the hull and envision what the complete Savoia would be like in flight. Aircraft to be salvaged included Buhl Air Sedan, Stinson Detroiter, and Waco Cabin, along with some others powered by the WWI rotary engines. The aircraft which had immediate use were repaired; duplicate aircraft of the same make and model were sold.

As the Great Depression continued, assets and capital were still very scarce commodities. The close proximity of Dad's office to the Dodge Garage across the street was to nurture a growing interest in aviation. It was an outlet for my long desired wish to fly. Through cannibalization of the various aircraft, Cap was able to construct some flyable airplanes. Licensed? At the time, it was the U.S. Department of Commerce which licensed aircraft. And licensed aircraft were the only accepted way to fly. However, if a plane flew, it was not always asked what the pedigree was. The garage basement was the assembly area. When enough compatible parts had been acquired, a large drive-out door to the rear made it possible for the parts in a semi-assembled state to be loaded onto a truck for transport to the airstrip.

The fact: you could only 'hanger fly' in the loft. To get airborne, an airplane and an airstrip were necessary. We rented a level patch of ground from a farmer on the outskirts of town to give the town its first and only airport. It was evident the farm owner received the benefit. In order for us to fly, the hay had to be cut. The hay crop was his. We were the 'gravy.' It was on these twenty-plus acres we built a sheet metal hangar from scrap. The hangar provided a place to finish assembling the aircraft and for storage of the resurrected planes. We flew from this airport without incident for several years. It was not a question of violation. Money was so very scarce; however, the desire to fly was great. The idea or thought of ever receiving money for this effort was never considered. True, there was some 'barnstorming' or flying the inquisitive public for very few bucks, but this was mainly done by those who did so as a full time effort. The fact; the legal status or being licensed was not the factor, flying was. If the airplane flew, looked reasonably well structured, we flew it. The end results were two sets of flying records; one log for the aircraft which were in license, another log for the unlicensed aircraft. The two shall never meet, as the unlicensed flight time had no recognition in the pursuit of a higher grade pilot's license.

Ownership of a Buhl Bull Pup, which had both wheels and snow skis, was an enjoyable experience. The "pup" was an open cockpit, single place airplane and fun to fly. Another favorite was a Hispano-Suizza powered Eaglerock, an open cockpit bi-plane.

The author is standing in front of a KR-21.

In time, the Department of Commerce was to become a full fledged aviation authority called the Civil Aeronautics Authority (CAA), a division of the Department of Commerce. The entire state had been under the authority of one U.S. Department of Commerce inspector. The expansion of the CAA brought an increase in numbers in the headquarters office. The lone Inspector of the Department of Commerce was aware of our operation. Small and insignificant, he did not give it any attention.

Flight Instructor

Time always brings change. A large change came about when the U.S. government started a civilian pilot training program. There was an immediate need for flight instructors. For the first time money was in sight. The requirement, of course, was a commercial license and instructors rating. All those qualified were quick to apply. However, the CAA inspector was quick to inform us he was aware of the past operation, and would not issue what we required. Fortunately, this position tempered with time. Written examinations were the first requirement for passage. The written examinations were lengthy, written in longhand in essay format. The multiple-choice examination was far in the future. Longhand essay examinations were subject to correction by the inspector. His interpretation of the answers was how the exam was graded, on a numerical scale. The examinations were long; there were few 'yes' or 'no' answers. And the lengthy answers were subject to his interpretation. The bad joke of the time by the Inspector was, "I don't correct 'em. I weigh 'em."

Flight checks followed the passage of the written exam. Upon completion, you were finally in the 'paid' column of aviation. Pilots involved in aviation at this time, basically had little hope of a flying career. The exception, perhaps, was the pilots in the service of the United States Military. The military flight operations were limited, most having restrictions of flight operation by fiscal appropriations.

During this time period, as a family, we had continued the business pursuit. Any flying position with reimbursement was the farthest thing from our thoughts, or even considered a possibility. Throughout this time, the positive attitude of Mother and Dad was extremely gratifying. For a questionable interest, their support was unfailing. The number of fatalities in aviation was not large, as aviation was a limited pursuit. However, the press gave extensive front-page coverage to the accidents which did occur. It was difficult for those not personally involved to give their approval, without reservations of a possible tragic occurrence.

The first full-time flying position made it necessary for me to leave the family business. This was not the lifelong plan Dad had intended or anticipated. As a result, there was much personal anguish for all concerned. The position of flight instructor was at the University of Wisconsin at Madison. Flight instruction programs were sponsored by the United States government and offered at the colleges and universities throughout the country. Participation was on a voluntary basis for the enrolled students. The basic purpose was to begin the process of building a pilot reserve.

The instructors were assigned ten primary students for the program. Assumption: three or four of the ten students would not progress as required, would be eliminated, washed out along the way. This procedure would then result in the instructor's student class reduced to six or seven, an acceptable work load. However, most instructors had 'come up the hard way', and had a positive view point. The general consensus: if motivated, nearly all the students could pass the primary course. If the students possessed the main requirements of desire and motivation, this analysis was correct. There was concurrence among the instructors that not all would progress at the same rate. If properly and patiently taught, nearly all would pass. This approach was successful. Nearly all classes with ten in them were completed. Instructors were not paid by the hour. Rather, they were paid by the month. If fewer students were retained in the program, the instructors' work load was reduced. The instructors, as a group, did not allow the payment method to influence their attitude relative to the student quota. Instructor's pay scale was $150.00 to $175.00 per month with a maximum of $200.00. The primary flight course consisted of forty flight hours before a final upgrade and a private pilot's license. The flight time until the student soloed was with instruction. After soloing, the flight time was divided into instruction periods, followed by solo flight to practice the maneuvers from the previous period.

The students were a fascinating cross-section of personalities, ability, and acumen. The method to teach flight successfully is not 'one method fits all.' The approach to arrive at the same result in a group of ten is a motivating challenge. An adept student reflected personal satisfaction, and was the instructor's personal the reward for the teaching effort. At the completion of the primary course, the top rated students were offered a secondary flight program. The secondary program was flown in larger and more aerobatic aircraft, and included aerobatic flight instruction.

A third program, offered at the completion of the second advanced program, was the instrument flight program. The instrument flight program was to teach flight exclusively by reference to the aircraft instruments. The desired result was for the pilot to make an entire flight by reference to instruments, and included an instrument approach at the final destination.

In order to be qualified to teach the instrument program, the instructors were required to have a Civil Aeronautic Authority Instrument Rating. This was in addition to the Commercial License and Certified Instructors Rating they possessed. It was the pursuit of this qualification which was to lead to a major change of my flying career.

Flying schools that had the aircraft equipped for instrument flight and qualified instructors were not commonplace. Consequently, it was necessary to go to a major city for this flight instrument course. For me, that city was Chicago. The school was located on American Airport at the intersection of Devon and Higgins Roads. This location was not important at this time. Orchard Airport was located across the road. Later, the airport was expanded for the purpose of building a large aircraft factory for Douglas Aircraft Company. The purpose of the factory was to build large numbers of Douglas DC-4s, AAF C-54s, and Navy R-5Ds. These models were different configurations of the same basic aircraft. In the 1950s, Orchard Airport would become Chicago O'Hare International Airport.

Stinson SM8A-Instrument Flight Trainer

Group of Instrument Flight Instructors standing in front of Stinson SM8A. The author is second from right.

This Stinson SM8A was powered by a Lycoming SR 680 radial engine, capable of developing 215 horsepower. The flight instruments were a primary group consisting of a sensitive altimeter, needle ball turn indicator, airspeed indicator, rate of climb-decent indicator, clock, a radio receiver for radio range reception and control tower reception, transmitter for control tower contact, navigation lights for night flight, and a moveable fabric hood to cover the pilot's side of the windshield for simulated instrument flight. The use of the Stinson SM8A was not limited to use as an instrument flight trainer. The aircraft was a popular general aviation aircraft.

This instrument flight school offered a program for an instrument rating on an installment payment method. The offer was taken up, as it was a necessary part of the planned requirement. The school also offered all types of flight instruction including primary. In light of this, it was possible for me to instruct flight students when not flying in the instrument program. However, there was a slight inequity. The cost of instrument flight in a Stinson SM8A was $15.00 per hour while the pay received for flight instruction was $3.00 per hour. Inequity or not, the rating had be accomplished.

The instrument flight school encompassed a remarkable collection of airplanes. The owner had a business relationship with a company which made cash loans on aircraft. These loans were usually made to make an aircraft purchase possible. As the world was still in the throes of the Great Depression, it was not unusual for the optimistic purchasers of these aircraft to suffer a financial problem. The holder of the loan would then repossess the aircraft. By agreement, the school owner would dispatch one of the pilots to fly the repossession to his location. In this manner, the instrument school became a 'one-of-a-kind.' By repossession, it had one of nearly every make and model aircraft, and became a location worthy of note. With our agreement relative to flight instruction, many different makes and models were flown. On any given day, it was possible to instruct students without flying the same aircraft more than once.

In addition, there were private owners who based their aircraft at the airport. On occasion, there were requests by these owners for instruction in their own aircraft. This added new types of aircraft, which we had not flown before. One of our well-to-do customers owned a Ryan with a Menasco engine. This was a very sleek, all metal, low wing aircraft with a sliding hatch over the two cockpits. This Ryan, popular as a racing airplane, was flown at the time by well-known racing pilots. The opportunity to fly this airplane was a great experience, as my financial situation at the time made the ownership of one impossible. There were other airplanes of considerable value based there. With so many types and models available for students to choose from, flying was always challenging and interesting.

The Stinson was flown on a schedule with other instrument students. As we became qualified, a check ride was scheduled with a Civil Aeronautics Authority inspector at Chicago Midway Airport, and we flew the Stinson there for this required check. Prior to the flight check, successful completion of a CAA instrument flight written examination was required and had been completed.

The Call-Transcontinental & Western Airlines

The timing turned out to be extremely beneficial. The owner of the instrument flight school called me into his office to discuss a telephone call he had just received. The call was from Transcontinental & Western Airlines, TWA. The nature of the call was their requirement to hire instrument qualified pilots. His question was, "Are you interested in going to the TWA office in Chicago for an interview for pilot employment?"

My reply was, "When?"

Handing me the telephone, he said, "It's up to you to make your appointment as they are on the line."

The call from the TWA Chicago office in produced an employment interview the same week. The meeting was conducted by the recruiting pilot from the home office. A written examination was given with an allotted time for completion. At the end of the meeting, the recruiting pilot politely stated, "We will let you know shortly if you have been accepted."

Two days passed. A telephone call advised a physical examination was required and asked when a flight to Kansas City could be scheduled?

The reply was, "How soon do you wish me there?"

The following day a flight took me to Kansas City where the home office was located and where the physical would be taken. After a nervous night in the hotel, the physical examination was taken the following day. Upon completion of the physical was the usual, "We will let you know how you made out," followed by my return flight to Chicago. The round-trip flight to Kansas City had been made in a Douglas DC-3. It is not necessary to note this was the first experience with an airplane that large. Previously, DC-3s had only been observed from behind the fence at Chicago Midway Airport. After anxiety had set in, a telephone call informed me the physical examination was successful, and asked when could my service begin?

My reply was, "Is tomorrow too soon?"

"Yes. Make it the first of the month."

This was in the 'too good to be true' category. Transcontinental & Western Airlines, TWA, was the airline that flew the large airliners; the Douglas DC-2s, DC-3s, and the Boeing Stratoliners. Those were the four-engine giants that had thundered over our heads as we stood behind the fence at Chicago Midway Airport. Never, in the 'wildest of dreams' category, had there been an opportunity for me to become a pilot for TWA. Now that dream was about to become reality. Transcontinental & Western Airlines was officially known as the LINDBERGH LINE, the airline of the Lone Eagle, Charles A. Lindbergh. The "LINDBERGH LINE" was proudly displayed on the fuselage of all TWA aircraft.

Corporate headquarters was located at the Kansas City Municipal Airport. A letter had been received from TWA advising a report time of 8:00 a.m. Monday. Also stated, if lodging was desired, a hotel would accommodate the new hires. Arriving in Kansas City on Sunday and proceeding to the hotel, already at the reception desk were three other pilot recruits in the process of registering. After completing registration and exchanging introductions, it was late afternoon. The foursome agreed food was in order, and proceeded to a restaurant just around the corner from the hotel. The group was made up of Amos from Los Angeles, Ed from New York, Ivan from Alabama, and me. After dinner, we returned to the hotel lobby to find it overflowing with U.S. Navy seamen from nearby Olathe Naval Air Station. They were dressed in summer 'whites', which included a large blue kerchief tied in a square knot in front. As we entered the lobby, Ivan, in a loud southern drawl, made the following statement, "Ah cain understands why them Germans are sinkin' all those ships. The whole Navy is in Kansas City!" Immediately after his objectionable remark was made, the entire naval contingent descended upon us. Most of the contingent was made up of late teenage to early twenty-year-olds. There was no desire on my part to engage in a violent confrontation with this group. However, self-defense was immediately required.

Confronted by three young men all swinging at me at the same time, the first was grabbed by his kerchief with his momentum easily carrying him to the floor. My foot was placed through his kerchief to keep him in that position while fending off the blows from the remaining two. As the thought flashed through my mind as to what could be done with this situation, the sound of long, shrill, sirens was heard as the police vehicles arrived at the front of the hotel. Fearing the arrival of the Naval Shore Patrol, the contingent immediately scattered in all directions. My concern was the possibility of being apprehended by the police and charged with a disturbance not of my making. Any exit through the main entrance was not possible, as it would soon be filled with police. We exited into a long, unknown hall. While running down this hall, the thought was, "What happens if there is no exit at the end of this hall?" Any arrest at this time would result in 'being fired before being hired.' Fortunately, at the end of the hall was an exit into an unlighted alley at the rear of the hotel. After a long walk, we returned to the hotel to spend the night.

Going for breakfast early the next morning at the restaurant around the corner, the same threesome was found together eating breakfast. Ivan was expressing no regrets for his 'near' disastrous foray the previous evening. He was reminded, the thought 'of being fired before being hired' was not a pleasant one. Still, Ivan expressed no remorse whatsoever. Consequently, he was told about an old saying back home, "When you are talking, you are not learning anything." Or, as perhaps he would have said, "When yr talkin', you ain't learnin' nothin!"

The group then proceeded to Goebel Hangar located at the Kansas City Municipal Airport. First order of business was to fill out applications for employment and associated documents. Manuals were then issued that covered aircraft engines, operations manuals, etc. There were many manuals to cover the study of all phases of airline operation and the duties of the first officer position. Thus began ground school, and employment by TWA, which was to last for 36 years. The year was 1942.

Captain Roger and the DC-3 Instrument Check

Captain Roger Don Rae was a division chief pilot of Transcontinental & Western Airlines in Chicago. Chicago was a small pilot domicile compared to other domiciles on the system. Roger and the six-month instrument check were an experience to remember. In flight in a DC-3 and under the hood, all the normal procedures were performed; it was the extra-curricular tests or activities Roger added that got your attention. Roger would have the pilot climb to 7,000 ft. During the climb, Roger would take his handful of suction cup cards, and place each one over the various flight instruments, leaving the airspeed indicator, turn and bank indicator, and the altimeter, the primary flight group exposed. While flying the primary group, Roger would take the controls with the command, "Cover up your eyes." Roger would then pull up the nose, push down the nose, slipping and skidding the aircraft, until he got it in an unusual attitude with nose pointing down and the airspeed such that the airplane was near stall. Roger would then say, "Recover."

It was then all right to look, recover to a normal flight attitude with reference to the primary instruments. Completing this maneuver, Roger would repeat the same procedure again with the 'Cover up your eyes.' This time, in another unusual attitude, Roger would cut the mixture controls on both engines. In this silence he would say, "Recover."

This time, recovery on the primary flight group was necessary, while closing the throttles before returning the mixture controls to cruise position (fuel again flowing to the engines). After recovery from this problem, Roger would say, "OK, make a range approach to Midway down to 1,000 ft," whereupon with his last suction cup, he would cover up the altimeter. This required an orientation on the Adcock radio range, while flying over the initial cone of silence, then outbound on the approach leg. This was followed by a procedure turn to the inbound leg. After passing over the low cone, we proceeded to the airport while descending on the engine boost instruments. The engine boost instruments had to be turned to the static position so they would indicate barometric pressure, and give an indication of altitude. That was why Roger gave you the 1,000 foot ceiling, as the uncorrected barometric pressure was being used. For those not familiar with the instrument check procedure, the pilot being checked cannot see out, while the check pilot has full view outside reference. After landing and taxiing to the hangar, the instrument check was complete. Roger would say, "See you later."

Before departing one afternoon, my comment to Roger was, "There is just one thing. If the pilot does not close the throttles first in that 'cut mixture' procedure before he brings the fuel mixtures on, those propellers are going to go full increased RPM, possibly past the governor set maximums. You could scatter cylinder heads all over the countryside."

Roger kept on walking back to the hangar. Via the maintenance grapevine, it was learned some weeks later that during this procedure, the pilot flying did return the fuel mixture controls to 'on' before closing the throttles. The engines came back to power; the propeller RPM went past the stops. The noise could be heard for miles. There was a rapid return to land before an engine failure could occur.

If you did not know Roger, it would have been simple to get the opinion Roger was trying to fail, or 'BUST' your check. However, that is not what Roger was attempting to do. It was his wish to remind you what could be flown under adverse circumstances. Fortunately, we had another interest in common, bird hunting. We both shot trap (clay pigeons) and as a result, often shot clay pigeons in a group. Roger and his wife Fran became and remained wonderful friends.

BOOK TWO

THE WORLD FROM THE FLIGHT DECK

Evolution of TWA

Transcontinental & Western Airlines evolved from a merger of Transcontinental Air Transport, TAT, and Western Air Express. Airline mergers and acquisitions were predominant in this period. The merger was contingent upon an air mail contract to be obtained by TWA. The airmail contract was to be awarded to TWA late in the same year. In July 1929, TAT had flown the first transcontinental air service, with a combination of aircraft and rail service, to operate from New York (Newark) to Glendale, California (Los Angeles). In this period of Ford Tri-Motor aircraft operation, Lindbergh served on the technical committee. It was necessary to implement weather and terminal facilities along the transcontinental route. This was accomplished by Charles A. Lindbergh.

Lighted airway beacons were located along what was to be called an airway. The beacons were spaced as closely as possible, approximately one every ten miles. A high powered electric lighted beacon was rotated by a motor, to shine a sweeping beam of white light in all directions. The light on the back side of the beacon, flashed in red, the Morse code identifier for the beacon location. As close as geographically possible, the beacon location identifiers repeated once every hundred miles. Emergency landing fields were established along the route. They were spaced as often as the topography permitted. These emergency landing fields had a rotating beacon with a lighted identifier to designate the facilities at the field. For example, on the back side of the beacon, a green light indicated a lighted field with lights along both sides of the landing area or landing areas. An amber or white identifier light indicated an emergency landing field, with unlighted landing areas. The green beacon light identifier became standard for all operational airports nationwide with lighted facilities. Where possible, manned weather observation stations were established at these locations along the route. The observers made weather observations, and reported throughout a twenty-four hour period to a central location for dissemination to pilots. Federal budget limited the number of hours per day the airports were manned for reporting.

The 'lighted airways' were established for night flight under visual flight conditions. Radio ranges were installed along the same routes to provide aircraft guidance under instrument weather conditions, and were also an additional navigational aid for night flight. The low frequency broadcast radio range consisted of a four quadrant transmitter. The radio range transmitted the Morse code alphabetical group for station identification, and to transmit Morse code signals to create an 'on course' audio path. The magnetic north quadrant was the N_. quadrant. Clockwise, there were four quadrants, alternating with N and A. The quadrants were so aligned on the 360 degree magnetic area to create an overlap of the N_. and A._ code signals. An 'on course' audio signal resulted. The courses created were magnetic compass course headings. The path along which the N_. combined with the A._ created a solid tone or hum. This was the 'on course' signal. These fanlike protractions extended out from the transmitter. The 'on course' signals were flown to the transmitter location. Directly over the transmitter, no audio signal was received. This was known as the "cone of silence", and was the manner in which position was established when over the transmitter. The 'on course' signal, which was created by the overlapping of the N_. and A._ signals, was the 'on course' hum and became known as "on the beam." A colloquial expression was created and is still used, "on the beam." Radio signal reception required pilots wear and listen to a headset. The operation of these radio ranges nationwide created the United States Civil Airway Network for Instrument Flight, and later would be applied world-wide.

Lindbergh flew the first eastbound Trans-continental Air Transport (TAT) flight with a Ford Tri-Motor from Glendale, CA (Los Angeles Terminal). TAT, the forerunner of Transcontinental & Western Air, was known as the "Lindbergh Line." Lindbergh's ongoing interest in TAT was shown by his participation in the company which continued with Transcontinental & Western Airlines, thus the title "The Lindbergh Line" prevailed.

Note: Jack Frye, Paul Richter, and Walter Hamilton founded Standard Airlines. With the merger of TAT, Standard Airlines, and Western Air Express, Jack Frye became president with Paul Richter, executive vice president. Upon the conclusion of the merger which created Transcontinental & Western Airlines, Jack Frye remained as president, and Paul Richter, executive VP.

The vision and lifelong pursuit of Jack Frye was to create an airline to circle the globe. The creative origin of this dream was the small airline which was to become Transcontinental & Western Airlines, later Trans World Airlines. Tragically, as often occurs in history, neither Jack Frye nor Paul Richter lived to savor the day Trans World Airlines became a global carrier when it inaugurated around the world daily airline service.

The key to the success of Transcontinental & Western Airlines under the leadership of Jack Frye, Paul Richter, and their staff was their recognition of what it takes to create an industry leading airline. That was their unqualified belief all personnel are an integral part of the airline. This belief became policy which contributed greatly to the success of TWA. All top management were licensed pilots, resulting in the airline being known as, "The Airline Run by Flyers."

In 1931, the evolutionary design of aircraft to be used in airline service continued. Jack Frye and Paul Richter with the assistance of TWA pilots drafted the specifications for the aircraft to be built by Douglas Aircraft Co., the DC-1. This aircraft was test flown for airline operation by TWA pilot, D.W. Tommy Tomlinson. There was a single DC-1 built. The production aircraft were DC-2s. Later, the DC-3 was to continue the line of Douglas commercial airliners. The DC-3 became the world-standard airliner or the 'work horse' of the airline industry of this time period. The popularity of the DC-3 would result in the greatest number of a single model transport aircraft to be produced in the history of aviation.

Captain

At this time, the expansion of TWA required the availability of more captains to fly the increased flight schedules. In as few as eighteen months, first officers advanced rapidly to captain flight training, very quickly as in my case. The rapid advancement to captain status required maximum application by first officers during the time served as co-pilot. The competency requirements for captain status were not reduced or lowered to suit the situation. Failure to successfully complete the captain status checkout was discharge. All the pilots involved were aware of this requirement, and conducted themselves accordingly. The end result was easily defined; total application by the individual would produce either success or failure. The individual pilot was required to qualify as captain or be terminated.

Expansion of the airline industry was greatly intensified by the addition of the International Division of TWA. During the years of World War II, aircraft were not available to expand the flight operation. Upon conclusion of the war, new aircraft became readily available. The Lockheed Constellation production, which had been allocated to the United States Army Air Forces as the C-69, had not gone into service. Consequently, all the great numbers of Lockheed Constellations on the production line at the Burbank facility became quickly available for commercial use. TWA immediately put these aircraft into service on both the domestic and international routes. Aircraft manufactured by other companies were available and also entered the operation.

First TWA Lockheed Constellation flight, April 17, 1944, from Burbank, CA to Washington National Airport non-stop; 6 hours 57 minutes. Flight was flown by TWA President Jack Frye and Howard Hughes.

In the background is a TWA Lockheed 049 Constellation at TWA International Division Headquarters, New Castle, Delaware in 1947. Four stripes on the newly designed uniform indicate rank of Captain.

First Industry Pilot Strike

During World War II, salaries of the airline pilots had been frozen to prewar levels. The hours per month and per year limitations flown by pilots had been increased substantially in the national emergency. There were no established pay scales for pilots flying the new, larger, and faster four-engine aircraft. The industry was faced with an urgent requirement to negotiate new wage contracts to cover the flight operation of these new aircraft. It was also necessary to establish an hourly flight time restriction. There was not an agreement proffered by any of the major airlines to resolve this problem. The Airline Pilots Association had met with the major air carriers without success to arrive at a basis to establish the new working agreements. The decision was made by the Airline Pilots Association that the threat of a work stoppage by the pilots of one of the major air carriers was necessary to arrive at a new contract agreement. This decision resulted in the unfortunate choice of TWA as the major target.

In October 1946, a complete work stoppage was executed by the pilots of TWA. The pilots' strike lasted several weeks before an arbitration concession was reached. After TWA flight operations resumed, a new working agreement was approved for the pilots. The concepts in this agreement became the standard for the airline industry. This was the first airline strike by airline pilots in the airline industry. While this strike or work stoppage was regarded as a necessary evil to arrive at a satisfactory working agreement, it was an extremely negative situation for TWA. The cessation of the entire flight operation at a time of great expansion greatly depleted the financial reserves of TWA. The ensuing financial crisis resulted in severe disagreement between the top management and Howard Hughes. The continued disagreement resulted in Howard Hughes dismissing Jack Frye as president. Paul Richter resigned from his position as executive vice president. With the departure of these two talented leaders, who had been driving forces from the inception of Standard Airlines to TAT, and finally to TWA, no one of their caliber was at the helm. This was an extremely difficult situation for TWA to have encountered at any time, but certainly not at this time of major expansion. The result was the offices of the president and chief executive officer became a revolving door, as no president served in the position for any length of time. In the years that followed, the other major air carriers were to benefit from stable leadership. American Airlines was under the direction of Mr. C.R. Smith. Delta had Mr. C.E. Woolman, United Mr. "Pat" Patterson, Eastern Airlines Captain Eddie Rickenbacker, and Continental Mr. Robert Six, just to name a few of the presidents of the major air carriers. These great leaders, with extended lengths of service, made possible stable, long standing policy for each carrier in the airline business. The changes in the leadership in TWA would evolve into a negative perception, which would ultimately result in the demise of the company.

Kansas City

The headquarters and main offices of Transcontinental & Western Air were located at 10 Richards Road, Kansas City, Missouri. Miss Ruby Jane McCully, the receptionist who also doubled as the plug-in key telephone switch board operator, greeted all arrivals with a smile as large as life.

Vice President of Operations, Mr. John Collings, had an office on the second floor overlooking the airport runways. The hallway to the left of the lobby served as access to the offices of Captain Swede Golien and Captain George Rice, who were in charge of the chief pilots' offices. Miss Helen Gunn was the chief pilots' secretary, regardless of who was chief pilot. Off the hallway on the right of the reception area were the flight dispatch offices, weather station, and associated services. The main office entry to Ruby's domain made it necessary for all, including flight crews, to pass through the lobby and greet the receptionist. All employees became 'first name' acquaintances of Ruby Jane.

Just inside the entry doors, two leather couches were aligned on opposite sides of the entry, directly opposite the receptionist position. These leather couches were used to seat people waiting to see one of the TWA officers. There were on occasions when one of these couches was occupied by a person who was asleep. This chap was badly attired, wearing wrinkled clothes, and appeared to have several days' growth of beard. It was an appearance not expected in the ma... entrance to TWA headquarters. When a person would uneasily quietly ask Ruby, "Who is that?" Ruby's straight faced reply was, "Oh, that's just Howard Hughes," or more often, "Oh, that's just Howard."

Author is wearing uniform of Transcontinental & Western Airlines. Two stripes indicate rank of Captain.

BOOK THREE

THE FORMATIVE FORTIES

THE DIFFICULT TODAY—
THE IMPOSSIBLE TOMORROW

Flight Navigator Training

In January 1943, TWA was awarded a contract by the United States Army Air Forces to train flight navigators for various services. Allocated by the USAAF, the aircraft flown were Lockheed C-60s, the military version of the commercial Lockheed Lodestar. The aircraft were powered by two Curtiss Wright G-205 engines, each rated at 1200 hp. The aircraft fuel capacity was just over 600 US gallons, which gave the aircraft good flight range. The aircraft cabin was modified into a flying classroom with plotting tables for navigation charts on both sides of the inside wall. The center of the cabin ceiling had been modified by the installation of Plexiglas astrodomes along the center of the ceiling. The purpose of the astrodome was to take celestial observations of the stars with an octant, or reflecting quadrant, during night flight. The celestial data was then entered on the charts to determine the position of the aircraft. During daylight, the astrodomes were used to take sun lines. A TWA navigation instructor presided over the class of AAF student navigators. The aircraft were flown by TWA captains and first officers. At the completion of the program, the USAAF flight navigators were assigned to overseas flight operations.

All flights were flown during the hours of darkness and were planned by the TWA captain and first officer. The course and destination were withheld from the student navigators as it was their ongoing problem to calculate the position of the aircraft at all times while being monitored, and later graded by the TWA navigation instructor. The flights were flown over as great a distance as possible. Landings were made at dawn at the nearest USAAF facility to refuel the aircraft. After refueling, the aircraft was flown to return to the main base to prepare for the next night flight. A different planned destination for each flight made participation in the program very exciting. After deplaning at the home base, the crew debriefing was often colored by comments about the previous night flight operation. One comment, which we did not want to hear was, "We were never worried, as we knew you pilots always knew where we were."

1946 – TWA International Division

The flight operation of the TWA International Division was made possible by the around-the-world routes awarded in 1945. In 1946, TWA inaugurated flights from the terminals on the East Coast of the United States: Washington, D.C.; Philadelphia, PA; New York, La Guardia Airport; and Boston Logan Airport.

There were terminals in Paris, France; Lisbon, Portugal; Rome, Italy; Cairo, Egypt; and Bombay, India. There were flights from Chicago Midway Airport to Europe. The intermediate terminals or cities served in Europe were: Geneva, Switzerland; Rome, Italy; and Athens, Greece. Later Zurich, Switzerland was served and in the Middle East; Tel Aviv, Palestine (under British rule). Cities served on the flight from Lisbon, Portugal to Cairo, Egypt were Algiers, Algeria; Tunis, Tunisia; and Tripoli, Libya. In 1947 service to Madrid, Spain was added. Later, service was added to Barcelona and Malaga. TWA flights from all the cities served within the United States were connected at the East Coast terminals.

In the spring of 1946, TWA inaugurated the first international flight from LaGuardia Field, New York to Orly Airport, Paris, France. The aircraft was a Lockheed Constellation. The route of flight across the North Atlantic was a Great Circle course to Europe. Along the Great Circle course fuel stops were made at Gander, Newfoundland and Shannon, Ireland. Fuel stops were made to conform to the range capabilities of the Lockheed Constellation and the Douglas DC-4.

The north latitude location of Gander, Newfoundland, makes the long winter weather conditions there a factor. The resulting low clouds and low visibility at Gander required alternate airports to be available within the range of each respective aircraft. The closest alternate airport is Stephensville Airport on the west coast of Newfoundland. Alternate airports in Nova Scotia and Goose Bay Labrador were used for Gander, Newfoundland. Winter flight operation into these Maritime terminals and the respective airports was made under conditions often involving heavy snowfall.

Sandy of Gander

The operation of the International Division of TWA during the time of the Douglas C-54s, DC-4s, and early Model Constellations required refueling along the route from the United States to Europe. Gander, Newfoundland is geographically located on the Great Circle Route, and is the shortest route from the eastern United States to Europe. Flight operations into Gander were not without winter challenges. Heavy snow fall and severe low temperatures made flight operations a challenge for flight crews, and ground crews who serviced the aircraft for flight arrivals and departures. The snow accumulations were deep, as the temperatures did not rise above freezing between the reoccurring weather systems, which caused the heavy snow fall. The snow was, in effect, pushed from the airport runways, taxiways, ramp, and buildings to form large piles of snow exceeding the height of the aircraft. The runways often had a solid line of plowed snow the complete length of the runway, with just enough room for aircraft operation. Further snowfall was pushed into the accumulation, making a higher and more extended drift. This winter occurrence was prevalent at all three refueling airports; Gander, Newfoundland; Goose Bay, Labrador; and Stephenville, Newfoundland.

Gander was the home of a large Newfoundland breed, far too majestic to be called a dog. Sandy was beautifully proportioned with long black hair, which grew fuller due to the cold climate. Sandy was an impressive 165 pounds of good nature, who was often found sitting in a snow drift at the entrance to the operations and passenger terminal building. As you might easily understand, Sandy became the mascot, or the 'image' most associated with Gander Airport. Sandy's great lumbering hulk was often seen anywhere in the area. His good nature made him the favorite of everyone, including the personnel at the commissary, who fed Sandy quite well. Sandy also became a favorite of the flight crews transiting Gander. It was common practice to seek him out after arriving there.

During an arrival at Gander following a snowstorm, which had resulted in large amounts of snow being piled along the runway, an incident involving Sandy occurred, which was frightening to the crew involved. Flying a Douglas DC-4 on final approach and landing, just as the aircraft touched down, Sandy lumbered up and over the snow drift to cross the runway. Fortunately, he was some distance down the runway from the landing aircraft, but the aircraft still posed a possible threat to his well being. The high drifts of snow did not allow for diversion in any direction. The DC-4 did not have reverse thrust to shorten the landing roll out. Braking on the snow covered runway was nearly non-existent. All possible effort was made to avoid hitting Sandy, coupled with the fact Sandy kept moving up and over the snow bank on the opposite side of the runway, injury to Sandy was avoided. After the incident was over, the flight crew expressed great emotional relief, as we all were fond of Sandy.

Later, when flying a flight making the usual fuel stop in Gander, and upon arrival at the terminal area, Sandy was nowhere to be found. In the operations office the first question was, "Where's Sandy?"

The dispatcher replied, "It's a long story."

While transiting Gander, a passenger from Switzerland had observed the handsome Sandy. He was impressed with his confirmation and good temperament. The large breeds of Europe, to include Switzerland and Germany, were suffering from a lack of new blood lines in their animals. The problems of continued 'in-breeding' are well known and undesirable. Without question, Sandy was an answer to this breeding problem. The person or persons quickly made a purchase of Sandy. The owner of Sandy was still in question, as he was airport property, but he was now gone.

The Swiss have long had a problem in obtaining new blood lines for the St. Bernard and the Bernese mountain dog. Sandy could now be Swiss. The German Leonberger has Newfoundland blood lines. Sandy could now be an adopted Leonberger. Whatever his destination, Sandy had traded his life in a snow drift to a life of a Lochinvar stud. It couldn't happen to a nicer friend.

After departing Gander, Newfoundland flying across the North Atlantic Ocean, a scheduled landing was made at Shannon, Ireland Airport. Prestwick, Scotland was used as an alternate airport for Shannon. The flights then operated from Shannon to Paris. Westbound flights from Paris to New York made the same schedule landings at Shannon and Gander. Due to the air mass circulation from west to east, the westbound flights from Shannon, Ireland to Gander, Newfoundland were of longer duration than the eastbound flights on the same route.

The fuel capacities of the Lockheed Constellation and the Douglas DC-4 were adequate to fly the distances involved. However, to have fueled these aircraft to their maximum capacity would have severely limited the payload remaining. Therefore, all flight planning was made to provide the fuel required to the destination, with adequate fuel to fly to an alternate airport, plus the required reserve in time. The west to east air mass movement resulted in the westbound flights taking longer to arrive at their destination. All flights across the North Atlantic required constant attention to their progress. During the elapsed time of 10 to 12 hours, flights often encountered extensive changes in the air mass movement, and the existing weather conditions at the destination. The common analogy was, westbound flights on the North Atlantic, at times, could be very interesting.

Winter flight conditions on the North Atlantic were subject to fast moving air mass circulation, which caused rapid changes in weather and air mass components. The result of the loss or negative component was often referred to as a 'head wind', causing long westbound flight time. There were occasions when a flight encountered higher than forecast component losses, which resulted in a course reversal and return to their airport of origin. This was not a common occurrence, but did occur.

At times, the high velocity negative component was so great, flight operations between Shannon, Ireland and Gander, Newfoundland were required to fly an alternate route across the North Atlantic. This route was much longer, flying from Shannon, Ireland to Santa Maria in the Azores Islands, thence to Gander, Newfoundland. When these air mass conditions prevailed, the westbound flights were often altered to fly from Paris to Santa Maria, Azores then on to Gander, Newfoundland, without the landing at Shannon Ireland. The Azores are an island archipelago, located off the west coast of the Iberian Peninsula.

As discussed in an earlier portion of the book, use of radio ranges were applied by the USAAF as an instrument flight navigation aid. These charts illustrate the typical radio range station (N_. and A._) associated with each airport on the islands of Terceira, and Santa Maria, and are used to locate them. Each radio range has its own frequency and identifier, and also transmitted weather sequence reports. Charts were prepared at the direction of the Commanding General, Army Air Forces, by the Aeronautical Chart Service, Washington, D.C. from best source material available November 1943. Scale: 1:1,000,000, 3rd Edition. The chart used for illustration purposes is for Sao Miguel Island (350), Azores, North Atlantic dated October 1945. Chart illustration pages 70-71.

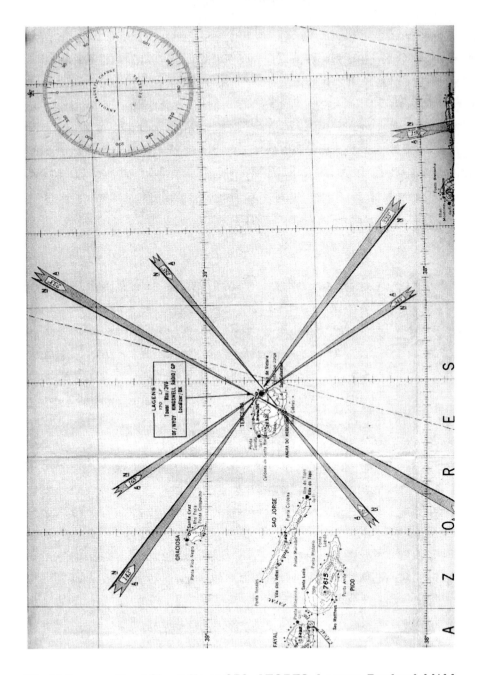

World Aeronautical Chart–Zone 350- AZORES, Lagens Revised 11/44

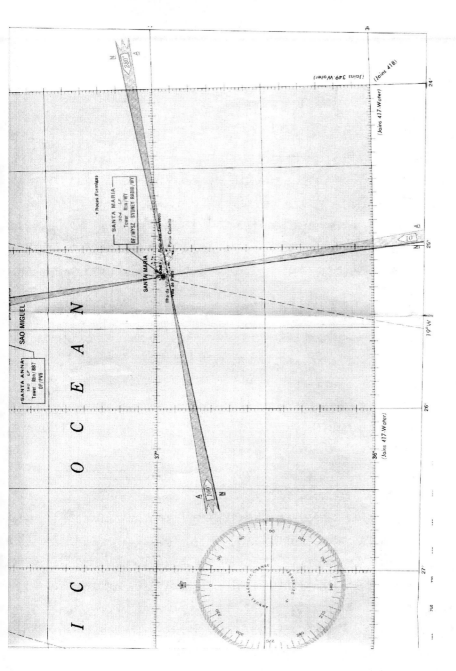

Santa Maria Island-World Aeronautical Chart Zone 350, Revised 11/44

Spain—1947

Initially, TWA flights from the eastern terminals operated to Gander, Newfoundland; Santa Maria, Azores; Lisbon, Portugal; Algiers, Algeria; Tunis, Tunisia; Tripoli, Libya; and Cairo, Egypt.

A request was made by the U.S. Civil Aeronautics Board for TWA to serve Madrid. Spain had been isolated from the rest of Europe following a very brutal civil war of the 1930s. As a result, the country had little air service with the rest of the world. The decision was made by the United States Air Force to establish air bases in Spain, to include the south coast on the Mediterranean Sea.

The reciprocity by the U.S. was to aid the Spanish government in badly needed water preservation, dams, and irrigation networks. Spain was devastated in the aftermath of their civil war, and urgently in need of economic assistance.

The request and opportunity to establish flight operation was not a difficult one to comply with; the only change to established flight operations was to extend the flights that had normally terminated in Lisbon, on to Madrid, a short flight of one hour and thirty minutes. Later, after the diplomatic agreements had been reached, the flights were extended from Madrid, Spain to Rome, Italy.

Barajas, the airport for Madrid was in the process of expansion. The available runway was short in length, and under construction to extend the runway length.

This did not pose a problem, as the short flights between Lisbon and Madrid required minimum fuel loads. Consequently, the takeoff gross weights were low and the available runway length was adequate. The flight operations procedures were interesting. The lengthening of the single runway was in progress daily. The work on the runway would stop for our landing arrival, then resume after we cleared the runway. The takeoff procedure was the same. The work would cease until we had taken off.

Most out of the ordinary was the aged method of runway construction. The cement or concrete mixer was a small one, commonly seen on household projects at home. The runway was constructed using the small bucket mixer, pouring one square meter of concrete at a time. The result was runway construction in one square meter sections. A square meter is a 39.37 inch dimension.

The method to extend a runway length several thousand feet was a long, slow process. The small square sections of concrete made it impossible to have adjoining each concrete square exactly at the same level as the one. Slightly different levels existed in all the areas of the runway. The aircraft landing gear and the wheels of the main landing gear had an irregular surface to roll on for takeoff and landing. The nose gear, which was located directly below the flight deck, made a loud singing noise, as the aircraft increased speed for takeoff. As soon as the nose gear touched down on landing, the same loud buzzing sound was heard. When it occurred, the vibration was not severe enough to cause damage, but it did get your attention. After the runway lengthening was completed, the only possible correction to make the surface level and smooth was to apply a thick coating of black asphalt over the entire surface. In Spain, work generally progressed at very slow pace, and it was several months later before the work was completed. Afterwards, the U.S. Air Force built the Air Force Base Torrejon in the Madrid region.

Ocean Station CHARLIE

The North Atlantic Ocean is often referred to as the cruel sea by those who have navigated its great expanse. The Great Circle Course, the shortest distance between the East Coast and Europe, is the great expanse of the North Atlantic. The sea conditions and above the surface weather are affected by the Gulf Stream; a large body of moving water, which has its origin in the Gulf of Mexico. Further warmed by the waters of the Caribbean, it flows up the East Coast of the United States, Nova Scotia, Newfoundland, ultimately to the western shores of northern Europe. The weather above the surface is created by the low pressure air masses which move east off the East Coast of North America. The variations in temperature, often great, cause the changing weather conditions to develop along the North Atlantic. The meteorological changes often result in heavy seas with violent swells, a rough surface for all to navigate. At the same time, the weather above the surface becomes more active with high velocity, air mass movement, precipitation, often icing conditions in the cloud formations. These active weather areas often extend along the coast, east of Nova Scotia and Newfoundland, extending out to sea. The storm areas tend to modify as the air masses move east. The cloud layers are inclined to stratify as the air masses move east of 30 degrees west longitude.

In order to observe weather conditions at sea, and to provide emergency assistance at sea, the stationing of ships at sea at a designated position was enacted in 1940, with several nations of the world participating. These ships were termed Ocean Station, locations identified by an alphabetic letter. Those ships, which were in service by the U.S.A., were of the United States Coast Guard. The U.S. Coast Guard vessels were 150 ft in length, were often cutters with a crew complement of over 100. The Coast Guard vessels were fully operational sea rescue ships.

The Ocean Station in the North Atlantic Ocean at 52 degrees, 45 minutes north latitude, 35 degrees, 30 minutes west longitude was designated Ocean Station Charlie. The United States Coast Guard vessels stationed at this position were on duty for 29 to 30 days, until relieved by another ship and crew.

Ocean Station Charlie was equipped with a full complement of radio transmitters and receivers, capable of contacting all ships at sea, and aircraft in flight in the area. There was a radio beacon, which could be used with direction finding radios, to plot the aircraft position relative to the position of the ship. The radio beacon identifier in Morse code, in addition to the station identification code, was transmitted in Morse code stating where the ship was located; if not 'on station', the position could be verified by referencing a grid, which was in our navigation information. Charlie was most helpful to establish a position fix, both eastbound and westbound on the North Atlantic.

Since the early 1940s, the Douglas C-54 and DC-4 had been in service worldwide to include the North Atlantic operation. The fuel capacity was adequate for flying this operation. The single shortcoming of the aircraft was lack of pressurization. In order to carry an adequate payload, the fuel on board was limited to less than the full capacity available. In all flight planning, the necessary fuel load was calculated; the fuel load included fuel burned to the destination, plus fuel required to fly to an alternate airport, plus required reserve fuel. After this calculation, the payload of passengers and cargo was available. It can be readily seen, the greater the fuel load, the lower the available payload. It can be easily recognized; the maximum fuel capacity of the aircraft could not be utilized and still carry a payload.

On March 8, 1948, TWA Flight 905 departed Shannon, Ireland at 21:48 Z (Zulu time) on the second leg of the flight, with an estimated flight plan time of 11 hours, 50 minutes to Gander. Shortly after passing over the west coastline of Ireland, instrument flight conditions were encountered. Instrument flight conditions continued, accompanied by snow and turbulence. The existence of continual instrument conditions and turbulence was not normal for this part of the North Atlantic, as this type of cloud formation normally stratified after passing approximately 30 degrees west longitude. During this instrument flight, the constant overcast conditions did not allow for a celestial observation. The low frequency radio beacons, Bushmils, located in the northern British Isles, and Lugo located on the coastline of Spain, were not receivable to adequately plot a radio position fix.

Loran stations had been installed under the direction of the United States Navy. The Loran stations on the eastern portion of the North Atlantic had been turned over to the countries where they were located. The Loran stations had not been well maintained. As a result, they were not functioning well enough to transmit reliable signals for position plotting. Consequently, the flight was flown by dead reckoning; a term used to define flight flown according to flight planned headings. At the arrival of a specific time over a planned longitudinal fix, a change of heading was made according to the flight plan.

The lack of aircraft pressurization limited the cruising altitude. Available oxygen supply on board was not adequate for extended passenger use. It was not possible for the captain to be aware of individual passenger requirement for respiratory oxygen. As a result, the maximum cruising altitude for passengers without the use of oxygen was not exceeded. The cruising altitude had been in instrument conditions. At no time had made a celestial observation been possible. The flight had now been en route for six hours without a celestial or radio position fix. Our position was only a flight plan reference estimate.

The DC-4 had a navigator plotting table immediately aft of the flight deck bulkhead. A Plexiglas astrodome was located in the same area in the ceiling of the fuselage. The navigator stool was also used as a means of elevation to use the Astrodome for celestial observation. The four legged stool had fittings at the bottom of each leg which, when snapped into the corresponding floor settings, secured the stool for use. Balancing on the top portion of the stool to make a celestial observation required skill and caution.

The navigator had become highly concerned about his inability to plot a position fix. The lack of a celestial observation was not due to a lack of many attempts on his part. The navigator had been recently hired by TWA for his position. Perhaps, it was the fact that he was new to the position, coupled with his youthfulness, increased his anxiety to perform his duties, which were hampered by the existing flight conditions. The constant turbulence made it difficult for me to leave the flight deck. However, it became necessary to advise the navigator to discontinue his attempts to take a celestial observation atop the stool. It was at this point, his demeanor was observed to be on the edge of loss of emotional control. He was assured his efforts were commendable, but he was risking personal injury. In fact, he was instructed to discontinue his attempts for a celestial observation until the turbulence subsided.

After returning to the flight deck, a further reference to our flight plan indicated we should be approaching the communicable range of Ocean Station Charlie. If we could make radio contact with Charlie, we could plot a fix from his radio beacon, and also make voice communication with the Ocean Station. Several radio contacts were attempted without any reply from Charlie. This indicated we had not progressed as planned. The snow static affected low frequency radio reception. We had not been successful in taking bearings on the console beacons, and now could not read the low frequency radio beacon aboard Ocean Station Charlie.

The high velocity air mass had moved in above the eastern portion of the North Atlantic. The result had hindered our progress to a greater limit than had been planned. This type of air mass movement occurred more often in the area off the coast of Newfoundland.

The forecasts and prognosis charts, which we had in our possession, indicated a deep low-pressure air mass approaching the south coast of Newfoundland. This type of air mass could make for low ceilings and visibility at both our destination Gander, and our alternate airport, Stephensville. This air mass movement could also cause high velocity westerly components on our course off the coast of Newfoundland.

Our position was not a desirable one. We were considerably behind our flight plan. We were unable to verify our exact geographical position. As captain, it became evident tensions were increasing among the flight crew. Despite instruction to the contrary, the navigator had continued an attempt to make a celestial observation, which was still not possible due to our instrument flight conditions. In his effort to do so, he had fallen from the navigator stool to the floor of the aircraft, striking the upper part of his body on the top of the stool as he fell. The flight purser and hostess had placed the navigator in the lower bunk, which was available for flight crew rest purposes.

An attempt to reach Ocean Station Charlie by radio contact was again unsuccessful. This repetition of negative contact verified our westerly progress was far behind flight plan. Further analysis indicated we were now well short of our planned progress. Forecast conditions farther along our course indicated the possibility of higher components and possible icing in clouds. The surface conditions at our destination and alternate were also deteriorating. We had now been in flight for nearly seven hours. The tension and concern of other flight crew members was building. After a thorough evaluation of our situation, and with great reluctance, the decision was made to reverse course and return to our original point, Shannon, Ireland. The return flight to Shannon required only 3½ hours which verified the lack of progress westbound we had experienced. After landing, the flight crew walked to TWA Shannon offices for debriefing. The crew had been on duty since the departure from Paris. A crew rest period was taken. The turnaround, while justified, still caused a great deal of soul searching to include the thoughts, "Would the high component losses have continued for the remainder of the flight?"

After a rest period and medical attention, the navigator appeared in satisfactory condition to return to duty. The high velocity components continued on the Great Circle course to Gander, Newfoundland. The flight was flown via Santa Maria, Azores to Gander, and then to New York. All North Atlantic navigation charts and data were audited by the TWA operations office. The flight was discussed with the chief pilot. My second thoughts were still there. In the past, we had dead reckoned all the way across the North Atlantic without difficulties. This flight had been fraught with running behind flight plan, in the portion of the flight that was forecast to be routine. The flight west of 30 degrees north longitude was usually the segment for adversity, to include aircraft wing icing. Our conference was without criticism from the chief pilot. Fortunately, it was the only course reversal of my North Atlantic operation.

On the way out of the offices, a stop was made at the chief navigator's office. We reviewed the flight log thoroughly. Upon completion he began to touch upon the emotional breakdown the young chap had experienced. My comments were that the emotional difficulty was understandable; however, the real concern was his decision not to observe a direct order to desist from attempting to get on the navigator stool in the turbulence, and his resulting injury. No pilot should suffer an emotional breakdown. Nevertheless, regarding his position, there was no critical comment on my part. If he wished to continue his employment, it should be his decision. Life is a learning process.

Mediterranean

Man first populated Africa an estimated 4,000,000 years ago. It is widely accepted Africa was the first continent to be populated. Recorded history refers to approximately the past 10,000 years, a relatively small period of time. Ancient history, as we know it, begins in the Middle East, as it was the beginning of written history. Early Babylon was situated on the Euphrates River, which is now part of Iraq; Persia, which is now known as Iran; the states of Arabia, which are now known as Saudi Arabia. Parts of Palestine and the principal city of Jerusalem now comprise Israel. In this period, man lived in what was, perhaps, the "Garden of Eden."

The flights operating to Rome; Athens; Tel Aviv; Cairo; Casablanca; Tripoli; Tunis; Algiers; and Lisbon resulted in flying over the Mediterranean Sea in its entirety. The route of flight over North Africa was from Lisbon to Algiers, Algeria; Tunis, Tunisia; Tripoli, Libya; ultimately to Cairo, Egypt. The coast of North Africa is an area stepped in rich ancient history.

The flight above the Mediterranean from the West over flies the Straits of Gibraltar, on the north the coastline of Europe, on the south the coastline of Africa, to the east the coastline of the Middle East. An entirely different perspective of any area to include the Mediterranean is experienced during extensive flights over the area. The aircraft flown during this period of time were flown at an intermediate altitude at which the area below was clearly visible.

The coast of North Africa extends from the Atlantic Ocean on the west, to a point beyond the Red Sea on the east. The country on the far eastern portion of North Africa is Egypt. This large portion of North Africa is a desert, which receives nearly all of its moisture from the Nile River. In reality, the great expanse of North Africa is an arid desert.

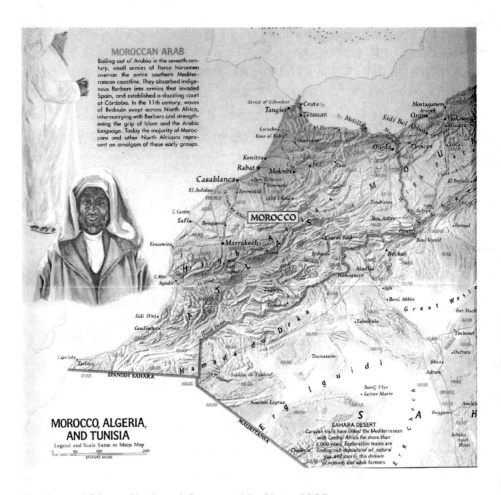

Northern Africa - National Geographic Map, 1982

Flight above this coast viewing the great expanse of desert provokes thoughts as to the cause of the great wasteland. The commerce and development of the greater Mediterranean civilizations, no doubt, resulted in a large depletion of natural resources. Present day Tunis is the location of ancient Carthage, founded by the Phoenicians as early as 9th century B.C. Carthage thrived for centuries until a third war with Rome when the civilization and the city were completely destroyed by the Romans. The destruction of Carthage, the "salting of the earth," and the slaughter of the populace, became known as the Carthaginian Peace. Syracuse (Siracusa) on the Island of Sicily to the north of Carthage was an early trading partner, later an adversary. Syracuse, founded by the Greek civilization, was the home of the Greek Archimedes. The early accurate calculation of Pi, the geometric formula to calculate the circumference of a circle, was a contribution by Archimedes. In this area of the Mediterranean is the Island of Malta, long famous in history to include the Crusades.

Carthage was a major trading center founded by the Phoenicians of Tyre. Thousands of ships were constructed for their commerce. Smelting of metals produced metal, which were made into instruments of war. In order to accomplish this, wood was the only source of energy available at this time. Both enterprises would have consumed large tracts of timber. Other nations of the Mediterranean area also had large fleets of military and commercial vessels, requiring tremendous amounts of timber in their construction.

The large temples and buildings of these early centers, such as Carthage, consumed extensive amounts of timber. After the conquest and burning of cities, more timber was required to rebuild the destruction. Large numbers of wild animals, lions, tigers, leopards, and elephants existed in the immediate coastal area. It seems unlikely the great centers could have been developed, and populated to the degree which they were, if they were on the edge of the now, great, arid Sahara Desert.

The Nile River Valley to the east provides for an appealing, thought provoking scenario. The Sphinx and the Great Pyramids of Giza appear to be a dichotomy in their lack of resemblance. While the Sphinx and the Great Pyramids are in close proximity, the erosion is dissimilar. The Pyramids show erosion from the drifting sands; the Sphinx shows early water erosion, which indicates a large amount of rainfall. The water erosion would have required periods of heavy rainfall. When considered, these factors indicate the existence of a rain forest in North Africa, which during many centuries of use reduced the soil to the existing desert. As man first existed in Africa, this factor becomes more likely. In the development of the race, it is only natural the populations would have to and did move north.

In Cairo, the principal city of Egypt, the window of the Hotel Heliopolis Palace overlooked the wide expanse of desert. The principal structures, which dominate the skyline, are the Pyramids of Giza and the Sphinx. An ancient monument, the Sphinx, incorporates the head of a woman and the body of a lion. When looking out across this great expanse and the ancient monuments, it often occurred to me the striking differences in the architecture between the great Pyramids and the Sphinx. While Egyptologists have insisted these structures are from the same time period, differences make these unlikely. It is the 'chap in the hat' who insists the Great Pyramids, the Sphinx, and other great Egyptian structures were built with volunteer labor, a very unlikely method in a time of widespread slavery. This is more likely a presentation to please the visiting, romantic tourist.

As stated earlier, the type of the erosion visible on the Sphinx indicates a time of considerable precipitation. For this type of the erosion to have occurred, a climate totally unlike that of the present climate would have to exist. The type of climate in all probability would have been that of a rain forest. With this analogy, it is entirely possible that North Africa was a large, luscious rain forest, totally unlike the arid desert of today.

With consideration to the enormous amount of time man has existed on the African continent, the environment has changed dramatically. The large gap in time is poorly documented due to the fact man did not have the capability to record events when they occurred. The first recorded history in this great expanse of time is the Egyptian hieroglyphics. The time frame of ancient Egypt and the surrounding area involves an era of approximately 5,000 years. The tremendous difference in the time involved results in a very lengthy period of time unaccounted for in history, relative to the original existing climate. These facts make it entirely possible the great expanse of desert on

the North African coast was man-made. The removal of
a great rain forest for the uses of man-made purposes
could easily have resulted in the defoliation of a rain
forest. It does not seem likely the great civilizations
such as Carthage could have existed in the current
desert expanse. Food requirements alone for this large
civilization would have required a large cultivatable
area.

During this time period, defoliation of North Africa
could easily have occurred when trees were the only
source of heating fuel. In addition, trees were the only
source of material to construct seagoing vessels. All of
the sea commerce so prevalent in early Mediterranean
history was dependent upon ships at sea. Instruments
of war through the Bronze Age and the Iron Age
required tremendous amounts of fuel to smelt and
create bronze, and later, iron. When all these factors
are considered, the destruction of the rain forest is
more easily understood.

Ancient Rome, in the earliest part of recorded
history, consumed tremendous amounts of natural
resources. Discoveries on the floor of the
Mediterranean Sea have yielded the remains of
seagoing ships in excess of 300 ft in length. Large
fleets of ships, constructed of wood throughout time,
consumed a tremendous amount of forest. When all
factors of the enormous consumption of timber by the
people of North Africa are considered, it is entirely
possible the area was once rich in natural resources,
and was devastated into the existing desert.
Excavations of this great expanse and into the depths
of the sand have yielded little to evaluate the past

civilization. Perhaps the amount of shifting sands throughout the period has destroyed what was once on the surface. Possibly, the importance of the Nile River as the source of water to cultivate the Nile Valley overshadowed other portions of Egypt.

In the time of ancient history, the Mediterranean Sea was referred to as the "Center of the World." In later times, it was termed the "Cradle of Civilization." If this terminology is correct, the cradle or crib must have been a 'Chinese import.' It is obvious the wrong infants fell from the cradle and did not survive. The infants who did survive were the most brutal in the history of the world. Basically, there were but three classes in society; the ruling class, the military, and the slaves. Later, religious subjects became part of this society. There is no geographical part of the world with more historical interest than the area which borders on the Mediterranean Sea.

Flight operations east of Cairo were above the Suez Canal to the north of the Red Sea. On the east shore of the Mediterranean are the countries of Palestine, Lebanon, and Syria. The area between Palestine and Lebanon is the location of ancient Tyre. To the east are the countries of Saudi Arabia, Jordan, Syria, Iraq, and Iran.

Flights from Cairo east made landings at Basra, Iraq and Dhahran, Saudi Arabia en route to Bombay, India.

Proposed Routing from East Coast Terminals

In the proposed original 'around the world' route, operations for TWA were to operate east of Bombay; Calcutta, India; Mandalay, Burma; Hanoi, Vietnam; Hong Kong to what is now Beijing; and Shanghai, China; Seoul, Korea; Tokyo, Japan; then by the great circle route with stops in Russia; Alaska; Seattle, Washington; to San Francisco and Los Angeles. The change in the leadership of China made this flight operation impossible. Consequently, all flights eastbound terminated in Bombay. Flights that originated in Bombay flew westbound.

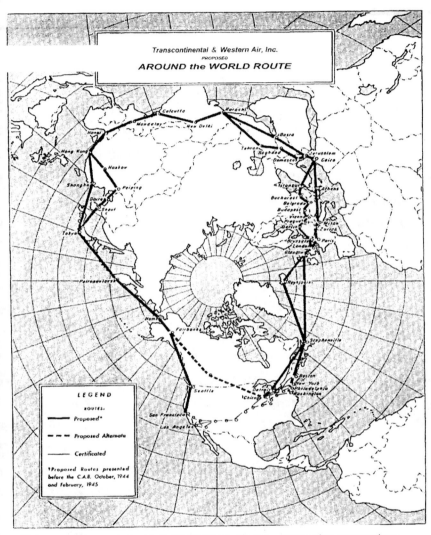

Transcontinental & Western Air, Inc.
PROPOSED
AROUND the WORLD ROUTE

LEGEND

ROUTES:

——— Proposed*

– – – Proposed Alternate

——— Certificated

*Proposed Routes presented
before the C.A.B. October, 1944
and February, 1945

This was the original Frye/Hughes dream. Note the extensive
European Captial coverage and the Middle East and Orient coverage. Frye told me they did not want Bombay and Colombo; neither
did he or Hughes like the Pacific crossing via Guam and Honolulu.
                                          - Larry Trimble

Transcontinental & Western Air proposed Around the World Routes

Political Impediments

During World War II (WWII), China had been allied with the United States. General Chiang Kai-shek had been the leader of the Chinese Nationalist government; in democratic terms, the president of China. Immediately following the end of WWII, a negative campaign was launched in Washington against Chiang Kai-shek. The major negative was that the general had been involved in monetary payoffs, amid other degrading accusations. In operating in this part of the world—Asia—perhaps the only people not involved in payoffs are those who do not have the opportunity to do so. Nonetheless, General Chiang Kai-shek and Madame Chiang Kai-shek were not in the good graces of Washington. Separately, negative accusations were leveled at Madame Chiang Kai-shek. As a result, the Chinese Nationalist government was not able to survive. The loss of the Chinese Nationalist leadership made the takeover of China an easy task for the Russian backed communists. There was no doubt an adequate supply of surplus military armaments in the Pacific to supply the Chinese Nationalist government if Washington had elected to do so. Later, most of this military surplus was sold for pennies on the dollar in the surplus market.

The Chinese communists organized in the north of China, equipped with military armaments provided by Russia, began their conquest of China. Lack of support for the Chinese Nationalists made the conquest by Cho

En Lai and Mao Tse Tung possible. The Chinese Nationalist government, led by General Chiang Kai-shek, was forced to retreat to the Island of Formosa, now Taiwan. The conquest and takeover of China by the Chinese communists was to result in serious consequences for the United States. With support from the Chinese and Russian communists, the North Korean military operation against South Korea was possible. Had the Chinese Nationalists remained in power, the North Korean military operation against South Korea would have been unlikely to occur. North Korea would not have had enough military support to take military action against South Korea. The current international difficulties created by North Korea would have been unlikely without the support of mainland China. A Chinese puppet, North Korea, creates an aggressive policy without being discouraged by China.

The Chinese communist takeover of China eliminated the possibility of TWA continuing the around the world operation as originally proposed. An alternate route structure would be required to complete the around the world service from Bombay. Adequate economic returns could be made with a schedule landing at Hong Kong, a British Colony. Landing rights required British Crown Colony approval. The approval for TWA to serve Hong Kong was not obtained until the mid-1960s. When approval was granted by the British, TWA flight operations began from Bombay; to Bangkok, Thailand; Hong Kong; Taipei; Guam; Honolulu, Hawaii, to Los Angeles, eastbound and westbound. This would complete the TWA Around the World operation.

Prior to WWII, there was little oil production in the Middle East, especially compared to present level of production. An oil production facility in Tehran, Iran was operated by British Petroleum Company. Following an agreement made with the king of Saudi Arabia, this would all change. The massive oil reserves in the Middle East were known, but had not been developed. All the principal governments knew of the existence of the undeveloped Middle East oil reserves. Hitler's conquest of North Africa, including Egypt and the Suez Canal were steps along the way to acquire the vast oil reserves of the Middle East. The German war machine bogged down for the lack of fuel. The successful stand by the British at the Battle of El-Alamein stopped the North African conquest by Germany. With Germany stopped there, they lost their conquest for North Africa and the Middle East oil.

President Franklin D. Roosevelt met with King Saud of Saudi Arabia aboard a United States Navy cruiser in the Red Sea off the coast of Jeddah, Saudi Arabia. The purpose of this conference was to obtain access to the oil reserves of Saudi Arabia. King Saud granted President Roosevelt permission for 'all the oil he wanted providing Palestine would not be partitioned.' President Roosevelt agreed and the agreement was consummated.

TWA was to play an extensive part in the development of the new oil fields and the pipelines necessary to make this oil available for ships at sea. The oil field workers available for this great expansion were, for the most part, from Texas. Great numbers of personnel were flown from the Texas area to New York, then to the Middle East oil fields. After arriving at LaGuardia field, the oil field personnel boarded TWA international flights for the Middle East. The development of these oil facilities required drilling of new wells, and all the required associated oil pipelines. These new oil pipelines were laid to terminals at ports on the Mediterranean Sea and the Persian Gulf.

These new oil fields were remote and, in most cases, did not have an airport serving the area. Accordingly, asphalt runways were constructed at remote points in the desert. These isolated facilities were used by TWA to fly the personnel to their final destination. It was a flight operation of a nature not flown before in the Middle East. The flights were comprised solely of these oil field workers. It was an exceedingly long flight for them from Texas to their destination—the Middle East.

In the late 1940s, the countries in the Middle East had, for the most part, one airport located in each principal city. The principal city in Saudi Arabia was Jeddah. The construction of airports serving the cities we know today had yet to be constructed. ARAMCO, Arabian American Oil was organized at this time. Headquarters were established in Dhahran. A large compound was also constructed to accommodate the American personnel. After the construction of the airport facility at Dhahran, it became part of the regular TWA flight schedule.

TWA headquarters for the Middle East at Cairo, Egypt was located at what had been Payne Field, the U.S. Army Air Force base. The airport was renamed Farouk Airport to honor King Farouk who ruled Egypt at this point in time. This facility housed the aircraft maintenance and overhaul operation for TWA Middle East operations. At this time, TWA proposed to make the facility a major aircraft overhaul base for the entire Middle East. There were many military Douglas C-47 aircraft stored at the facility during WWII. TWA used the facility to modify these aircraft to a DC-3 configuration; to equip many new Middle East airlines, such as Ethiopian and Saudi Arabian Airlines, for their flight operations.

TWA had acquired one of these military C-47s, which was flown in support of the Middle East operation. On many occasions, TWA flew to Jeddah to meet with King Saud and to fly him to any desired destination in Saudi Arabia. Many of these destinations had very limited airport facilities. The pilots flying this operation found the king to be very amicable and enjoyed the association with him. At this time, airport facilities were few and improvised points of landing were necessary. As such, either the Douglas C-47, or DC-3 was capable of these operations. It was this early association with the king of Saudi Arabia that resulted in TWA organizing and supervising the operation of Saudi Arabian Airlines.

TWA modified a fleet of C-47s for the use of Ethiopian Airlines. TWA personnel managed Ethiopian Airlines until the demise of King Haile Selassie I (the little king) at the hands of terrorist forces. The king was very fond of TWA personnel and they remained there until after the advent of the Boeing 707.

Prior to the departure of President Jack Frye from TWA, General T.B. Wilson served as chairman. During his tenure, a new military surplus B-17 was acquired. The B-17 was returned to Boeing Aircraft Company in Seattle, Washington for modification to an executive configuration. After modification, this particular aircraft was flown to the TWA base in Cairo, Egypt where it was then based. General Wilson's tenure was brief. TWA later sold the aircraft to the Shah of Iran. A TWA pilot, Captain Richard "Dick" Colburn, an old personal friend, instructed the Shah of Iran for an extended period of time and qualified him to fly the Boeing B-17. Needless to say, the Shah of Iran thoroughly enjoyed flying the B-17 as his personal executive aircraft.

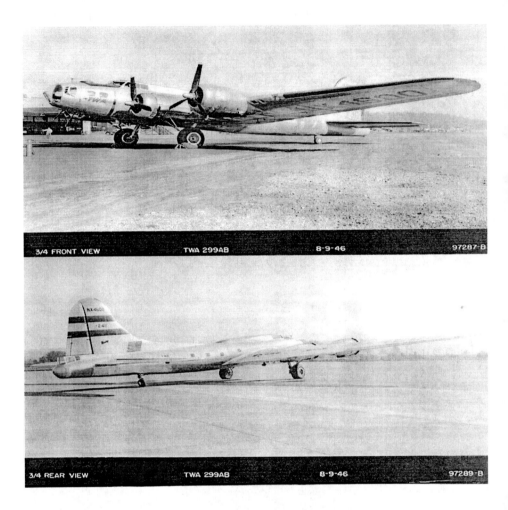

3/4 FRONT VIEW   TWA 299AB   8-9-46   97287-B

3/4 REAR VIEW   TWA 299AB   8-9-46   97289-B

B-17 TWA aircraft modified to executive configuration and located at TWA Cairo, Egypt base was later sold to the Shah of Iran.

and aft lavatory installed in proximity to the entrance door. Directly forward of these facilities was the only area with floor space large enough for the group to conduct their crap game. Unfortunately, the large concentration of the players' body weight had dangerously shifted the center of gravity aft, to where the horizontal elevator correction had been reached, and had passed the maximum aft correction. The participants of the crap game ignored the pleas of the steward to return to their assigned seats.

Rising from the left flight deck seat, the flight engineer was instructed to take the seat vacated by the pilot, and to assist the co-pilot with utmost forward pressure on the control column. A rapid walk to the rear of the passenger cabin confirmed the steward's report. A large number of the passengers were centered in the rear area; the crap game having their undivided attention. An appeal to the participants to disperse was ignored, followed by the command to move forward immediately, as the safety of the fight was in jeopardy. This resulted in the chap with the dice looking up over his shoulder with blood shot eyes stating, "Whooshe the f___ing bellhop?" In these situations, it is obvious command authority is not a factor.

The next command was, "Break it up or the flight will land immediately," in an attempt to establish some form of order. In reality, it was not possible to land as our position over the Mediterranean did not make a quick diversion possible. However, one in the group hanging over a seat in the last row aft said, "Better do as the bellhop says." With that, the game quickly broke up with the participants filing back to their respective seats.

Upon returning to the flight deck, the out of balance condition was easily corrected. Our observation of the situation; there was a condition where the aircraft was close to an uncontrollable aft center of gravity. If it had not been corrected, eventually the aircraft would have gone out of control, striking the waters of the Mediterranean. The circumstances which caused the loss of control would not have been found by any investigation. The report would have noted: aircraft struck the water in a nose down attitude; examination of the power plants indicated they were performing normally, no other structural failure prior to striking the water. Cause of accident: Unknown. Another day and night—another learning experience.

The flight operations in the Mediterranean involved flights originating at the East Coast terminals of the United States. The westbound flight operations either originated in Bombay, India or Cairo, Egypt. In the Mediterranean flight schedules served Rome, Italy; Athens, Greece; Tel Aviv; Palestine; and Cairo, Egypt.

Upon arriving at Farouk Field, Cairo on July 22, 1948, to fly TWA Flight 925 to Athens, Rome, Geneva, and Paris, the TWA station manager advised me officers of the United States Embassy wished to discuss a situation. The meeting took place in the TWA station manager's office. The United States Embassy attaché advised Mrs. Frederick Haas of Philadelphia was to be a passenger onboard the flight to New York. He conveyed the Embassy's concern for the safety of Mrs. Haas. Mr. Frederick Haas had been killed by a mob on the 19th of July during their Cairo visit. The attaché expressed his wish Mrs. Haas be given personal security while on board the TWA flight. His desire was for the captain to personally take charge of Mrs. Haas during the flight.

In order to comply with such a wish, it would be necessary for Mrs. Hass to be carried in the flight crew section of the aircraft. This possible solution was explained to the members of the embassy. As this was the only possible solution to their request, all parties concurred. Prior to the boarding of the other passengers, it was planned for Mrs. Haas to board the aircraft and be escorted by the captain to the flight crew section. The aircraft to be flown on this flight was a DC-4 with a crew section, in addition to the flight deck. There was an additional area to accommodate a navigation plotting table, and a crew rest facility. These additional quarters were necessary as the aircraft was operated on flights over the North Atlantic. It was in this area that Mrs. Hass would be accommodated for her flight to New York.

Once airborne, there was time for individual attention and discussions with Mrs. Haas. The story of her tragic encounter, as well as her husband's fatal encounter, was as follows. While in Cairo, Mr. and Mrs. Hass had gone on a sightseeing excursion, which included a visit to the university section. While in this section of Cairo, they came face to face with a large violent group. In this malicious and brutal encounter with the mob, Mr. Haas was stoned to death before Mrs. Haas' eyes, and his body dragged off by the mob. The murder occurred before any Cairo police arrived on the scene. This tragic confrontation was rapid and violent, without any opposition to the offenders. Following the murder of her husband, Mrs. Haas was taken to a police facility in Cairo. She was held captive by the Cairo police and, during this captivity, was not allowed to communicate with anyone. The situation became extremely frightening to her as she feared she was being held while a plan was developed for her demise. If she disappeared, there would be no account of this tragedy. The conclusion: Mr. and Mrs. Frederick Haas would be missing. Approximately two days after the murder occurred, an officer of a British oil company heard what had happened, and that Mrs. Haas was being held by the police. The officer of this British oil company advised the British Embassy, which in turn advised the United States Embassy of the situation, and her ongoing unlawful detention. The result was the immediate release of Mrs. Haas to the personnel of the United States Embassy. At this time, the remains of Mr. Haas had not been recovered.

The partitioning of Palestine had occurred creating the state of Israel and immediately the armed conflict with the Arab states had erupted. The state of war between Egypt and Israel served to inflame the university students. The Haas tragedy was a result of this mob action.

The entire TWA flight crew made every possible effort to extend their greatest sympathy and attention. The flight from Cairo involved scheduled landings at Athens, Rome, and Geneva, before arriving Orly Airport Paris. Upon arrival at Paris, a scheduled flight crew change was made with a new crew flying the DC-4 to New York. Before the departure from Paris, a conference was held with the outbound flight crew to advise them of the requirement for those remaining flights, in support of Mrs. Haas, to complete her flight to Philadelphia, PA. Under the direct supervision of the flight crew, there were no further threats to Mrs. Haas during the flight from Cairo. Upon arrival in New York, the distraught widow refused comment to the press.

To prepare for another TWA flight from Cairo, Egypt, the procedure was to perform preflight planning procedures in the TWA dispatch office. While in the process of filing the necessary data for the scheduled flight from Cairo to Paris, a message came over the communications radio. Philippines Airlines advised us their flight arriving in Cairo had feathered (shut down) an engine. As a result, the flight would cancel upon arrival. Their immediate question was, "Could TWA accommodate their passengers from Cairo to their Rome destination?"

The question presented the following; our TWA flight was scheduled to operate non-stop from Cairo to Paris. Would we consider landing at Rome en route to accommodate the Philippines Airlines passengers? Personal concurrence was immediately proffered with flight plans and associated changes made. The TWA flight would now operate from Cairo to Rome, then Paris, and then as previously scheduled to New York, N.Y.

The difference in the customs of the people from the Middle East often created situations worthy of note.

While approaching the boarding stair located at the rear entrance of the aircraft to board the flight for departure, a loud, unfriendly conversation was taking place. The difference of opinion was between a TWA passenger and the TWA passenger agent, who was in the process of boarding passengers. Tucked under the passenger's arm was a burlap sack with an Airedale's head protruding from the sack. The argument had occurred because the passenger wished to board the aircraft with his pet Airedale in the bag. The TWA passenger agent was insistent the dog be placed in the baggage compartment. Of course, this was company policy which the agent had to enforce. In addition, the agent, of Arabic origin, regarded a dog as a very lowly form of life. After listening to this long, unpleasant encounter, the passenger agent was advised to allow the passenger to board with his pet. This was not accomplished without considerable objection by the agent involved. However, the captain usually prevails. With the boarding problem resolved, the flight prepared for departure.

The aircraft had one boarding entrance at the rear of the aircraft through which both passengers and crew entered. It was necessary to walk the complete length of the cabin to reach the door to the flight deck. Walking up the aisle to the flight deck, a brightly attired passenger with a colorful Niqab on her head was noted sitting in the forward section. In greeting her, the woman identified herself as 'Syrian' of Arabic origin. The lady had beaming eyes, representing a radiant personality, exuding great enthusiasm. In addition to this enthusiasm, her greeting was an outstretched palm passed in an arc before her face. The motion of her hand over her face was similar to the well known 'high sign.' This manner of greeting was not only pleasant, but particularly interesting. Her presence on board would prove more fascinating as the flight progressed.

While en route, the extremely gratified passenger with his Airedale, "Curry," upon numerous occasions expressed his thanks to the cabin crew. Before arriving at his destination, he presented a paper with his name, address, and telephone number in Switzerland. In addition to this personal information was an invitation to contact him at any opportunity when in Switzerland. On one of many later visits to Switzerland, Hans was contacted. The result has been a long, lasting friendship with him and his family. Differences in cultures often lead to situations, if properly addressed, can result in the most positive conclusion.

The flight was flown with a Lockheed Constellation aircraft and departed Cairo for Rome. Shortly after over flying Alexandria on the north coast of Egypt, the sun was setting in the west over the Mediterranean. At midpoint over the Mediterranean, just west of the island of Crete, an engine failure occurred and the propeller was feathered. This procedure is followed to stop the rotation of a failed engine. The fact the flight was now in total darkness, the decision was made to divert the flight to land at Athens, Greece. After landing and arriving in Athens, the engine failure required the flight be delayed. This made it necessary to find overnight lodgings for the passengers and the flight crew.

At this time, Greece was under siege by the communists from the north. Salonika, the principal city of northern Greece, was under the control of communists. As a result, after sundown Athens was under curfew and martial law. This made finding accommodations at that hour extremely difficult. After some delay, accommodations were found in a remote rural lodge and all proceeded there to spend the night.

The following morning a Constellation aircraft was flown to Athens to replace the out of service aircraft, and to proceed with the flight continuance. All passengers reported in, including the lady from Damascus, who promptly greeted us with her open palm moving sweepingly in front of her face. The flight then continued on to Rome, where our accommodated passengers from Philippine Airlines, along with Hans and his Airedale still in the bag, deplaned. The flight departed from Rome for Paris. During takeoff, shortly after leaving the ground, the control tower operator excitedly and loudly exclaimed over the radio, "TWA, you are on fire!"

At that moment our instrumentation did not indicate any fire. The controller's excitement, together with his heavy accent, made further reception difficult. However, by a sudden indication on the instrument panel, it was ascertained his reference was to an engine. During our takeoff roll, just as we left the ground, a large black cloud of smoke and flames had erupted from an engine. The engine, which was the source of the problem, could not be determined from the controller's transmission. With some delay, the flight instruments indicated which engine had failed and was on fire. Immediately upon this detection, the engine was shut down, and the propeller feathered.

While returning to land, the fire was extinguished. Landing was made as soon as possible and the aircraft taxied to the terminal building. Once again the flight was interrupted.

The following day the aircraft was made available to resume the delayed flight. The failed engine had been removed and replaced by a newly overhauled Wright 3350. Upon arrival at the TWA Rome dispatch office, the first question was, "What goes between you and the lady from Syria?"

After our flight interruption the previous day, the passengers were rebooked on another TWA flight bound for Paris and New York. Apparently, after boarding the aircraft, the lady from Syria opened the flight deck door and entered. She immediately stepped down into the flight deck and looked at the captain. When discovering a change had taken place, she deplaned and declined to proceed further on the flight. Of course, this was the subject of much humorous ridicule, and as the saying goes, a good laugh was had by all at the captain's expense. Upon boarding the aircraft for departure from Rome, we were once again greeted with the 'high sign' by our beaming, delightful lady from Syria. The flight proceeded from Rome to Paris, where a normal crew change was to occur for the flight to New York. Due to the two engine failures we had experienced while en route to Paris over a two day period, crews had been moved up to fly the flight we would normally have flown the previous day. As a result, there was no crew in Paris to fly the flight to New York. The only solution was for our flight deck crew to continue flying the flight from Paris, France with fuel stops at Shannon, Ireland;

Gander, Newfoundland; and then to New York. This made for a slightly longer flight, but necessity dictates decisions.

The fact we were continuing on to New York did solve one problem. As we re-boarded the aircraft, the jovial lady was happy to see us. There would not be a problem for the continuation of her flight with a new captain. We flew on to New York, and as our gracious lady departed for the customs and immigration offices, we were greeted one final time with the same 'high sign.' If ego was served, it would have been possible there was some personal reason for the lady from Damascus to wish to reach her destination with me. In reality, ego aside, it was obvious in her mind; she had attached the face of the original captain with her arrival in New York. Simply put, the original caravan leader would take the caravan of passengers to their destination without a change of that leader. In this case, due to the engine failures, the leader had returned the following day to continue the caravan. Also, it was an old custom to present the caravan leader with an expensive gift. But in this case, it did not happen. While often trying, flying in the international division was also extremely appealing.

At this time, the Lockheed Constellation had been in airline operation less than two years. The Curtiss Wright BA-3350 engines were causing a great deal of irregular flight operation due to failures of several internal parts. Engine fires were not uncommon. This failure of the Wright 3350 engine had been prevalent in their use, powering the Boeing B-29 long range bombers. As more flight operation followed, the engine would reach a more acceptable operating level. The later model BD-3350 would prove to be a more reliable power plant. As such, the original BA-3350 would pose reliability problems for the duration of the Constellation flight operation which continued until the Jet Age.

On another flight operation, we had flown a TWA Trans-Atlantic flight from New York to Shannon, Ireland. Upon landing and taxiing to the terminal, we parked next to another TWA Constellation. After deplaning, there was considerable activity around the other aircraft, which attracted our attention. We walked to the other Constellation and were advised the westbound flight had been delayed. There was a mechanical malfunction in the hydraulic system. The gauge on the instrument panel had indicated the supply of hydraulic fluid in the reservoir was low. Hydraulic fluid had been added to the reservoir tank to bring the level up to the desired level. However, when the engines were started, the reservoir indicator quickly dropped to a low indication level. The obvious problem; there was a leak somewhere in the system, which was not found visually. There was no external presence of red hydraulic fluid, which would have been easily seen. In order to detect the hydraulic leak, the decision was made to start an engine with an operating hydraulic pump. Hydraulic fluid would be constantly added to the system until the leak was found. This procedure was in progress when we arrived on the scene. After the addition of several gallons of hydraulic fluid, a small amount of red fluid was seen dripping from the aft baggage compartment door, which had remained closed. When the aft compartment door was opened, a deluge of hydraulic fluid drenched the person opening the door. The leak had been in a hydraulic line located at the top of the compartment. This line supplied hydraulic pressure to the control boost system located in the tail section.

In the process known as 'trouble shooting,' some fifty-five gallons of hydraulic fluid had been added to the system. The cargo compartment was full of passenger and crew luggage. It had taken sometime for all the luggage and contents to become fully saturated before the fluid was seen dripping from the aft compartment door. Since the entire contents of passenger luggage were now completely saturated, the passenger service people were given a real problem to cope with. All contents, including the luggage, had to be replaced. Just recently, a TWA crew member had a complete wardrobe tailored in Rome. His entire luggage complement, to consist of three, fully filled suitcases, had been in the aft cargo compartment. His dilemma: personal belongings, including his new clothes, would not be replaced by the company. While there have been many "goofs" in the airline industry, this one ranks high on the list.

Israel Re-Inauguration of Air Service

TWA flights in the Middle East, the Mediterranean, were flown Rome, Athens, Tel Aviv, Cairo, eastbound; the same cities were served westbound in the reverse order. Prior to World War I, Palestine had been a part of the Ottoman Empire. For over 700 years, the Ottoman Turks had ruled the Ottoman Empire. The Ottoman Empire was ruled by those of the Muslim faith. However, others with different religious beliefs also occupied parts of the empire. Since World War I, Palestine had been a British Protectorate. In 1948, Palestine was partitioned giving sovereignty to Israel. As a sovereign nation, conflict erupted immediately between Israel and the Arab nations.

When the hostilities began, the fighting encompassed the entire area surrounding Lydda, the airport serving Tel Aviv. The military conflict resulted in the immediate cessation of flight operations to Lydda by all international air carriers. These airlines included TWA, British European, Swissair, and Air France among others. As a result, there was no air service for Tel Aviv, Israel.

In the spring of 1949, the United States Department of State determined scheduled flights into Lydda Airport, Tel Aviv, should be restored. Through the U.S. Civil Aeronautics, the State Department contacted TWA to restore this air service.

TWA was operating the International Division under temporary authority granted by the Civil Aeronautics Board. In 1947 Congressional hearings had been held in Washington, D.C. Howard Hughes had personally appeared to defend the Hughes Aircraft Company, which had been charged with irregularities in the development of the eight-engine flying boat. The investigation had been chaired by Senator Brewster of Maine. Howard Hughes and Senator Brewster had engaged in acrimonious conversations. The hearing was the centerpiece of Washington news. Howard Hughes had noted Senator Brewster's close association with Juan Trippe, president of Pan American Airways. Hughes had established the connection to be of political importance to the TWA International Division, which Trippe strongly opposed. The situation was intensely volatile as the future of the TWA International Division was at stake. As president of Pan American, Juan Trippe had asked the Civil Aeronautics Board to revoke TWA's temporary certificate to operate the TWA International Division. The re-establishment of air service to Tel Aviv was made a central issue.

During this time, TWA was without a president, since Jack Frye had not been replaced. The operational leadership was in the hands of Warren Lee Pierson, who was chairman of the board of directors and acting president, as well as the chief executive officer of another major American corporation. Key policies were to be pursued by the acting president. Authorization to add London, England, and Frankfurt, Germany, to the International Division system was on file with the Civil Aeronautics Board. From a purely political position, this proposal was opposed by Pan American Airways. Adding further fuel to the fire of this politically charged issue, Pan Am had stated to the Civil Aeronautics Board, "Why give TWA more when TWA does not serve the cities they currently have?" This reference was to the termination of the Tel Aviv, Israel service. At this time, TWA was the only United States carrier serving Rome. Pan American had applied to the Civil Aeronautics Board to add service to Rome as part of their European network. The political infighting had involved many government bureaus. As Pan American possessed a permanent authority while TWA was operating on a temporary certificate, the situation made the TWA position more difficult. In January of 1949, Mr. Ralph A. Damon became president of TWA; Mr. Pierson remained as chairman of the board. Mr. Damon left American Airlines when Mr. C.R. Smith, president of American sold their international division, American Overseas Airlines (AOA), to Pan American. Mr. Damon had opposed the "chosen instrument" policy advocated by Pan American. The chosen instrument policy would have made Pan American the only American international carrier serving the international flight operations. Mr. Damon fully concurred with Mr. Hughes in the opposition to the policy advocated by Pan American, which was to eliminate TWA from international flight operations.

This request to restore air service to Israel was a difficult one for TWA to comply with. Restoring air services under the existing conflict presented many problems. However, all TWA people recognized this request had to be put into motion immediately.

The conflict involved all of the Arab states, regardless of the fact that not all were involved in the actual fighting. Nevertheless, the Arab states not currently involved in the fighting were in sympathy with those who were involved. The center of TWA Mediterranean flight operations was at Cairo, Egypt.

In 1948 the partitioning of Palestine by the United Nations occurred with the approval of President Harry S. Truman. This was contrary to the agreement made by President Franklin D. Roosevelt with King Saud of Saudi Arabia.

When the conflict began, the Air Line Pilots Association (ALPA) and the International Air Line Pilots Association immediately instituted a policy which directed all member pilots not to fly into the area of conflict. This policy was established with regard to the safety of the passengers, as well as the flight crews.

The policy of Airline Pilots Association was not the only difficulty to be faced in order to re-establish airline service into Lydda Airport. The TWA facility there had been closed; all personnel had been dispersed, along with the necessary ground support equipment. The aircraft to be flown would require insurance coverage on the passengers, as well as the aircraft. In itself, this was a major undertaking. Since the request to reinstate service was from the Civil Aeronautics Board, and in spite of numerous obstacles, TWA proceeded accordingly.

Flight Assignment-Israel

In order to fly the inaugural flight proposed for July of 1949, it would be necessary to assign a flight crew to fly the flight. Cairo, Egypt, was the domicile of the Middle East based TWA flight crews. It was only natural to have the Cairo based flight crews fly the proposed flight from Rome to Tel Aviv. The Cairo based crews could be flown on a TWA flight from Cairo to Rome. The fact ALPA had advised all pilots concerned <u>not</u> to fly in this area of conflict, and the fact the Cairo-based crews had family living in Cairo, the Cairo based crews declined. Whereupon the chief pilot of TWA International Division based in New York was given the assignment to provide a flight crew to fly this operation.

Captain Harry E. Campbell was chief pilot of TWA International Division. The official title: Superintendent of Flight Operations, Atlantic Region. Harry was well known to all in this division. The chief scheduler for all the pilots in this operation was a gregarious Irishman, Jim O'Malley. As the plans for these Middle East operations were in progress, the telephone rang.

"Hello, Lyle. This is Jim. We need a captain for Rome assignment to fly the Rome to Tel Aviv flight operation."

The immediate reply was, "Jim, you are aware of the ALPA stand on this matter. And secondly, why call me?"

The reply was, "Well, Lyle, you have flown the route and are qualified to fly the route."

"Who told you all of this, Jim?"

The reply, "You know who Lyle, Captain Campbell."

"Jim, you are a fine person and are well regarded. But, the answer is, NO!"

"Lyle, Captain Campbell isn't going to like this."

"No offense, Jim. It is quite possible he will call back."

This was the understatement of the day as the phone rang shortly thereafter. It was Captain Harry Campbell with the same dialogue; the number of any qualified crew was relatively small at this time. To more fully understand the situation, a full complement of captains in the International Division was quite small by today's standards. The contention by Captain Harry; there were few captains in the New York domicile who were qualified in the Middle East. A known fact; there were not any radio navigational facilities in the Tel Aviv area. Further statements by Captain Harry were made relative to the fact past experience was necessary. When talking with Captain Harry on one occasion, it was brought to his attention the operation could easily be flown by any one of the Cairo based captains. The answer to this statement was already known. The reply was made by a highly irritated respondent. The telephone calls from the chief pilot's office continued.

As a further complication, TWA had applied to the Civil Aeronautics Board to add service to London and Frankfurt, both of which were currently served by the competitor, Pan American Airlines. Not surprisingly, as stated earlier, Pan Am had objected and had countered with, "Why give TWA more cities when they do not serve what they have?"

Obviously this meant Lydda Airport–Tel Aviv, Israel. The timing of the Pan Am counter was embarrassing and put more pressure on TWA to resume service. Under the existing industry competition, the dialogue was familiar and the Pan Am requests were denied. Later, TWA was granted approval by the Civil Aeronautics Board to serve both London and Frankfurt.

The last week in June arrived, with plans to fly regular schedules, and enjoy the summer at the lake. Another telephone call was received from Captain Harry. This time Captain Harry advised the inaugural schedule was set for 5th of July and someone had to fly the inaugural. At this point, it was suggested all previous TWA inaugural flights had been flown by the front office pilot, who were management personnel. Why was this inaugural flight operation any different? Ignoring the question, Captain Harry persisted that the flight had to be flown, and the deadline was rapidly approaching. At this time Captain Harry was advised, if concurrence was reached to fly the inaugural flight from Rome to Tel Aviv, and return flight to Rome, it would be highly unlikely the assignment in Rome would end at that time. It was also suggested once in Rome, appeals to be relieved would be ignored. Captain Harry assured me this would not be the case. Harboring strong suspicions to the contrary, an agreement was reached to fly the inaugural flight.

On July 2, 1949, in command of the flight to Rome, the flight departed from LaGuardia Field, New York, and arrived at Ciampino Airport, Rome, on the 3rd of July. Accommodations for my stay during the inaugural flight operation had been made by the TWA Rome office. The temporary residence was a suite on the top floor of the Albergo Continentale. To be occupying a suite gave the first clue the assignment was not to be of short duration. This had been suspected during the initial discussion, though a single flight had been assured.

The suite did turn out to have difficulties. Often, when arriving back at the Albergo, a card would be hanging on the elevator cage, "non funzonia." This meant a climb up all the stairs to reach the top floor suite. In many ways, Italy had not recovered from WWII. Repairs and spare parts were not readily available. Air-conditioning was non-existent. The climb to the top of the hotel during the day, with a temperature of 100 degrees Fahrenheit, was a trifle fatiguing. The cause of the equipment malfunctions was the interruption of electrical power. The lights would repeatedly flicker on and off; then, go off, for extended periods.

The plan of operation in the re-instatement of air service to Lydda Airport was to fly from Rome to Lydda; then originate a return flight to Rome, which was to be a connection point with other TWA flights. The procedure at this time regarding all transport aircraft; each aircraft carried an individual logbook assigned to the specific aircraft, and its identification numbers. This logbook was in addition to another logbook, which dealt with maintenance matters. The logbook was a carryover from the ships at sea, and by law, must be presented at each port of call. This procedure posed a particular problem for this flight operation. When presented at the ports of call, the log books were stamped with the port name and country therein. The armed conflict, which was taking place in the Middle East, created a challenging situation. If an aircraft landed in Israel, the logbook entry would show this landing as a permanent part of the aircraft records. If the aircraft later landed in one of the Arab countries, it could be subject to detention.

In order to cope with this problem, it was decided to designate one aircraft for use in this operation. Upon the completion of this operation, it would be returned to service in TWA's Domestic flight operation. Consequently, we used a new Lockheed Model 749 Constellation. This new aircraft offered the possibility of a maintenance-free operation. The decision was also influenced by fact there were no maintenance facilities at Lydda, Israel.

Flight scheduling set up a departure from Rome at midnight local time. The approximate six-hour flight plan to Lydda made the arrival of the flight just after sunrise. This was important as all passengers traveling to or from Lydda Airport to Tel Aviv would be part of an armed convoy. The armed convoy was necessary as the conflict was taking place in all directions surrounding the airport. The convoy was made up of armed vehicles and Sherman tanks, which had been brought in from Germany. The elapsed time transporting passengers in both directions in an armed convoy would take most of the daylight hours. The schedules had been set up accordingly with a proposed departure for Rome after sundown. Flight operations were conducted day or night as this was not a limiting factor. If electrical power was interrupted or unavailable, which frequently happened, flare pots were located at the ends of the runway for flight operations during darkness.

Communications between Lydda Airport and Tel Aviv were limited to one telephone line for use by both civilian and military. The telephone line often suffered interruptions due to the ongoing ground conflict. Later, TWA was to obtain a VHF radio unit for communications between the TWA office at Lydda Airport and the TWA office in Tel Aviv. Under the existing difficulties, departing passengers could not be manifested until the armed convoy arrived at the airport. Of utmost importance, the ongoing conflict made armed convoys mandatory. This operation could only be carried out during daylight hours. For this reason, the original plan called for arrival operations at daybreak, in order to give both convoys a full period of daylight in which to operate.

Food service, usually an accepted fact by the passengers, was difficult to provision aboard the flight departing Lydda for Rome. Food was in extremely short supply for the entire country of Israel. The populace was literally starving, to include the TWA personnel. A consideration to place adequate food aboard in Rome to service the return flight was given long examination. Due to inadequate food galley space aboard the aircraft, the plan had to be discarded. Further consideration had to be given to the fact it was the month of July. Daytime temperatures in both cities were in excess of 100° Fahrenheit. The flight time from Rome to Tel Aviv, plus the long turn-around period, made the possibility of food contamination highly likely. Therefore, there was no food service for the Tel Aviv origination. As the outgoing passengers from Tel Aviv to Rome fully understood the food scarcity in Israel, this did not cause a problem.

Zionist goal, a national home for Jews in Palestine, won British support in the 1917 Balfour Declaration, which also promised that nothing would prejudice the rights of Arab residents. Jewish immigration increased during the mandate, becoming a tide with Nazi persecution in Europe.

Conflict grew as Jews acquired more land and Palestinian Arabs resisted the newcomers. Extremists on both sides resorted to terrorism. Seeking a peaceful solution, the newly formed United Nations adopted a plan to divide the country. Jews accepted partition; Arabs did not.

Britain withdrew in 1948, and the State of Israel was proclaimed. War broke out as Arab armies supported Palestinian claims to the land. Israel won three-fourths of Palestine, and Jordan annexed the West Bank. More than 600,000 Arabs left Israel, many to live in U.N.-supported refugee camps.

Clashes escalated between Arab neighbors and Israel. In the six-day war of June 1967, Israel occupied the land shown; some 250,000 Arabs fled from the West Bank. Conflicts among the Arab nations, the Palestinians, and Israel complicate resolution of the quarrel and feed international tensions.

Evolution of Palestine 1920 to 1967 National Geographic Map, 1982.

On July 5, 1949, at 22:10 local time, TWA Flight 912 departed from Ciampino Airport, Rome, on the inaugural flight to Lydda—Tel Aviv, Israel. The aircraft was TWA709, CAA N91209, a new 749 Model Constellation christened, "THE STAR of LYDDA." Some of the flight crew had been assigned to the operation using inverse seniority. The flight hostess, Miss Adele Kaczlowski, had volunteered. It was her desire to spend her 'off duty' time in Rome sight-seeing.

A management decision had been made for the inaugural flight to make a schedule landing in Athens, Greece. It was their logic to make this a diversionary appearance in the operation of the flight. There was no personal concurrence. The flight would operate to Tel Aviv in any event. Air traffic control existed within the vicinity of the airports in use, usually a 50 kilometer radius from the major airport. There was no airway traffic control in the Mediterranean; radar was not installed at any point. The presence of an aircraft could only be established if that aircraft made radio transmission, advising their position. Three hours later, during early morning hours, TWA Flight 912 landed in Athens. The Athens bound passengers were deplaned. Because there was no high-octane aviation fuel available at Lydda at this time, the aircraft was refueled in Athens, with sufficient fuel for the continuation flight to Lydda, and the return flight to Rome. Future flights departing Rome for Tel Aviv were fueled with a maximum fuel load for the round-trip sequence. This fueling procedure would remain in place during the entire operation.

After departure, the flight from Athens over flies the islands of the Aegean Sea, then above the island of Rhodes to include the famous Harbor of Rhodes. This is the location of the Colossus of Rhodes, one of the seven wonders of the ancient world. The flight passes south of the island of Cyprus, long famous in ancient and recent history. After crossing the coastline just past daybreak 3 hours 10 minutes later, TWA Flight 912 landed at Lydda Airport on the morning of July 6, 1949, completing the re-inaugural flight from Rome to Tel Aviv.

Immediately after landing, military ordinance was present everywhere. While parking the aircraft at the terminal building, U.S. Sherman tanks could be seen surrounding the terminal building. The dignitaries of Israel warmly greeted the arrival as it ended the isolation of Israel by air from the outside world. The entire crew was greeted by the Israeli dignitaries and was invited to attend the inaugural ceremony. In addition to the ceremonies, every effort was made to offer food. Considering the food shortage which existed in the entire country, this was a supreme effort.

One of the items of particular interest in the buffet setting was beer in bottles. There were no breweries in Palestine to brew any malt beverage. The bottles of beer on the buffet were easily recognized as 'home brewed,' a brew easily identified by the presence of the yeast in the bottom of the bottle. In the home brewing process, the yeast is allowed to remain during bottling in order to carbonate the beer. During Prohibition, home brewing was a common practice. This process had not been observed since my youth. There was great temptation to sample the Israeli homebrew. However, partaking of alcohol in uniform was forbidden and the temptation dismissed.

There were many necessary technical problems to be discussed during the time at Lydda. Consequently, time spent at the inaugural reception was short. The meeting with the minister of aviation had been scheduled first. As a result, the TWA staff meeting would be delayed accordingly.

The meeting with the aviation minister was conducted in his office on the second floor of the operations building. First on the agenda was the discussion regarding the status of the non-directional radio beacon. The non-directional radio beacon, frequency 415 kcs, was not in operation when we arrived. It was the only radio facility for the Lydda Airport. The CAA Form 511, which had been assigned for my signature, called for the radio facility to be in operation as part of the Form 511 specifications. In reality, the operation of this radio facility was not expected to be operating when we departed Rome. However, the regulations were in place. The armed conflict around the airport often caused destruction of some of the facilities. It was a full time military priority and operation to keep the road to Tel Aviv open.

The minister advised the radio transmitter had been damaged during the early military conflict and repair parts were on request. The requirement of the non-directional beacon relative to the CAA 511 Form, which approved flight operation in the airport, was a definite requirement. In order to avoid cancellation of the 511 approval form, it was suggested to the minister he advise the Paris office of the U.S. CAA that the radio beacon was temporarily out of service. The minister concurred and the next subject regarding air communications began.

The Israeli requirement to contact the Lydda control tower prior to entering the approach corridor made the use of high frequency radio mandatory. It was certain the Farouk Airport, Cairo control tower was monitoring these radio frequencies. Since a state of war existed between Israel and Egypt, our flight operation into Lydda could be considered a covert operation by the Egyptian government. The TWA flight to and from Lydda was at times only 100 miles offshore from the Egyptian coastline. The Egyptian Air Force possessed British Spitfire fighters, and their bases in northern Egypt made our flight path easily reached. However, our flight path was not in the control tower airspace. Thus, we were not required to contact Cairo radio. It was correct to assume our radio contacts with the Lydda control tower had been monitored by Cairo. Consequently, Cairo radio stations would be on alert to monitor our communications with the Lydda control tower during our proposed departure for Rome. Under the circumstances, it appeared advisable to use a light gun for ground clearance and takeoff clearance, instead of radio communication. The minister of aviation did not concur, citing the ongoing military conflict and the required use of the departure corridor. There were other issues discussed, but were to remain unresolved at this point. The meeting was then concluded.

Next, a lengthy meeting was held with the TWA station manager, Mr. Stan Swank, his staff of ground supervisors, and the flight crew. Mr. Swank was the sole American representative at the airport. The first subject was flight security.

From the time of origin of the TWA International Division, there had always been an awareness of subversive, fatal activity. In later years, TWA Middle East flight operations were to suffer; the loss of aircraft, passengers, and flight crews, due to skyjackings and explosives put aboard by various methods.

There was a long history of fatal dirty tricks by malcontents or dissidents. One particularly nasty procedure: to place a stick of dynamite with a percussion cap attached, in the nose gear compartment in such a position where, as the nose landing gear retracted, it would make contact with the percussion cap, triggering an explosion. The location of the nose gear housing directly below the flight deck resulted in the fatal destruction of the aircraft.

There were no passenger security checks in effect at Lydda Airport. As a result, the question of baggage inspection was a major concern. The fact there would be no baggage inspection by the airport personnel required our participation. After much discussion, all concurred that matching passenger baggage to each individual passenger would be required.

Under these circumstances, a policy was developed to have all passengers personally identify their luggage before it was allowed to be placed aboard the aircraft. The bag matching was accomplished by placing the loaded baggage carts at the rear of the aircraft, close to the passenger boarding stair. Everyone, including crew members, had to board the aircraft using the aft entrance door. As the passengers approached the boarding stair, they were required to personally identify their luggage. Not until every piece of luggage had been identified by the owner would it be placed aboard the aircraft. This procedure was lengthy and added much time to the flight origination process. Under the circumstances, it was the only possible plan. Some years later, the Israelis would claim to have originated "bag matching." However, it was here at the TWA office at Lydda Airport that the "bag matching" plan originated.   There were many other issues to resolve and operations procedures requiring review. The meeting was lengthy.

Shortly after arrival, the remainder of the flight crew was taken to a rest area. The ongoing armed conflict made leaving the airport impossible. The only rest facilities available were exceptionally small rooms on the second floor. These rooms contained a single cot.

The size of the room was slightly larger than the size of the cot. Therefore, it was necessary to be on the cot in order to close the door. The airport administration building had been built by the British to be a combination of military and civilian aircraft operation for Palestine. As a result, there were no overnight billeting facilities available.

The fact the TWA Flight 912 had made a scheduled landing at Athens before arrival at Lydda, the flight arrived one and one-half hours later than if the flight had operated Rome to Lydda nonstop. This hour and one-half delayed arrival was critical. The daylight time available, during which the armed convoy needed to operate, was reduced. The difficulties in operating a secure convoy required the full daylight period. The return convoy, transporting the outbound flight passengers for Rome, arrived at Lydda as the sun passed below the horizon. If there had been any further delay, the convoy would have been detained in Tel Aviv until the following morning.

The meetings and other situations required nearly all of the time at Lydda and made for a very short rest period in the spacious one cot room. A shave was accomplished in the station manager's office; the water was neither hot nor cold.

The departure for Rome was delayed by many operational problems to include the necessity for matching baggage to each individual passenger. This delay was anticipated and dealt with accordingly.

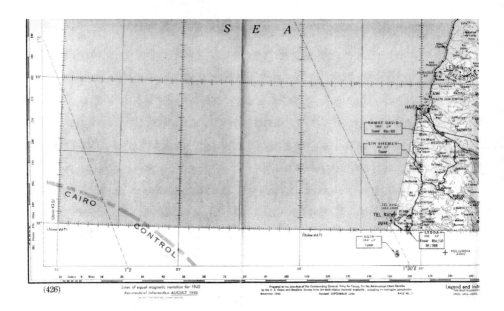

Cairo Control Airspace and Tel Aviv, Israel-AAF Aeronautical Chart, August 1946.

TWA Flight 915 of the 6th of July departed Lydda at 23:06 local time. The departure was made using radio contacts with the Lydda control tower as requested by the Israeli minister of aviation. The airport is situated 20 miles east southeast of the Mediterranean coastline. Shortly after takeoff, approaching the coastline, and still on the same radio frequency, a transmission from Cairo radio; "TWA Flight 915, what was your time off Lydda?"

We had anticipated Cairo radio had monitored our radio transmissions on the inbound flight. The Cairo radio requests went unanswered. The same requests by Cairo radio were to follow. The designated Farouk Airport air space did not project north of the coastline of Egypt far enough to be entered into by our flight. Airway traffic control over the Mediterranean was nonexistent. Consequently, any such position reporting was not required.

Apprehension about the request by Cairo radio for our time off Lydda was one of concern for our safety. Since a state of war existed between Egypt and Israel, the reaction by the Arab states to TWA restoring air service to Israel was unknown. The true airspeed of the 749 Constellation was known by the Cairo aviation centers. Many flight plans for departures from Cairo had been filed indicating the true airspeed, and other performance data of the airplane. Given the time off Lydda, it would be simple to calculate our positions along the course to Rome. In the initial stages of the flight, our position was as close as 100 miles from the coastline of Egypt. It was a known factor the Egyptian Air Force possessed British Spitfire fighters. The interception of our flight along our course could be easily accomplished by Spitfire fighters.

Requests for our radio contact by Cairo radio continued. In addition to the radio silence, the flight remained on course at low altitude, with all exterior and interior lights turned off. Since TWA Flight 915 had departed in darkness and continued to fly at low altitude without any lighting to identify the aircraft, the operation could be reasonably safe. In the evening sky, the aircraft would show as a silhouette. The higher above the surface the aircraft flew, the more significant the silhouette would be. Flying as close to the surface as possible would create the least profile to be observed. The flight continued at low altitude until we approached the coastline of the island of Crete, Greece, at which point the flight was reasonably beyond interception. The aircraft then climbed to cruising altitude. After over flying a point south of the island of Crete, the course over flies the Adriatic Sea, crossing above the south coastline of Italy in the vicinity of Bari approaching Rome. The flight was just off shore above Naples, the island of Capri, before landing at Ciampino Airport, Rome. TWA Flight 915 arrived in Ciampino at 04:21 local time on July 7th. It had indeed been a long day.

After deplaning, the TWA Rome flight dispatcher made his presence known to me by presenting a teletype message from the TWA Paris operations office for Europe. The message requested the captain of TWA 915 proceed to Paris on a connecting flight departing from Rome. In light of the long period of time it had taken to fly the required operation, this was indeed a questionable request. The message stated a debriefing meeting was necessary in order for the Paris operations office for Europe to review the existing operations situation in Lydda. This was necessary in order to plan the next flight. At times, unusual and unreasonable requests had been a known factor. With much disgust over this request, expressed to the flight dispatcher who was only relaying a message, the connecting TWA flight was boarded for Paris.

En route to Paris, the flight made a scheduled landing at Geneva, Switzerland. While on the ground, TWA personnel of Geneva were anxious to know about the re-inauguration of flights to Tel Aviv, Israel. Many of these people had become friends over the years. A pleasant discussion was held before continuing on to Paris.

Upon arriving at Orly Field, Paris, the operations meeting was conducted as had been requested. The war-related operation problems at Lydda were reviewed. The lack of telephone communication between Lydda and Tel Aviv made the procurement of ground VHF radio equipment an immediate requirement. TWA had been advised by the Arab states, in light of our operation into Israel, there would be immediate changes in our future flight operation in the Middle East. Any, and all, TWA flights operating into Israel would not be allowed to fly in the air space over any Arab state. This did not pose any problem for the current operation as all flight approaches to land at Lydda were conducted over the Mediterranean. However, if in the future, flights were to operate from Tel Aviv, Israel, to Bombay, India, there would be a serious problem.

At the time Bombay, India, was the far eastern terminus for the TWA International Operation. TWA flights were flying from Cairo, Egypt, to airports in Saudi Arabia and Iraq, en route to Bombay. This restriction of air space above the Arab states would pose difficulty for the Lydda to Bombay flight operation. In relation to TWA's other operation into Tel Aviv, there was no comment. There was not any statement relative to the TWA flight crew flying the Rome-Tel Aviv flight operation. As the captain flying the operation, my opinion regarding the terrorists' operation; the Arab nations recognized the captain of all ships was required to make all ports of call. After all, the Arabs had been traders for centuries, and at this moment, it appeared this would be their policy. The interception of our radio contact by Cairo radio was discussed at length. The future reaction on their part was unknown. As long as the current state of war existed, their future reaction could be subject to change.

Since beginning the operation in Rome, this requested appearance in Paris had now begun the third day of duty. With regard to my fatigue, the meeting was terminated. A flight from Orly Airdrome, Paris, was boarded to return to Rome.

After arrival in Rome a long nap was taken at the Albergo Continentale. There was still a day or so before the next scheduled flight. A group of TWA people from the United States, based in Rome, was extremely interested in discussing the recent flight operation into Lydda. Joining this small group, we proceeded to the Restoranté Borgesé in the famous, beautiful Borgesé Gardens. Once seated at our table, the conversation was interrupted by persons unknown to most of us. It rapidly became evident these people were employed by other airlines serving Rome. As relative strangers, their questions were most pointed and under the circumstances, highly amusing. As Americans, we accept inquisitive people without resentment; a characteristic uncommon in most other countries. It became obvious the airline companies, which had terminated air service to Tel Aviv, were anxious to reinstate their flight operations. While we did not know them, they had made it their business to know who we were. The conversational bantering continued in jest. However, knowing their intent, there was not any pertinent information discussed. After our competitive airline group found their efforts to be fruitless, they departed. At last, we were free to order and our own conversation followed.

The restoranté was a delightful place. Accompanied by music, the dinner was most enjoyable. Many of the patrons were dancing. Later, during our conviviality, a most slender, attractive young lady appeared at our table. For a young woman to be unattended was most unusual, so we invited her to join us. She spoke excellent English, with almost an indistinguishable Italian accent. As soon as the pleasantries were over, which included a self introduction, 'Jeannie' turned the conversation towards the flights to Israel. This was a repeat performance of the group who had just departed. The humor involved made the conversations interesting to all. After her questioning, we proposed, "Jeannie, why don't you just ask us what you wish to know? Perhaps we will tell you."

Blushing, Jeannie smiled and changed the subject. Attractive, pleasant, and a graceful dancer, Jeannie spent the remainder of the evening at our table. Her abode was on our way back to the hotel, so we dropped her off on the way.

During previous time spent in Rome, the commanding officer of the United States Military Air Transport Service, MATS, had been present at a social function. The commanding officer was a pleasant chap and we had exchanged introductions. The following morning, a call was made to the commanding officer's office. After the usual pleasantries were exchanged, the question posed to him was, "Who is this girl Jeannie?"

After much laughter his question was, "Why do you ask?"

The encounter of the previous evening was related to him. Still highly amused his reply was, "It is not who Jeannie is, but where she is. Jeannie is at the top of our VD list."

We both enjoyed the humorous situation, and after much laughter, he was told we had merely dropped her off at her apartment the previous evening. The C.O. was somewhat skeptical of this explanation. He did add he hoped our story was true. However, with a degree of doubt in his voice, he stated if it became necessary, MATS had a clinic and medical staff on the base. An expression of gratitude was extended for his most pertinent information. The usual "ciao" ended our talk. At times, skepticism with unknown attractive girls is the best policy.

The TWA Flight 912 which followed was delayed departing Rome due to the late arrival of the connecting flight from New York. The flight operated from Rome to Tel Aviv non-stop, as had been planned. The flight time of 5 hours 38 minutes was considerably less than the initial flight with the Athens' landing. Local conditions at Lydda Airport were still difficult as the conflict continued. Food shortages remained prevalent throughout the entire country. Armed convoys continued to transport the passengers to and from Tel Aviv. It was also necessary for the TWA personnel to utilize the protection off the airport. The time on the ground was taken up by a repeat meeting with the minister of aviation. The 'out of service' notation was still in effect for the radio beacon, the single navigation facility for Lydda. The CAA did not react well to the continued use of the airport operations specification, without the radio facility in service. The time remaining without the radio facility being repaired, could not be estimated. Therefore, some positive correction was necessary. The minister made his proposal: a radio beacon of lower power output had been obtained. It was not compatible to replace the failed beacon. However, the minister proposed to install the lower powered beacon on a small truck, similar to an American pickup truck. The truck would be positioned at the end of whichever runway was in use. At the time, Lydda had two runways. With reciprocal use, that made four useable runway directions. The control tower would advise the inbound flights as to the runway location of the beacon transmitter. In his presentation, the minister personally thought this was a great idea. Our position was difficult. It did not bode well in a situation such as this to be too direct, as the country was in state of war. However, it was an obvious situation that the CAA would not buy, or approve, as any associated radio facility must have a definite fixed location, defined in longitude and latitude. A moving, unfixed, navigational facility would not be approved. For example; the airport weather conditions are overcast, the pilot cannot visually see the airport, and the beacon must be used to locate the airport. Where on the airport the beacon is cannot be assumed. The truck may have been taken in for an oil change, or the driver forgot to turn off the transmitter, and the beacon was not located where it was thought to be. During the hours of darkness, it could be difficult for the control tower to positively identify where the truck-transmitter was located. There could be many other possible deviations. All things considered, the CAA would not sign off on it. This was an unusual situation. The CAA normally had their own inspectors to check and approve airport installations. In this case, due to the conflict, the decision had been delegated to me. There was no reason to be put into an embarrassing situation by submitting an approval, which would make your judgment appear less than intelligent. With this in mind, the only attitude was non-committal, not a position normally expressed. The minister was doing the best possible under these circumstances, and there was no useful purpose to offend.

In walking through the passenger boarding area, a gentleman approached me and made his presence known. He presented identification verifying his position as an officer of American Export Shipping Co. He stated his trip had taken him to the Port of Haifa, Israel, to establish shipping facilities there. It was imperative he return to the office in Genoa, Italy. TWA operated the only air service. The agents had told him the flight was fully booked. It was explained to him we were unable to book a reservation beyond the number of seats of the configuration of the aircraft, as a passenger must be in a seat. However, we would examine all aspects. The only possible solution was to make an additional seat with a seat belt available.

The original Constellation configuration had been built with a bulkhead immediately aft of the flight deck; then a compartment of eight seats facing each other, followed by the food galley. Aft of this area was the main passenger cabin and lavatories. In order to fly the International Division with flights across the North Atlantic, this configuration had been modified. Instead of the forward seats, the compartment had a navigator's plotting table for celestial navigation. An astrodome was located in the ceiling. The opposite side was set with two bunks, upper and lower, for crew rest facilities. If the two bunks were disassembled, there would be room for four seats, two and two, facing each other. In this part of the operation, neither the plotting table nor the bunks were used. The configuration was changed to make four additional seats available.

The gentleman with American Export Shipping was contacted, and it was explained the only possible additional seat we could provide would be in the flight crew section. Due to the food shortage in Israel, food service would not be available. The gentleman was quick to accept the seating as offered. Three more distressed passengers were accommodated in the remaining seats. These seats were used only when positive identification of the passenger was made. Later, the TWA vice president of operations humorously related, this was the only time any TWA flight operation had over a 100 percent load factor.

The required armed convoy consumed all of the daylight hours, and fortunately, was successful in having enough daylight remaining to transport the departing passengers from Tel Aviv. TWA Flight 915 departed at 21:00 for Rome. Almost immediately after our takeoff from Lydda, Cairo radio called asking, "TWA, what was your time off Lydda?"

Having occurred on the previous flight, this communication had been anticipated and the request was ignored. As a result of the communication, the climb to cruising altitude was stopped and the flight leveled off at a low level. All interior and exterior lights were again turned off. Flight 915 continued to receive calls from Cairo radio.

Approaching Crete, the aircraft resumed climb to cruising altitude, proceeding on to Rome. TWA Flight 915 arrived at Ciampino Airport, Rome, 02:14 local time. The passengers in the crew seating area, including our new friend, Mr. Horace Craddock of American Export Shipping, were effusive in their personal thanks for the special accommodation we had made. A letter of thanks from American Export Shipping Co., New York was received at a later date.

Rome

The following morning the Roman sun rose early and hot. Air conditioning was non-existent. A cool environment was a must. Rome possessed but one country club, the Cicola de Golfa, located on the Appian Way to Naples. The Circola de Golfa was not far from Ciampino Airport. We had noticed it on the drive to Ciampino; 18 holes of golf, a restoranté, bar, and an Olympic size swimming pool. The constant flowing water to the pool came down from a spring in the mountains above. It was cold enough for your heart to miss a beat or two when diving in. However, in 100 degree Fahrenheit plus heat, it seemed delightful.

The early arising made for an early arrival at the Circola de Golfa. A plunge into the pool, followed by a refreshing swim, got the heart in motion. As in most clubs, the pool was surrounded by umbrellas, tables, and chairs. One of the chairs next to the pool was occupied by a very down cast looking American. After exiting the pool, a greeting to him of, "It can't be as bad as all that," was abruptly returned, "The h___ it isn't."

As one American greeting another, the chap said, "My name's Mc Whorter. I'm a Hollywood producer and I'm here to make a picture called "September Affair." The two principals, Joe Cotton and Joan Fountain are arriving today to start shooting. But all my equipment, cameras, film, everything is tied up in Italian customs."

Thinking for a moment, my retort was, "That is quite a bit for one sentence. Don't bother to repeat. Stay right here while your problem is reviewed."

A telephone call was made to the TWA office at Ciampino. Fortunately, the desired person answered the phone; the station manager for Rome, Memphis Cole, an old TWA friend from Kansas City. Mr. McWhorter's dilemma was explained to Memphis. As it was approaching the lunch hour, Memphis was invited to join us for lunch at the Circola de Golfa. Memphis concurred saying, "See you in about an hour."

Returning to Mr. McWhorter with, "Hope you planned to stay for lunch," was greeted with an abrupt retort, "Without my equipment, what else is there to do? I may as well."

By the time Memphis arrived, it had been established, it was "Dick" McWhorter and my name was "Lyle." After being seated and with the usual libation, Memphis said to Dick, "About your customs problem; recovering your cameras, film, etc., would 2 o'clock do?"

After swallowing, Dick recovered with, "You're kidding."

Memphis replied, "I've been known to, but not this time."

An elated Dick hurried his lunch, then with Memphis guiding the expedition, departed for customs at Ciampino Airport.

The next morning a call to my room at the Albergo Continentale, "Captain, this is the desk. A Mr. Mc Whorter is in the lobby."

One very happy person was waiting in the lobby. Dick greeted me with, "You have to be the smartest guy in Rome."

"Not true, Richard. Just know the right people."

Dick had recovered all of the errant film equipment. His crew was setting up to begin the filming of "September Affair." We walked out the main entrance of the hotel. Parked in the drive was a former U.S. Army military jeep. While getting in, Dick said, "This is all I could come up with at the moment." While driving, Dick advised there was work to be done at the Italian film studio. They were going to use only part of it. Was there time for both of us to drive to Cine Citta? The day was free and the drive continued.

Prior to WWII, Cine Citta had been the main Italian film studio for Italy. As we drove, it turned out the studio was located just off the Appian Way, about a block north of Ciampino Airport. Later, this location turned out to be a problem when "Quo Vadis" was filmed there. It was a bit difficult to film a chariot race when you have a Lockheed Constellation appear in the sky above, or have a Constellation landing at Ciampino. Driving into Cine Citta, the entire studio was in shambles. It had been closed during the war. Everything had fallen into disrepair. After a walk about, it was evident Dick had his work cut out for him; to clean up and reorganize enough of the studio for their use. Driving back to the Albergo, Dick commented on the rough riding jeep. He was reminded a jeep was not a stranger to my posterior, as it had seen a lot of jeeps. Chuckling, Dick commented he would have to try again to see what was available for hire.

The next morning the desk called to say Mr. Mc Whorter was waiting down stairs. Walking out the entrance door under the marquee was an Alfa Romeo limousine. In the back seat was a grinning Dick with the greeting, "Is this more to your liking?" The humorous situation was well covered when Dick asked, "What are your plans for the day?"

"It's hot, Dick."

"How about playing golf at Circola de Golfa?"

"No, Dick, just the pool. You know what they say about mad dogs and Englishman."

"Good. I must do some things at Cine Citta. I'll drop you on the way." On the way to the club, the transition from an army jeep to an Alfa Romeo was discussed with the notation the world of McWhorter covered a lot of territory. In the chauffeured Alfa, we rode to the Circola de Golfa. Dropping me off, Dick said, "See you for lunch and is there anything else?"

"Yes, bring Joan Fontaine."

Hollywood had discovered Rome. "September Affair" was perhaps the first of the post war movie productions in Italy, to be followed by many more including "Roman Holiday" among others. In the process, many aspiring starlets flew to Rome to be 'discovered.' The Circola de Golfa, the only golf course in Rome, plus the other amenities the club offered, became a popular daytime American hangout. The movie crowd attracted people from all walks of life.

One day at lunch an American with a very attractive wife of Philippine extraction introduced themselves to the group. Without a lot of emphasis, he indicated he had been in the Pacific engaged in purchasing surplus American items left over from WWII. It was assumed, if he bought military surplus, he also sold military equipment. Of all the different talents present, there was no emphasis put on anyone in particular.

Dick showed up for lunch as planned and broached the subject of the Constellation. "You are in charge of that new Constellation which you are flying to Israel."

"Yes, that is correct, Dick. Why do you ask?"

"Well, as you know, we must photograph a four-engine aircraft to use in "September Affair" and the Constellation would fit in very well with what we need."

"Richard, having looked at the script the fact is, this aircraft disappears and is not to be found. Allowing the use of a TWA airplane is verboten, unless you'd like me to look for other employment. Not wishing to be in that position, the answer is, no."

With a smile he said, "Thought you would be unreasonable," and the subject was dropped.

To be party to photographing a TWA Lockheed Constellation in a motion picture for the entire world to see fatally disappear would be a sure fire way to terminate my career. However, the Constellation was photographed later on for the final scenes in the picture where Joan Fontaine and Joe Cotton were happily seated together in the airplane.

Note: the principal stock holder of TWA, Howard Hughes, also owned a motion picture studio, RKO which was competitive with Dick's studio. Dick enjoyed the thought of using one of Howard's aircraft in his production 'gratis.' No doubt, Howard was happy about the use of a TWA Constellation in "September Affair," as the world-wide exposure was good publicity. The aircraft, which disappeared in the picture, turned out to be an Italian military aircraft. Who took the heat for that one remains unknown.

The next TWA Flight 912 departed Ciampino, Rome, at 03:42 local time, arrived at Lydda, Tel Aviv, at 09:33 local time for a flight time of 5 hours 51 minutes. The slightly earlier arrival allowed more daylight for the round trip armed convoy to Tel Aviv.

Another meeting was held with the minister of aviation. He made his displeasure known we had not used his idea of a mobile radio beacon. There was no satisfactory reply for this question. An unpleasant exchange was to be avoided at all cost. The same operational problems existed. However, previous decisions were in place to deal with them. As a result, a rest period in one of the small cot equipped rooms was in order. After lying down on the cot, there was just room enough left to close the door. There were no shower facilities anywhere in the area. Consequently, disrobing was not realistic. After a brief period of shut eye, there was a knock at the door. Struggling to stand up and open the door, a stranger was standing outside. He identified himself, and then made reference to my meeting in Rome with the chap and his attractive Philippi no bride. He said, "You know the man in the surplus business. We are business associates."

Recalling this meeting, my response was, "Yes, what do you wish?"

Still in the hall, the chap replied, "I have a small package I would like you to take to Rome to deliver to

ACA511A

Operations Specifications
AIRPORT D/F INSTRUMENT APPROACH PROCEDURE

Name of Air Carrier

City T.W.A.   is authorized to operate into and out of
                          Airport   Elevation above sea level
Lydda Israel   Lydda   144'
Authorized as
    Regular   ... Refueling   Alternate ... Provisional for
                              Ceiling and Visibility Minimums
                                              Landing :
      Aircraft   : Take-Off : Regular   : Straight-in :
                  :   : Approach   : Approach   : Alternate
                  : Day : Night: Day : Night : Day : Night: Day : Night

Douglas C-54 DC   :   :   :   NA :   :   :
Lockheed L-749   : 300-1 : 1000-2 : 500-1½ : 1000-2 :   : 800-2 : 1000-2

If an Instrument Approach Procedure is conducted, it shall be in accordance with
the following specifications:
1. Initial Approach to D/F station Lydda Rdo Bcn Frequency 415 Identif. LY

  From Primary Radio Fix : Degrees : Minimum: From Secondary :Degrees :Minimum
                         : Mag.   : Alt.   : Radio Fix   : Mag.   : Alt.
                         : 070   :   :
                         :   : 4500   : from 20 miles from coastline **

2. Shuttle   None
3. Final Approach Track outbound 270 Degrees Mag. Inbound 090 Degrees Mag.
4. Procedure turn Left (Right) side of Track. Min.Alt. 2000 within 25 miles feet
5. Altitude over D/F Station on Final Approach 640 feet
6. Magnetic Track D/F Station to Airport on airport degrees
7. Distance D/F Station to Airport on airport miles
8. If Visual Contact not established within 0 miles after passing
   D/F Station, or if landing not accomplished, climb to 2000 feet on track
   of degrees magnetic within 25 miles of D/F
   station.
Notes:

    Radio beacon "LY" 415 kcs operating 0500-2000Z
                              (see over)

ACA Form 511A for Lydda Airport, Israel, June, 1949.

Mr. F.E. Busch,   W.L. Trimble,
General Operations Manager,   Director of Operations, Europe,
Kansas City, Mo.   Orly Field, France
                                                        AS.G.9.235
                                              2 8 JUIN 1949
                Lydda Operation - Form 511A

Reference (a)   Director of Operations, Europe, letter AS.G.9.225
                dated June 17, 1949

Enclosure (A)   Revised Form 511A
         (B)   Digest of Airport and Facility Information, Lydda

          Under cover of Reference (a) Form 511A for
     Lydda was forwarded to your office for processing. The
     limits as specified therein were for VFR operation since
     no radio facility was available.

          As indicated, a check of the installation of the
     radio beacon and the operation thereof was being conducted
     by Mr. Helfert, CAA Coordinator, Paris, through State
     Department channels. This check has been completed and
     confirmation has been received that the radio beacon has
     been reinstalled and is in operation in accordance with the
     information contained in Enclosure (B). Accordingly
     Enclosure (A), Revised Form 511A for Lydda utilizing radio
     beacon is forwarded herewith for processing. Simultaneously
     Mr. Helfert is being furnished with a copy of this procedure.
     He has indicated that his recommendation will be with-held
     until the procedure has been observed on the inaugural flight.
     Captain Bobzin will likewise be furnished with a copy of
     this procedure for flight check. His comment will likewise
     be forwarded by cable at the earliest possible date.

          Enclosure (b) is forwarded herewith for your
     information as to the data upon which Form 511A was pre-
     dicated. A copy of the same enclosure has been forwarded
     to the Manager-Manuals, in order that the relative publications
     may be revised accordingly.

                                   W.L. Trimble,
                                   Director of Operations,
                                   Europe.

cc Mr. H. Helfert,
   Capt. Bobzin

Correspondence regarding Form 511A Lydda, Israel operation.

To which Harry replied, "Cannot help that Lyle. The orders came down from the top." The conversation with Harry ended with, "All right hardhead, I'll call you back."

The following day Jim was on the telephone. "Lyle, you win. You are set up on a round trip via Paris to Cairo."

"Jim, it is not a matter of winning anything. If incorrect, it could be my posterior."

The TWA operation of the International Division required many flight crew members. All crew members were required to have United States passports and the required visas for each country to be served. Therefore, TWA maintained a passport office in Washington, DC. It was the duty of this office to examine from a list of departing crew members; the passport requirements for each individual crewmember, including the required visas for each country their flights were scheduled to serve. When the passport office received the flight pattern assignment for our flights to Cairo, Egypt, the passports were objectively examined. The result was an urgent telephone call from Miss Judy Cox, supervisor of the TWA Passport Office.

"Lyle, we require a set of new passport pictures immediately. You must have a new passport, including visas, for the next flight assignment. As a result of your last flight assignment involving the flights into Israel, your current passport contains visas to both the Arab states and Israel. The Israeli visa could pose a problem on your next flight to Cairo. Please expedite a complete set of passport pictures in order we may have a new passport issued for your future flight operation."

The request was promptly fulfilled, and the new passport was waiting for me at the TWA office at LaGuardia Field before we departed. The canceled passport was returned, and is in a personal collection. It is perhaps one of the few passports of the 1940s to include visas to all of the Arab states and Israel.

TRANSCONTINENTAL & WESTERN AIR, INC.

Cable Address "TWAIR"

August 17, 1949

Mr. Lyle D. Bobzin
Mansion Apts. - Apt. #5
Kiamensi Road
Marshallton, Delaware

Dear Lyle:

Enclosed herewith is your canceled passport #28992, which is returned to you for a souvenir.

It was necessary to obtain a new passport for you in order to make you available for flights into Cairo inasmuch as your old passport contained an Israeli visa prohibiting travel to Egypt.

The Israeli visa in your old passport was secured for your entry into Israel on the provisioning flight before the new regulations were in effect.

Very truly yours,

Judy Cox
Passport Representative

JC:dt

Letter from TWA Passport Office dated 8/17/1949.

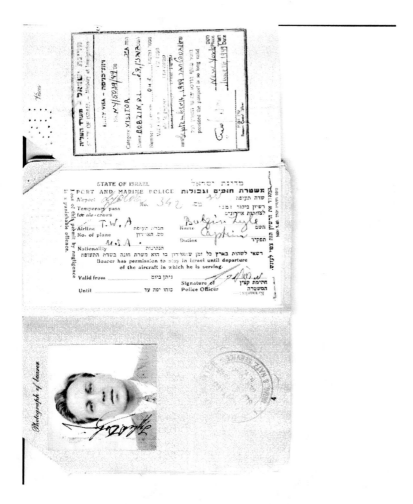

US Passport #28992 showing Israeli visa.

US Passport #28992 showing Egyptian visas.

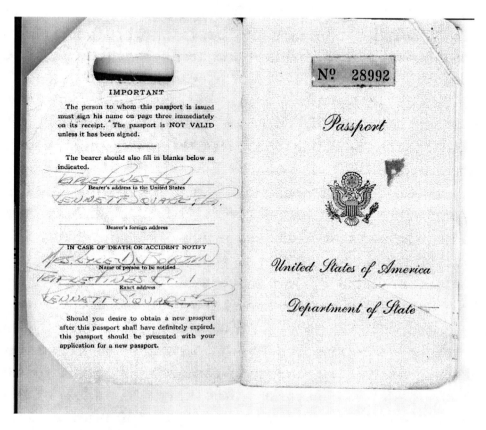

US Passport #28922.

The flight assignments to follow were two DC-4 flights to Cairo. TWA Flight 976 departed LaGuardia Field, New York, and landed at Shannon, Ireland, for 15 hours 7 minutes actual flight time. After refueling, the flight proceeded to Orly Airdrome, Paris. The following day TWA Flight 922 departed Paris, landing at Geneva, Switzerland; Rome, Italy; Athens, Greece; and Farouk Field Cairo, Egypt. As was customary at all airports upon arrival, the captain was required to sign the documents. After arrival in Cairo, the Egyptian public health office was a mandatory visit to sign the required forms. Upon entry to the office, a greeting from all of the officers concerned was, "Captain, it has been some time since you were last in Cairo. Where have you been?"

The greetings were made by the smiling officers, and with great humor. This was the well-known 'needle,' and was accepted in the same humorous manner. It was obvious to all why there had been a long absence since the last flight to Cairo. The next required office, immigration, was to be a repeat performance with the same humor. The customs office was next with the routine repeated, as were those to follow. As was customary, after all forms were signed as required by the captain, the normal call at the TWA office was made to pick up the hotel authorization. Even here the greeting was the same by the Egyptian employees of TWA. This subject had now reached the point to be terminated. It became necessary to advise the employees, it could possibly be difficult if overheard by others, who may not be sympathetic to our situation.

We arrived at the Heliopolis Palace Hotel and the usual pleasantries were exchanged in the same humorous manner. After a normal layover, we departed from Cairo on TWA Flight 929 making scheduled landings at Athens, Greece; Rome, Italy; and Paris. The following day TWA Flight 941 departed Paris making scheduled landings at Shannon, Ireland; Gander, Newfoundland; and terminating at LaGuardia Field, New York.

The scheduled flights had gone as previously planned without any operational difficulties. Our operation into Cairo was routine. The concern by management over the difficulty of the flight operations failed to materialize. The reaction by the Egyptian government had been cordial. They had accepted the facts as had been personally expected. With the continued war, the Egyptian government wished commerce to remain as normal as possible.

The flight operation of the inaugural flight and others to follow to Tel Aviv, Israel, was conducted with the caution previously defined. Precautions developed to prevent radical individuals from making unauthorized adverse decisions, which could have been serious, were a result of the resumption of the service to Israel. The Israeli government became aware of the problem of requiring an Israeli visa for flight crew members when later flying into Arab states. Consequently, the Israeli government changed its policy and no longer required visas for flight crew members. Thus, the future flight crew scheduling policy for the Middle East was changed accordingly.

The flight pattern from New York had positioned us in Rome to fly a flight to Tel Aviv. The flight operated as a DC-4. The Italian meteorological services had been restored at Ciampino Airport. As a result, a routine visit was made to this office. It was midnight local time when we discussed with the meteorologist the planned route of flight from Rome to Tel Aviv. The meteorologist defined weather conditions as, "Captain, you gotta nica night." With the usual, "bona sera," we left the office.

TWA Flight 976 departed Ciampino Airport at 01:44 local time in the excellent weather conditions so described. The route of flight was above the south of

Italy over flying the 'heel of the boot,' in the southern portion of the Adriatic Sea flying above the island of Crete. After over flying the island of Crete, the course would be above the Mediterranean passing south of Cyprus, then crossing above the coastline of Israel before landing at Lydda.

The flight above Crete was in clear weather conditions, and the lights of the principal city of Khania were visible through breaks in this scattered cloud deck. The highest mountain in Crete is located south of Heraklion. After passing over Crete, though instrument flight conditions were encountered, the flight was smooth. There was no indication in the sky conditions to show the development of convergence air mass activity.

Without warning, the aircraft became enveloped in violent, turbulent conditions accompanied by severe lightning. It was obvious the cold air mass from overhead Russia and Turkey had converged with the warmer air mass from North Africa. Resulting cloud buildups were developing as the flight progressed. A course reversal, or turning back, was not an acceptable procedure, due to high terrain on the return course. There were no reliable radio aids or facilities in the area. Consequently, the flight continued into the area with lower, not higher terrain. The indicated airspeed of the aircraft was reduced to provide for a greater safety margin of the aircraft. The turbulence was accompanied by violent lightning. The aircraft incurred several lightning strikes, and as a result, several static discharges. The static discharges caused blue, flame-like flashes down the interior of the aircraft, starting at the nose and exiting at the tail. It was difficult to maintain a constant altitude throughout this area. The zone of weather convergence had developed over the Mediterranean, south of the island of Cyprus, and west of the coast of Lebanon and Israel. Off the coastline, the flight finally entered good weather conditions and proceeded to Lydda. A total flight time from Rome had been 7 hours 21 minutes. The total flight time from our origination point, Paris, was 11 hours 31 minutes. The time in Lydda was 19:08 local time. It had <u>not</u> been a "nica night," as so defined in Rome.

The history of commerce in the Mediterranean area required ships at sea. Continued exploration on the Mediterranean Sea floor has revealed thousands of shipwrecks, which met their fate while navigating the Mediterranean. These shipwrecks give credibility to the fact the Mediterranean is not always a calm and docile sea. No doubt, unforeseen or changeable weather conditions contributed to the cause of many of these past shipwrecks. The cold air masses moving south from over Russia converged with the warm air masses moving north from the deserts of North Africa. The area in which these two air masses converged over the Mediterranean was subject to violent weather conditions. The wood sailing ships were no match for the rapid violent storms which developed. Therein lays the premise as to the cause of the sea floor being littered with wooden ships, which met disaster during those rapidly forming violent storms.

The weather and flight conditions that had been encountered called for a thorough examination of the aircraft after arrival. Static discharges often exit at points along the wing and tail section. As a result, lightning strikes and the resultant static discharges caused burn areas on the aircraft where the static discharges exited.

The Douglas DC-4 is an all metal aircraft, except for the flight control surfaces. The wing ailerons, the rudder, and the elevators are an aluminum framework covered by linen fabric, which in turn is covered with nitrate dope and pigment. In the past, this type of construction had been used for the whole aircraft. An inspection of the flight control surfaces showed several exit points of the static discharges. When this occurred, a small portion of the trailing edge of the flight control was burned away. There had been exit points on all of the flight control surfaces. The tail cone, a streamlined aluminum fairing, had been an exit point of one of the static discharges. As a result, the tail cone had been split open and was missing. This condition was noted by the TWA ground personnel, and their reaction was one of dismay. Maintenance and repair facilities at Lydda were extremely limited.

Past personal experience in the rebuilding, and maintenance of aircraft, had given expertise in dealing with fabric and structural repair. During the inspection process, the ground personnel were advised repair materials had to be located. It was suggested perhaps the Israeli Air Force base south of Lydda would have some of the required materials. The materials listed for them were; linen fabric, nitrate dope, welding rod, small bolts and/or metal screws.

As in fabric covered wings, fabric covered flight controls have a similar structure. The trailing edge of aluminum material is in the shape of a 'V.' In order to repair the burned out areas, it would be necessary to insert a length of welding rod into the V. The rod would be cut, with loops added at the ends, for the proper length to fill in the void. The rod would be secured in place by the screws inserted through the loops on the ends. Thus strengthened, the framework would be recovered with the linen fabric adhered to the existing fabric with the application of nitrate dope, and adhered to the control surface, and stitched where necessary.

A further examination revealed the high frequency radio antenna had been torn from the aircraft by the static discharges. The high frequency radio antennas were long, and extended from a mast above the flight deck to a connection at the top of the vertical stabilizer. This long, high frequency radio antenna was connected to the radio transmitters by a copper lead, through a large circular Plexiglas insulator in the top of the fuselage. A copper lead wire from the insulator was connected to the radio transmitters and receivers. The static discharges set up by a direct lightning strike, arced the connection points of the antenna. As a result, the antenna had separated from the aircraft. The copper lead, one-quarter inch in diameter, had arced, thus separating from the insulator, falling onto the seat cushion of the additional crew member seat below, and finally burning its way to the metal frame. Fortunately, the seat was not occupied at the time. The replacement of the tail cone would not be possible since this item was not available. The explanation of how to repair the control surfaces completed, and a discussion of the inability to find a replacement antenna also completed, it was time to get some rest.

The re-inauguration of TWA fights to Israel had taken place just weeks previously. As the military conflict was still in progress, operations remained difficult. The small cot in the closet-size facilities was still the same. After a rest period, TWA personnel came to discuss the departure of the flight to Rome. The materials to repair the damage to the flight controls had been obtained, and the required repairs had been accomplished. The replacement of the lost radio antenna was not possible. The replacement would require a new antenna be flown in on a future flight. The scheduled departure of TWA 927 was now close at hand. The lack of a high frequency radio antenna made communication over long distances impossible. It was explained to the TWA personnel the DC-4 had a seven channel VHF transceiver with an undamaged antenna. The VHF radio was fully functional and could be used to contact control towers at all airports. In view of this, we would operate Flight 927 on schedule.

"But, Captain, you will not be able to transmit your estimated time of arrival to Rome dispatch."

"In this case, Rome dispatch will have our time of arrival when we contact Ciampino Tower for landing. Unless, of course, you can call Rome by telephone, which you tell me is not in service." The ongoing conflict had interrupted telephone service once again to and from Lydda.

The area of severity in the eastern Mediterranean had cleared and the thunderstorm area had dissipated.

TWA Flight 927 departed Lydda Tel Aviv at 03:30 local time. It was a "nica early morning." We arrived at Ciampino, Rome at 10:45 local time for a flight time of 8 hours 15 minutes.

The permanent repairs to the DC-4 were to be performed by TWA maintenance at Ciampino, which had adequate replacement parts. TWA Flight 927 was scheduled to continue on from Rome, with an intermediate landing before arriving in New York.

Another 749 model Constellation was put in service at Ciampino to continue Flight 927 to New York. We departed Rome on Flight 927, making a scheduled landing in Geneva, Switzerland and proceeded to Orly Airdrome, Paris, arriving at 15:10 local time. The total flight time for the day was 12 hours 15 minutes.

In the future, there were changes in the international procedures. Long a problem, the ship's log was eliminated from the documentation requirements. The aircraft log had always been a part of each individual aircraft documents. The aircraft maintenance log book then in use, is still in effect today, as this log has the current maintenance records relative to all parts of the aircraft. The captain was relived of signing volumes of documents at each airport of landing. There had been reams of paper to sign; e.g. waybills, bills of lading, a multitude of items which the captain had to assume were in order and sign.

The entire overall picture in the Middle East was to change after the 1967 conflict. During this conflict, the uncontrolled distribution of weapons of war became prevalent. The result; many fragmented activists became armed with an array of weapons. In abundance Russian AK-47s became the standard weapon of the extremists. The fragmentation of liberation units was uncontrollable by the governments of the respective countries. Airlines, including TWA, became victims of these terrorist organizations. The period that followed was one of violence, in which lives were lost and aircraft destroyed. The violence occurred without authorization of, or by the governments of the countries in which they occurred. The incidence of skyjackings was exacerbated by these extremist organizations. The clandestine use of explosives placed onboard aircraft produced a most critical time in airline flight operation.

In the late 1940s, TWA received the business of a large contingent of Japanese passengers. These Japanese passengers flew in large groups on their around the world flight, as ambassadors of goodwill to the world. In reality, all of the people were involved in a study of goods produced by all the countries visited. Individual groups departed on different days over a long projected period. In this manner, one group would have completed their mission at each city, to be replaced by another group on the same flight. It was worth noting that upon arrival at each airport, one group would deplane only to be replaced by another group departing that city. This procedure was taking place at all of the cities served by TWA, in both the international and domestic flight operation. The TWA personnel became accustomed to this long term program, and enjoyed their participation. It is of note, after the flights were completed by these goodwill ambassadors, that these passengers were most likely engineers. In their around the world flights, the principal cities of Italy, Switzerland, Germany, Britain, and the United States were part of the agenda. There were many humorous observations by TWA personnel during this program.

One story: the Swiss, unable to start one of their automated machines, removed the cover of the machine to investigate and found a small Japanese man inside, a visitor from the previous day!

Soon after this extensive program was implemented, Japanese industry began to develop all types of electronics, watch making, photographic equipment, and an extensive automobile industry. Also, there were many lesser production developments. The Japanese goodwill teams observed the methodology of many things produced in the countries they visited and were able to duplicate the products. The purpose of these expensive flights had been to study the manufacturing techniques of most of the major industrialized countries of the world.

Included in the world tour was Scotland. The Scots were only too happy to show them the distillation process of their favorite Scotch whiskey. The Japanese had long been drinkers of Scotch whiskey. To satisfy this taste at home, the Japanese went to great lengths to duplicate the world famous Scotch whiskey. The product was a reasonably good whiskey, but by no means close to the original. The whiskey project was, perhaps, one of the few failures of this world-wide project.

At this time, passenger boarding of the aircraft was done by the means of an 'air stair' placed at the rear boarding door. The DC-4 was parked at the departure gate at Rome Ciampino Airport. Approaching the boarding stair, two Catholic priests were standing at the foot of the boarding stairs. One of the smiling priests extended his hand saying, "This is Father John and I am Father Lorenzo. You must be the pilot. I am a sky pilot."

After completing the introductions, we continued to board the aircraft via the air stairs. While proceeding along the aisle to their assigned seating, a very humorous conversation continued. Both expressed their interest in the aircraft and were invited to view the flight deck area. An immediate friendship developed. To satisfy their great interest, they were invited to be seated in the unoccupied, additional crew member seats. The flight departed Rome for its first schedule landing at Geneva, Switzerland. The two additional 'sky pilots' thoroughly enjoyed their flight to Geneva, as they had been supplied with headsets to listen and observe all communications. After arrival at the TWA gate at Geneva Airport, Father John commented, "Wouldn't you sometimes just like to tell them to go to hell?"

Father John's comment was made in jest and we enjoyed a good laugh. The TWA flight departed Geneva, Switzerland, and next schedule landing was made at Orly Airport in Paris, France.

A complete crew change was made in Paris for the continuation of the flight to New York. After deplaning in Paris, the conversation with Father John and Father Lorenzo continued. We explained our departure and that another TWA crew would fly them to New York. During the goodbyes Father Lorenzo stated, "I am Father Lorenzo Spirali. My parish is in Havana, Cuba. If you ever visit Havana, please call me."

This statement was sincerely made as he presented his card of identification. Jokingly he stated, "You fly quite well for one of the 'other' following." Religion had never been discussed. Father Lorenzo had deduced the captain was a Christian but not of his persuasion. Father Lorenzo was thanked and assured that on our next flight to Havana, he would hear from us.

When winter arrived in the cold Northeast, we then made our usual vacation flight south. Our destination was Havana, Cuba. After arriving at our hotel, we called Father Lorenzo. His reception was enthusiastic and jovial, stating he would visit us at the hotel the following morning.

The next morning Father Lorenzo arrived in his standard two-door Chevrolet, much the same as the favorite mode of transportation for Howard Hughes. When advised his austere mode of transportation was the same as Howard Hughes, the major stockholder of TWA, he was highly amused. His early morning arrivals continued throughout our stay in Havana as Father Lorenzo insisted he be our personal guide during our island stay. The dedicated attention by Father Lorenzo changed what could have been an ordinary visit into an outstanding one. A thorough knowledge of Havana and the environs gave us an insight into what otherwise would have remained an unknown. During this extensive and objective insight into Havana, we

observed the major program of Father Lorenzo; the
establishment of medical dispensaries and clinics for
the poor, which was Father Lorenzo's passion. A
dedicated priest, he pledged his life's work to these
programs to benefit Cuba's poor. After several days of
especially enjoyable sightseeing, it was time to return
home. The parting conversation with Father Lorenzo
was an emotional one. Sincere and devoted, such a man
as he is seldom encountered. He left an indelible
memory with us for the remainder of our lifetime.

Day of the Cheval

A flight assignment had been flown from New York with the intermediate landing in Paris; the flight assignment was then flown with intermediate landings to Cairo, Egypt. The return flights had been flown to Paris, France. We were now positioned for our return to New York, with intermediate landings in Shannon, Ireland; Gander, Newfoundland; and terminating in New York. The overall time to complete the flight assignment was just over twenty-four hours. This included time on the ground for refueling at the intermediate airports.

We had arrived at Orly Airport, Paris, for the departure time of 03:00 local time. The aircraft was a Douglas C-54 air freighter. The flight crew had checked in at the Orly Office and completed the necessary flight planning for the proposed flight. We arrived at the aircraft parked on the ramp to observe more than the normal activity in progress around the aircraft. The activity was centered at the rear loading door. A mare in a box stall was in the process of being loaded aboard the C-54.

The loading of the horse in the box stall had been in progress for some time. The horse was confined to a box stall, which was just long enough and wide enough to contain the mare with her head well above the top of the box stall. The mare was not taking the proceedings with a receptive attitude. In fact, she was outwardly disturbed and had been mildly sedated. The Supervisor of TWA cargo, Paris, came to advise us this is the first horse to be flown by any airline. As the attempted loading of the mare continued, this fact became very evident. The C-54 had a large, cargo loading door located at the rear of the fuselage. The height of this door was limited to the height of the fuselage. The door width was wide enough to allow the box stall to enter the aircraft. The door height was not high enough to allow the horse to enter with her head erect, as she would be in her normal stance. The box stall was being elevated by a fork lift, which in reality was not large enough for the loading. The mare obviously resented the noise of the gasoline engine powering the fork lift, which was lifting her off the ground. When the box stall was raised high enough to allow the bottom of the box stall to pass onto the floor of the aircraft at the entrance door, the mare's head was well above the top of the C-54 cargo door. At this point, efforts to lower her head were met with stiff opposition on her part.

While observing this study in futility, it was easy to agree with the mare. The horse was being hoisted off the ground with a noisy contraption. When she could not be loaded in the door, she was lowered to ground level, then to be hoisted again in another attempt to get horse and box stall aboard the aircraft. This 'not so funny' fire drill went on for hours. The same procedure; up and down, with accompanying conversation as to how to try it next time. There were coffee breaks taken, time for more planning, and with some luck by the time our four-legged girl was loaded, some five plus hours had passed.

The French have bred some of the most noteworthy breeds of horses, 'cheval,' the Percheron among others. However, our personnel at TWA had much to learn about loading them. The sun had risen during the procedure. The "Day of the Cheval" was photographed with my 35mm German Robot camera.

Figure 1

Attempt to load mare on C-54 rear cargo door.

Figure 2

Continued attempt to load the mare while the TWA French load
supervisor looks away from this prolonged effort.

Figure 3
Loading attempt continues.

Figure 4

After nearly 5 1/2 hours the mare is moving towards inside of the cargo bay.

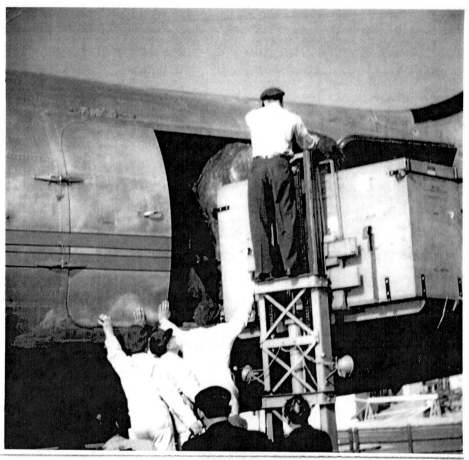

Figure 5

Success! Much to the relief of everyone the mare finally moves into cargo bay.

We departed Orly Field, Paris 5 hours 30 minutes late. This is not a way to begin a flight which would take an overall twenty-four hours plus to complete, under normal conditions.

The beautiful mare was being shipped to Ireland to be bred. After breeding her to an Irish stud of racing fame, there were high hopes for a foal of racing promise. Taking into account the long delay loading our equine cargo, the entire crew expressed great anxiety about how long it was going to take to unload our cargo at Shannon, Ireland.

As soon as the C-54 arrived on the ramp, the Irish plan was put into motion. With great apprehension, we all gathered at the rear of the C-54 to wait for the unloading of our prize cargo. An airplane incline ramp was pushed up to the cargo door. An Irish stallion was led to the lower end of the incline ramp. The Irish groom looked at the horse box stall with distain. He dropped the front panel of the box stall and promptly led the mare from her stall. She obliged with lowering her head to pass through the door and walked down the ramp to greet her Irish counterpart. Much to the relief of the flight crew, the entire deplaning process consumed less than 15 minutes.

The flight time from Paris, France, to Shannon, Ireland, had been 3 hours 11 minutes. The flight time Shannon to Stephensville, Newfoundland, was 10 hours 38 minutes. Flight time Stephensville to LaGuardia, New York, was 5 hours 29 minutes. Upon termination at LaGuardia, the crew was required to ferry the aircraft to the overhaul base at New Castle, Delaware. The flight time was 1 hour. We arrived at Newcastle at 04:00 local time of the second day. Total time for the flights was 20 hours 18 minutes. The flight times were under the scheduled time. The air mass above the North Atlantic created favorable components. The air mass above the Maritimes, the northeast coast was also favorable. The flight time Shannon, Ireland, to Stephensville, Newfoundland, was over two hours less than schedule, and the flight time to New York was over one and one-half hours less than schedule.

The story did not end here. The following flight assignment was a flight to Paris. After arrival at Orly Field, the flight was routinely met by the maintenance supervisor, Roy Davis. After we discussed the status of the aircraft we had flown to Paris, the conversation quickly changed to the previous flight, and the delay in loading the mare for her flight to Shannon, Ireland.

Laughing Roy said, "Lyle, you don't know the whole story. The previous day that mare was Pan Am Cargo. When they attempted to load her aboard the Pan Am C-54, she bucked and kicked the fuselage area at the loading door. There was extensive airframe damage and Pan Am had to cancel the flight until they could repair the aircraft. Pan Am gave TWA the shipment to Shannon. We thought it best not to relate this to you."

"That's wonderful, Roy. This item will be filed in my mind to 'even things up', as some would say. Is there anything else which might be well to know?"

This was a TWA 'first' which would have been best missed.

Christmas—1949

The necessity for this North Atlantic routing occurred in December 1949. We had departed from LaGuardia Airport on the 18th of December on a flight pattern we would fly via Paris to Lydda Airport serving Tel Aviv, Israel with a return flight pattern via Paris to LaGuardia Field, New York. This was a most favorable flight pattern at this time of year, as the schedule called for the flight crew to return to New York well ahead of the Christmas holidays.

Originating at LaGuardia Field, New York, this flight pattern was normal with landings at Gander, Newfoundland; Shannon, Ireland; and Paris, which was the flight crew layover point. The following day the flight departed Paris landing at Geneva, Switzerland; Rome, Italy; and Lydda Airport serving Tel Aviv, Israel. After a crew rest layover, the westbound flight making landings at Rome, Italy; and Geneva, Switzerland; and Paris was routine. This flight pattern had now positioned the flight crew in Paris on the 21st of December, in a position to be westbound and home well before Christmas.

The negative weather pattern, which frequently occurs in Western Europe during the winter months, took place immediately upon our arrival in Paris. The winter Azores high pressure area moved in over Europe, completely enveloping Western Europe. The Azores high pressure area causes air stagnation over its entirety. In the winter, temperatures are slightly above the freezing mark. Due to stagnation and temperatures near freezing, the lack of air movement results in dense fog weather conditions.

Weather conditions throughout all of Western Europe deteriorated rapidly, remained with a low ceilings and poor visibility. The weather reports for Orly Airport and all other airports in the area were; ceiling zero, visibility zero. The long-standing effect of this Azores high pressure area brought flight operations to a halt.

Our proposed departure for New York on December 22nd was delayed to the 23rd, then the 24th, and finally to the 25th at 06:00. The first westbound flight to arrive in Paris was a C-54 cargo flight. Our return flight aboard a schedule passenger flight was now changed to a C-54 freighter.

We received a call at 03:30 hours for the 06:00 departure. We arrived at the breakfast room to find the door locked with a sign saying, "Merry Christmas." This "Merry Christmas" was our only notice breakfast would not be available. We arrived at Orly Airport expecting to partake of a delayed breakfast. We informed the personnel of our lack of food, which we had not expected to occur. The reply from operations personnel was, "Captain, today is Christmas."

Our rapid retort was, "We're well aware of that, but that answer does not solve the problem!"

The conversation ensued relative to the necessity for a reasonable meal before departing on a long flight. The alibi continued the same, "But, Captain, this is Christmas."

After having been delayed several days in Paris, the crew was eager to return to New York. It was obvious there was no food service available for the flight crew at Orly. The next subject for discussion was the lack of crew lunches normally placed aboard the aircraft. The same unacceptable attitude persisted, "But Captain, this is Christmas. There is no one in the commissary."

Our nutritional requirement had been completely ignored. In the present situation, it meant the crew was to fly the flight without any food of any kind. The crew could have refused to fly until food service was available. However, during the ensuing delay, weather conditions might return to zero ceiling, zero visibility. The result would be a further delay in Paris. The crew elected to fly without food.

As a result of the high velocity negative component on the North Atlantic, the flight would operate from Paris to Santa Maria in the Azores, then on to Gander, Newfoundland, and New York. The lack of any food of any nature at Paris suggested the flight crew would fly over eight hours to Santa Maria without any food. The original plan, faulty as it was; the crew would receive food service upon arrival at Santa Maria in the Azores.

Flight 941 departed Orly Airport, Paris, at 06:00 and after a flight of 8 hrs 14 min. arrived in Santa Maria. But, as the old saying goes, you will not believe what happened next. The flight operations office had been abandoned, as it was Christmas. The only ground service available was for aircraft refueling. It was not necessary to be reminded again that 'today is Christmas.' Perhaps it would be understandable, even tempting to say, the crew would fly no farther without any meals available.

Upon arrival, a negative confrontation ensued. Again, due to the holiday, no food service was available. It was obvious, if the crew refused to fly before food service was available, the departure of the flight was in question. After a heated discussion with the ground personnel, the flight crew agreed to continue on without food. While it was an extremely undesirable situation, the wish to get home on Christmas Day prevailed. There had been nothing, not anything as little as a cup of coffee available, and the only liquid onboard the C-54 aircraft was water.

It is perhaps necessary to remind all at this time how austere conditions were at Santa Maria airport. Any elaborate form of terminal building did not exist. The regular scheduled flights involved mail service for Santa Maria. On occasion, westbound flights were boarded by Portuguese men immigrating to the United States to work as sheepherders in the western states. The fact it was a holiday only led to the lack of any personnel at the airport. The island of Santa Maria was sparsely populated, with the airport taking up most of the acreage on the west side of the island, and a few windmills and pasture lands on the east side.

The hard fact: the crew could refuse to fly until food service was available. But under the circumstances, what could be accomplished by doing so? It was doubtful the sheepherders possessed any food to share. It became obvious the flight would depart for Gander in the same 'foodless' state as it had departed Paris.

After refueling the aircraft and with water as the only food service, Flight 941 departed for Gander, Newfoundland. The proposed flight plan called for a 10 hour flight to Gander. After some time aloft, leg stretching was required and an inspection of the cabin made. At the far aft station, a large dog kennel was observed having a sign on top stating, "This is the property of Army Air Force Colonel 'XXX.' " Inside the much too small kennel was a large male Boxer dog with his head touching the top of the kennel. The Boxer was seated on a long metal can of Spam. This was the largest can of Span packed by Hormel, and had obviously come from the U.S. military commissary near Paris. The can of Spam was removed from the kennel. The Boxer was then more comfortable, as his head was no longer touching the top of the kennel. It was obvious the good Colonel had meant the Spam as nourishment for his fine Boxer, but the situation called for other distribution. The large, long can of Spam was taken forward to the flight deck and consumed in a most "gauche" manner, without bread. We were not entirely thoughtless. We shared some with the hungry Boxer. What had to be a first in aviation; Christmas dinner aboard an aircraft, Spam, 'sans pain,' or without bread! Spam! Nothing else. After departing Santa Maria, some 10 hours later Flight 941 landed at Gander, Newfoundland.

At this time, Gander Airport was host to many military and civilian flight operations. The commissary had not taken the day off and a most welcome food service was supplied for the crew. Once the provisioning for the C-54 had been accomplished, we continued the flight to La Guardia Airport, New York. Flight 941 landed La Guardia Airport, New York 6 hours 51 minutes later. It was 02:05 local time in New York, on the 26th of December. Christmas Day had been spent in flight. The food had been sumptuous, Spam. Perhaps everyone has heard Spam mentioned in the most derogatory manner, but never as the main and only course for a Christmas dinner.

The flight on the 'long way' across the North Atlantic had taken 24 hours, 46 minutes from Paris to New York. The crew was now only one day late for Christmas. After everyone in the crew wished each other, "A Merry day after Christmas" on December 26th in the wee morning hours, all headed for our homes.

There had been much acrimonious conversation with those who did not take proper action to provide the necessary commissary which should have been a routine service, regardless of the Christmas holiday. The lack of proper commissary at Santa Maria Airport in the Portuguese Azores was explained away, as "an occurrence of a non-scheduled landing as a fuel stop." In each incidence, however, the desire to be at home with our families overcame the lack of the usual food service. Most flights are routine. Then, there are others which are not. You can rate this one....

BOOK FOUR

THE FIFTIES

INTERNATIONAL DIVISION–
THE EXPANSION CONTINUES

The Constellation Years

The TWA International Division continued to expand with the addition of London, England; and Frankfort, Germany. On June 23, 1950, we were transiting Shannon, Ireland; on Flight 925 from Paris, France; to New York, NY. While walking through the terminal, a gentleman approached me to inquire in which direction my flight was heading. When advised the flight was westbound, he asked if there was any space available for him and his traveling companion, since their flight had been indefinitely delayed. He was advised in the affirmative and escorted to the TWA ticket counter where the agent told us the flight was closed. The agent was then directed to "re-open" the flight manifest and board the two passengers in question. While en route, the passengers advised of their appreciation. This encounter and the positive outcome set the tone for the coming decade.

Unnoted- cc: Captain Lyle D. Bobzin
P.O.Box 338
Hopatcong, New Jersey.

THE AMERICAN DISTILLING COMPANY
PEKIN, ILLINOIS
Office of Samuel Rothberg

July 6, 1950

Mr. Ralph S. Damon, President,
Trans World Air Lines,
10 Richards Road,
Kansas City 6, Missouri.

Dear Mr. Damon:

On June 23 I arrived at the Shannon Airport on A.O.A.
from London, the last leg of a round-the-world flight.
We were advised of engine trouble and that there would
be an indefinite delay. In making inquiry at your
ticket office at the Shannon Airport we were advised
no space was available on westbound flights.

It was then that I noticed a TWA captain and asked him
in what direction he was heading and was informed "westbound". On inquiry as to whether there was space available
on his flight, he advised me there was and proceeded to
use his good office to see that space was made available
for myself and an associate.

Captain Lyle D. Bobzin certainly did his best to see that
we were quickly accommodated on Flight 925, even though
it meant delayed departure of this flight.

I should like you to know that I am the owner of more
that 2,000 shares of Trans World Airlines Stock (street
names) and have owned this stock for many years. The
courtesies extended by Captain Bobzin make me feel certain
that if this spirit is carried out through the entire
organization, the stock will eventually turn out to be a
very good investment.

Very sincerely yours,

SR-lz

Commendation letter from Mr. Samuel Rothberg, American Distilling Co.

In the 1950s, a program by Lockheed to enlarge or 'stretch' the Constellation resulted in the Model 1049. The purpose was to lengthen the fuselage to make room for more payloads, and to increase the fuel capacity to extend the range of flight. New higher horsepower Wright 3350 engines were installed. Increased fuel capacity was necessary to extend range of flight. One of the desired results of the modifications would be the elimination of fuel stops in the North Atlantic operation at Gander, Newfoundland; and Shannon, Ireland. The new model would enable TWA to fly non-stop from the United States terminals to the major cities of Europe; in the operation of the flights in the United States, to fly all flights from coast-to-coast non-stop, both eastbound and westbound.

The leadership or presidency was to change several times during the 1950s. Howard Hughes continued to dominate in the selection of top management of TWA. Jack Frye had left in the late 1940s to be replaced by Ralph Damon, who had served as president of American Airlines during World War II, while C.R. Smith was serving in the Army Air Forces during the war. At the end of the war, Ralph Damon had served as president of American Overseas Airline, which was owned and controlled by American Airlines. C.R. Smith sold American Overseas Airline to Pan American, which left Ralph Damon free to assume the vacant office of president and CEO of TWA.

The Constellation had become the major aircraft in number in the TWA fleet. The DC-4 was replaced by the longer range and pressurized Constellation, in both international and domestic flight operations. The reliable, but unpressurized DC-3 was replaced with the Martin 404. The C-54s remained in service in the air cargo operation.

Postwar TWA expanded rapidly in both international and domestic operations. After the departure of Captain Jack Frye, there had been long periods during which TWA had been without a president. During 1948, Mr. LaMotte Cohu had served as president for a brief period of time. TWA personnel often made reference to the fact that "we can operate without a president." The fact: Jack Frye and Paul Richter had made the people of TWA so well aware of their self-worth and individual importance in the functioning of the airline, TWA was able to do just that, function well. It was timely Mr. Ralph Damon came aboard on January 25, 1949, and was a valuable addition to the company as president and CEO.

During this time, Howard Hughes began an aircraft ownership plan previously unknown to the airline industry. Later, the procedure was to become widely accepted by the industry. Mr. Hughes conceived the process whereby Hughes Tool Company purchased the aircraft to be flown by TWA. In turn, the Hughes Tool Company leased the aircraft to TWA. The accelerated depreciation schedules were more favorable, allowing the Hughes Tool Company to take advantage of depreciation schedules, while TWA obtained the aircraft for operation. For years to come, a plaque on the bulkhead just aft of the pilot's seat stated, "This aircraft is the property of Hughes Tool Company."

Hughes' interest in aviation had always made him a major factor in all TWA aircraft purchases. The policy of the parent leasing to the subsidiary was universally adopted by the industry.

In the service of TWA, the Lockheed Model 1049 was the first of an L-1049 series. During the 1950s, the L-1049 was followed by the Models L-1049G, L-1049H–an all cargo version–and the last Constellation, the L-1649A, which was placed in service in June 1957.

The L-1049 was the first stretched version of the original L-049 series. With increased fuel capacity, the larger aircraft would accommodate more passengers and payload. The newer version Wright 3350 engines produced increased horsepower. The wing span remained the same overall. In order to increase the fuel capacity, it was necessary to add an additional fuel tank to the wing structure. The additional fuel cell was incorporated into the center section structure of the wing. In previous aircraft, this area had been what was called, the 'dry bay.' It was the area directly below the fuselage, and was designed not to contain fuel. The long-standing practice had been not to have a fuel tank directly below the fuselage. The theory was to have no fuel there in the event an accident ruptured the wing proper. The proposal to change this long-standing policy was met with immediate opposition. The pro: to build an aircraft with range to fly non-stop coast-to-coast, both eastbound and westbound, this was the only available area in which to carry more fuel that was needed. The con: the objection to having a fuel cell below the cabin area.

As the TWA air safety representative at the time, this controversy came home to roost. Meetings with the TWA pilot groups were consistent; objecting to the combustibility of the fuel in the center wing section. Meetings with the Lockheed engineering people; insistence the center section could be structurally enhanced to make the area resistant to fuel spillage in case of an accident. TWA engineering was aware of the objections. However, the desire was to make a new aircraft with the range required for non-stop coast-to-coast flight operation. The design with a stronger, redesigned center section prevailed.

At one of the meetings with Lockheed engineers, the proposal was made; build the center section with 75ST aluminum, instead of 24ST aluminum, as used in previous aircraft. The 75ST aluminum is considerably stronger and would make the whole box section more distortion resistant. My immediate reaction to this proposal; 75ST aluminum, while considerably stronger, has a much higher resultant metal fatigue factor than 24ST aluminum. This caveat was overruled based on the increased strength of 75ST aluminum. As a result of this decision, the life span of the Model 1049 Constellation would be shortened considerably.

The entire flight operation was brought to a halt by a FAA safety bulletin calling for the replacement of the center section of the aircraft. Metal fatigue had developed in the 75ST structure. It was not economically feasible to replace the center section. Therefore, the flight operation of the L-1049 stopped in the early 1960s. The number of aircraft involved was not great. TWA had only purchased ten of the Model L-1049s. Two had been destroyed in fatal accidents not related to the center section problem. The remaining eight aircraft were scrapped. The fate of the two L-1049 aircraft; both were tragic, and both involved mid-air collisions resulting in total loss of life. The first was a mid-air collision with a United Airlines DC-7 overhead the Grand Canyon, as the DC-7 had overtaken the TWA Super Constellation, causing the greatest loss of life in an aircraft accident to that date. The second fatality occurred when the Super Constellation was overtaken by a United Airlines DC-8 jet overhead Staten Island, New York. Both aircraft were destroyed with a large loss of life. The strange coincidence in both accidents was; neither flight crew of the Super Constellations saw what hit them. They only knew the aircraft was out of control, beyond their ability to avoid a fatal crash.

The additional range of the L-1049 was not adequate to fly routes non-stop, as desired on domestic and international schedules. TWA modified the schedules accordingly, with most domestic westbound flights scheduled to land in Chicago. The westbound international flights still required the Gander, Newfoundland fuel stop.

As in a previous Christmas season, the annual effort to spend Christmas with the family was once again derailed. The flight was an eastbound L-1049 Super Constellation scheduled from Los Angeles to New York Idlewild Airport. In flight above Pennsylvania approaching Selinsgrove, PA the entire airplane filled rapidly with dense smoke. The operations procedure was for the crew to immediately don full face masks connected to an oxygen supply tank. These masks were cumbersome, but were donned quickly. Simultaneously, electrical power was removed from all the electrical systems, as the source of the fire was unknown. At the same time, the aircraft was depressurized, and immediately descended to a safe altitude above the existing terrain. Passengers and cabin crew were provided oxygen masks and donned them accordingly. We desired a landing as soon as possible. While performing all the required procedures, it was fortunate the ground beneath the aircraft was visible. The geography of the United States was well known because years of flying had fixed it in memory. The Susquehanna River was visible below. As a result, the flight was altered to fly above the river to the south until visually sighting Harrisburg, PA and the Harrisburg Airport. An unannounced arrival and landing was made. Our arrival at Harrisburg on Christmas Day was neither scheduled nor expected. All station and control tower personnel were surprised and taken off-guard. During our rapid decent and short flight to Harrisburg, there had not been any sign visible fire, which would require immediate evacuation. Accordingly, after landing and with both aircraft doors open, we taxied a short distance to the terminal building. The surprised personnel quickly placed the boarding stairs at the open doors. Passengers rapidly deplaned without injury. Although those onboard had been exposed to the dense smoke during the short flight, no one had suffered any adverse effects due to the use of oxygen masks. The emergency landing of the Super Constellation at Harrisburg was an unusual event. This was the first time this type of aircraft had landed there.

Due to the Christmas holiday, it was difficult to find other air service for our passengers to continue on to New York. While undamaged, the aircraft was out of service until the cause of the dense smoke could be ascertained. We did our best to properly extend all service to our passengers, with the hostesses doing everything possible.

There were the usual, not so well thought out questions put to us such as, "Why didn't you contact us of your diversion?" and so forth. When deactivated, the electrical system removes the power from all radios. Later, systems were designed so one radio would remain active under these conditions.

TWA Vice President of Operations, Paul S. Fredickson called to inquire what had taken place. His Christmas had been interrupted by our diversion. We had become well-acquainted in the past as Paul had been a check airman, and had been part of my captain checkout program. The conversation was cordial. His only request was to advise him of the cause of the malfunction.

Once the passengers had been taken care of, the male flight crew directed their attention to the aircraft. Due to the holiday, no maintenance personnel were on duty. Since Harrisburg had no scheduled Constellation service, there were no Constellation trained mechanics based there. After many phone calls to TWA maintenance in New York, we advised at no time had there been any visible fire. Consequently, there was no damage to any part of the aircraft. An examination of the engine areas of all four-engines showed a visible oil stain on one of the engines, which had a turbo-compressor installed to pressurize the cabin. Further examination indicated a possible failure of seals on this turbo-compressor. This had resulted in the complete lubricating oil supply being blown, under pressure, into the aircraft air ducts, while at the same time passing over the cabin heaters, and then into the cabin. The cabin heaters had burned the vaporized compressor lubricating oil, therein causing the dense smoke. The oil supply sump on this compressor was empty, verifying the failure. After disconnecting the failed turbo-compressor, we started the engine and made a ground run-up. The engine functioned normally. The decision was made to fly the aircraft to New York Idlewild Airport. The cabin would not be pressurized; however, the flight was short, and this was not a factor. On what is termed a 'ferry flight', the entire crew flew to New York late in the evening of Christmas Day, 1952. The flight delay on Christmas Day made it impossible for me to attend Christmas dinner with family, as normally occurred. Unknown at the time, this Christmas Day would have been the last holiday to spend with my father, who passed away in September 1953.

CAA Hearings for Jet Powered Aircraft

In late summer of 1953, the Civil Aeronautics Authority, forerunner of the Federal Aviation Administration, began hearings on the project of January 1, 1953, termed–"The Proposed CAA Policies for Airworthiness Certification of Turbine Powered Transport." Serving as the TWA Air Safety & Accident Investigation Representative for TWA pilots, my presence at the hearings was required.

The hearings conducted by the CAA were attended by airline captains representing; American, Continental, Eastern, Pacific Northern, Pan American, National, United Airlines, as well as TWA. In language understood by all, the purpose was to make recommendations for required options for the operation of the jet powered transports currently in the process of design. During these meetings, we spent long days together with everyone contributing personal suggestions to be incorporated into this program. One at a time, my suggestions were entered.

The first proposal was to simplify or streamline communications. Radio communications of aircraft while en route were made from the respective airline flight to the radio network operated by each respective airline. All pilot communications first went to the airlines radio station for the area. Then the radio operator reported the same information or request to the respective CAA Airway Traffic Control Center. If the request was for a change in the flight operation, the

ATCC would either confirm or deny the request to the airline radio operator, who would then relay the information to the airline flight. It can be easily understood this was a cumbersome process involving numerous delays, at a time when the top speed of aircraft was approximately 300 miles per hour. To project this type of communication procedure into the jet age, with aircraft projecting to double in air speed, was not acceptable.

The second proposal was relative to airborne radar. In the recent period, airborne radar had been installed on some of the Constellation aircraft. Bulletins issued to pilots had explained the 'how to' and, in a self taught manner, pilots had become proficient in the operation of the airborne radar. The principal purpose was to project weather areas ahead of the aircraft on a cathode ray screen of the radar unit. The return on the CRT was extremely helpful when flying on instruments in the areas of thunderstorm activity. There had been two different types of installations on TWA aircraft: C band manufactured by RCA; and X band manufactured by Bendix Aircraft. It was only common sense to recommend airborne radar be made mandatory for turbine powered aircraft.

Both suggestions were accepted, entered into the record, and later applied to jet transport. As is nearly always the case, the result is not necessarily the original intent of the proposal. The communication network became a function of the FAA and an integral part of the FAA Air Traffic Control system. At this time, it was not the intention to create the largest bureaucracy in the FAA. However, direct communication from air to ground did become operational procedure.

The combined data from the hearings was published by the CAA in a document of January 1, 1954. All participants' names were noted. It is, perhaps, noteworthy all personal time devoted to this project was done on 'off duty' periods, without any monetary compensation.

The Trojan DC-4

In the 1950s, the Lockheed Constellation comprised a major portion of the fleet along with the Douglas DC-4, with the Martin 404 rounding out the fleet.

In the early evening hours a Constellation flight terminated in Chicago, Illinois. While in the pilots' ready room turning in the flight papers, Captain Marvin Horstman came by and greeted us. Captain Horstman was the chief pilot of the TWA Chicago flight crew domicile. After Marvin's cordial greeting and a few pleasantries, we asked what kept him at the airport past normal hours. He informed us the TWA mechanics had engaged in an unplanned and unauthorized walk-out that morning. Crew chiefs normally taxied the aircraft to and from the TWA terminal to the maintenance hangar, but they were too busy to perform this task. As a result, Marvin had been taxiing the aircraft to and from the terminal since early morning. It seemed logical he should have some relief from his duties. At this time, my services were volunteered to complete the remainder of the evening for him. In fact, it was suggested perhaps his dear wife, Jane, would appreciate his arrival home.

Before he departed, Marvin explained the situation that had created this personnel problem. It appeared one of the agitators had abused his sick leave and was disciplined accordingly. The disciplinary action had resulted in a walkout, termed a "wildcat" strike. After

Marvin departed, several aircraft, which had terminated flights, were taxied to the TWA maintenance hangar.

Taxiing the Constellation involved an interesting procedure. The procedure: occupy pilot seat to apply parking brake; check off the required items on the 'before starting' check list; move to the flight engineer station to start the engines; then return to the left pilot seat to taxi the aircraft. After arrival at the hanger, final step was to apply parking brake; return to F/E station; and shut down the engines.

There was a respite between arrivals which allowed for a visit to an old friend, Passenger Service Representative, Miss Virginia Jones. We adjourned to her office for a cup of coffee. Shortly thereafter, we were advised several TWA mechanics were at the ticket counter. This was an unusual occurrence, so we both went to the ticket counter. A large group of TWA mechanics greeted us; one of them addressing us by our names, since we both knew him well. The entire group was extremely upset, and explained they had not been permitted to begin or take part in their normal work shift. The leader of the group was an old friend and addressed me by name stating, "Lyle, we do not want to strike."

Their emotional outbreak and distress was most upsetting. As a result of the morning shift initiating an illegal work stoppage, the TWA maintenance director locked out <u>all</u> the mechanics. It was now approaching midnight. The last TWA terminating flight would soon arrive. We discussed their dilemma.

"Ginny" Jones knew them all as working associates. She had been aware of the work stoppage throughout the day and the resultant irregularities. It appeared the only logical course of action was to somehow get this group of well intended employees back to work. After considering several options, the following course of action was explained to the group. The last flight termination was a DC-4 aircraft that would be taxied to the maintenance hangar. The procedure would be to start only the two inboard engines to taxi the aircraft to the maintenance hangar. The current plan, made with the maintenance supervisor, was to taxi the aircraft up to the doors of the hangar before shutting down the engines. This procedure was necessary as the aircraft required overnight maintenance before a flight assignment the following morning. The aircraft would be moved into the hangar by tow to accomplish this requirement.

Personally conceived, the proposed plan was based on ancient Greek mythology. We would perform a Trojan DC-4. In addition to the original plan to taxi the airplane to the maintenance hangar, the revised plan was explained to the group of mechanics. After the aircraft had been vacated by the arriving passengers, they would board the aircraft and be seated in the passenger cabin. After taxiing the DC-4 to the hangar and the hangar doors were opened, the aircraft would be taxied directly into the hangar. There was no threat of injury to any ground personnel, as the aircraft was taxied with only the inboard engines operating. When the aircraft was inside the hangar and the hangar doors closed, they would all deplane inside the maintenance hangar.

The plan was performed accordingly, and as anticipated, the arrival of the aircraft in the hangar with engines running brought the chief of maintenance storming out of his office. His presence there was known as we had conversed with him when taxiing previous aircraft to the hangar. The boarding stand was placed at the forward door of the aircraft. All deplaned only to be greeted by one furious Chief Frank Toyne, who exploded with, "What the hell do you think you are doing?"

At the head of the column my reply was, "Just trying to get these men back to work. It is what they wish to do."

Frank's anger could not be ignored. After several glaring moments, he then addressed the group of mechanics with his opinions about the early morning walkout. It was obvious nothing constructive was going to be accomplished with this negative conversation. Addressing him face-to-face, "Frank, for once in your life, try listening to what these people are telling you. They do not wish to continue the strike!"

After a few moments of silence, Frank motioned for the entire group to join him in his office. As is often the case, once the animosity was removed from the scene, everyone returned to their respective duties. The early morning shift arrived on time. Work began on schedule and TWA Chicago operations returned to normal.

The news of the difficulty in Chicago had reached President Ralph S. Damon at TWA headquarters in New York and the situation had been monitored from his office throughout the day. When news of the TWA Trojan DC-4 operation and favorable outcome reached New York the following morning, along with the routine operation, the reports were met with gratitude. Mr.

Damon was relieved and happy to hear of the friendly and productive results. President Damon extended his thanks for the measures taken, and later followed up with a personal letter, indicating a check for $100.00 would be forthcoming. In this letter, he extended his thanks with an apology for not delivering his wishes in person. It is interesting to note the check was to be for $100.00. When Mr. Damon found out there would be IRS withholding taxes of $25.00, the check was revised to $125.00.

TWA

TRANS WORLD AIRLINES Inc.

January 27, 1964

Dear Lyle:

The other officers of TWA join with me in sincerely thanking you for your fine work during the recent trouble in Chicago.

It is unfortunate that such an incident did occur but it is gratifying to see such an exhibition of loyalty and willingness when your company needed your help.

It would be impossible for me to place a value in dollars and cents on the service you rendered your company at Chicago, but as an expression of our sincere appreciation, you will soon receive a check in the amount of $100.00. It was my hope that I could send you shares of TWA stock but I find that we as a corporation cannot buy and issue our own stock. Please accept this check in lieu.

Sincerely,

R.S. Damon

R. S. Damon
President

Ralph Damon Thank you letter.

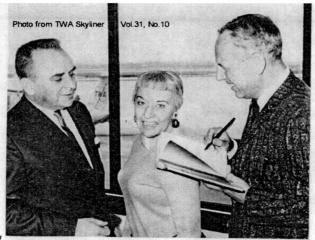

"AIRPORT" AUTHOR Arthur Hailey uses shoulder of O'Hare PRR Ginny Henline to autograph a copy of his new novel for maintenance foreman Roy Davis. Roy is one of the leading recognizable characters in the book, under the name of Joe Patroni. The only real name used in "Airport" is Ginny's.

Ginny Jones Henline - ORD PRR Extraordaire.

Rubinoff and his Violin

On Thanksgiving Day 1952, the flight was between two major cities of the United States. A hostess entered the flight deck to complain of a passenger making a lot of noise in the cabin. To examine the situation, an immediate cabin inspection was made to determine the problem. Alone in a row of three seats, next to the window sat Mr. Rubinoff playing Chopin's Polonaise on his 'muted' violin. This was the reported unbearable noise.

There was a quick and satisfactory manner to cope with the situation. After self-introduction, Mr. Rubinoff was asked if he and his violin would care to visit the flight deck. He smiled and followed me to the observer's seat on the flight deck. After tactfully informing him of the feminine complaint, he smiled saying, "But I was practicing with the violin muted." He was quickly informed to continue playing the violin without the mute. He obliged with many favorite compositions. During a break in the enjoyable renditions, Mr. Rubinoff would tell many humorous stories.

Most appealing and humorous was his association with Will Rogers, a comedian of world-wide recognition. Mr. Rubinoff explained: "I was fond of Will. We spent much time together and Will's favorite pastime was to play checkers. Will always took so much time to study his next move, I would pick up my violin I had placed by my elbow and play. During one such game of checkers, after a long delay during which time I had picked up my violin, Will finally made his move saying, 'Fiddler,' it is your move."

Indignantly I replied, "I am not a fiddler. I am a violinist."

Will's reply; "Rubinoff, when a violinist plays, he stands up. When a fiddler plays, he sits down. You're playing sitting down. Fiddler, it's your move."

This is the best display of a personality–one who tells humor about himself. It is hardly necessary to comment how extremely enjoyable this encounter was. When we reached our destination sooner than wished, with a gracious smile and violin case in hand, Mr. Rubinoff departed. Life does have its rewards.

Unique business card of Rubinoff in the shape of his classic violin.

Lockheed Super Constellation – "Super G"

The Lockheed L-1049 aircraft was unable to provide the required range for the non-stop flight operation. The L-1049G was built to fulfill the range requirements necessary for the long non-stop flights. The aircraft power plants were the new Wright Turbo Compound 3350 engines. The engines were rated at a higher horsepower than the previous W-3350. The wing was now internally carrying all possible fuel. Consequently, wing tip tanks were added. The additional fuel did provide some, but not all of the desired operational range.

The flight deck was updated to include further enhancement of the flight deck windows. The windows had been enlarged on the 1049 from the original 049. Flight deck windows on the 049 had been small as a consideration of cabin pressurization. The 049 was the first of Lockheed's commercial pressurized aircraft; 049 windows were so small pilots referred to flying the 049, 'like flying a house looking out the keyhole.'

Airborne radar was standard on the L-1049G. It had been necessary to install radar on the previous models. The radar installation called for a new, extensive nose cone which was quite distinctive, and added to the overall length of the airplane.

The L-1049G interior was completely redesigned. The new interior was most attractive with the newly designed seats upholstered in leather. The term "G" in the G model number became synonymous for glamour.

The quality of the in-flight food service was elevated to a point of excellence. Now capable of coast-to-coast non-stop flights, both eastbound and westbound across the United States, the "G" was well received by the flying public. TWA flew many publicity flights for TWA Ambassadors Club members and frequent flyers. As captain, it was my pleasure to fly several of these flights.

A large sign, constructed as a model of the TWA Lockheed 1049-G complete with rotating propellers, was erected atop a building in Times Square, New York. This large, illuminated likeness of a TWA "G" with turning propellers was an advertising sensation in New York City. Dedication of this outsized advertisement was conducted at night to maximize the value of the illumination. In January 1956, President and CEO Ralph S. Damon made the dedication on the roof top below the sign. There was a sizable group in the party and motion pictures were taken for the desired publicity. Unfortunately, the night was a cold one and not appropriate for the formal attire worn by the dedication party. Dressed only in formal attire and without a top coat, Mr. Damon suffered a severe chill as a result of the inclement exposure. After a short illness, he passed away. The premature death of Mr. Damon, who had brought successful management to TWA, ended an airline career well respected by all. Mr. Carter L. Burgess succeeded Mr. Damon as president.

Under the Burgess administration, a much needed complete redesign of the flight crew member uniform to include captain, first officer, and flight engineer was accomplished. This basic uniform concept remained in place throughout the rest of Trans World Airlines operation. At the direction of President Burgess, all captains were presented with an Ambassador Club membership. The purpose of the membership was to make it possible for a captain to invite selected guests or individuals to enjoy the hospitality of the private lounge prior to their flight. In addition, it also made it possible for the captain to enter the club to meet guests, if so directed by a public relations representative, or by directive from the office of the chief pilot. At this time, an Ambassador Club membership was by invitation only and was a very exclusive honor. Later, a lawsuit forced the airlines to open their club membership to the general public. A membership to these exclusive clubs could be purchased for a fee on an annual basis, or a lifetime membership for a substantial one-time fee.

TRANS WORLD AIRLINES

Ambassadors Club

Whereas the development of Air Transportation, by bringing the peoples within these United States and of the World closer together, fosters the growth of unity, amity and good will, not only within our own borders —East, West, North, South—but also among nations and peoples throughout the World, and whereas

Capt. L. D. Bobzin

by his use, recommendation and support, has contributed importantly to the expansion and progress of air transportation, be it known, therefore, that he qualifies as an "AMBASSADOR" and is hereby elected to the TWA Ambassadors Club, with full privileges of membership.

DATE   April 17, 1957

Carter H Burgess
President

Copy of TWA Ambassador Membership Certificate for Captain L D Bobzin.

USAF General Carl Spaatz – USAF General Ira Eaker

Generals Carl Spaatz and Ira Eaker were passengers aboard a TWA Super Constellation flying a transcontinental flight from New York to Los Angeles. The first Super Constellation had reverse seating arrangements with the first class compartment in the aft portion of the fuselage, and the coach section forward. The first class lounge was located in the far aft portion of the cabin and consisted of a large oval lounge to conform to the aft area.

After flying for some time, a customary cabin inspection was made. Seated in the aft first class lounge engaged in a game of gin rummy were General Carl Spaatz and General Ira Eaker. Both looked up from their game to acknowledge my greeting and thanking them for flying TWA, as we considered it a great honor they had chosen TWA for their flight. They thanked me for the statement, after which they returned to their gin rummy game. The flight had been in clear weather conditions and without incident.

We were approaching Palm Springs, California, flying at 20,000 ft. The sky was clear and it was early evening. In clear fight conditions, the rotating beacon identifying Desert Center Airport was visible just ahead of our flight. At this moment and for no apparent reason, the flight deck filled with dense black smoke, accompanied by a strong burning odor. Immediately, all three flight deck members donned the emergency smoke masks and turned on the oxygen for survival from the acrid smoke. The throttles were retarded and an emergency decent was made to position the aircraft for an emergency landing at the Desert Center emergency airport. Or, if conditions did not deteriorate too rapidly, a landing farther ahead at Palm Springs, California Airport. The pungent, acrid smoke gave a definite indication of an electrical fire somewhere.

During our decent, Ernie, the flight engineer had been pulling circuit breakers to trouble shoot the origin of the burning odor. The lights had been turned off in the aircraft as part of the emergency procedure which deactivates all electrical power. The cabin pressure was reduced to aid in smoke dispersal, and for the aircraft to be fully depressurized for landing. Suddenly, in a rapid transmission over the smoke mask intercom Ernie's voice was heard, "I found it. I've got it, Lyle."

This meant he had found the source of the shorted circuit and deactivated it by tripping the circuit breaker. He was precisely correct as the smoke began to diminish. The emergency decent was stopped and the aircraft put into a climb attitude to return to cruising altitude. The efficient, rapid action Ernie had taken to diagnose which circuit had failed, and to disable it quickly, avoided the necessity of making an emergency landing. The flight soon returned to normal operation and all lighting was restored. After advising the passengers the flight conditions were now normal and the flight was proceeding to land at Los Angeles, a cabin inspection was made. Arriving at the rear to the first class lounge, General Carl Spaatz and General Ira Eaker were still engaged in their game of gin rummy. An apology was made to them for turning off the lights, which interrupted their gin game. Both took my apology with a grin, knowing it was a necessary action, and with some kind comments returned to their game. After over flying Palm Springs and the San Gorgonio Pass, we arrived on schedule at Los Angeles International Airport.

Flying Lockheed Constellations on scheduled flights, John Clark served with me as first officer and co-pilot on many of these flights. John was a personable chap of Midwestern origin, an enjoyable addition to any flight crew. In his pre-employment interview, John had come face-to-face with Captain Harry Campbell, that is, AAF Colonel Harry Campbell, now returned from service in World War II (WWII). Captain Harry was now in charge of pre-employment interviews for prospective pilots. Having known Captain Harry for several years, the story of John's interview was particularly entertaining and out of the ordinary. John had appeared in Captain Harry's office for his interview. After presenting his qualifications for employment, it was apparent John possessed all the requirements for the position as first officer. During the interview, Captain Harry leafed through the flight time records. TWA requirements for flight time certification were; up-to-date flight log books to verify the total flight time and the aircraft types flown. John had been somewhat lax in his record keeping, and had not transposed his total military flight time from his AAF Form 5 records to a log book. He presented Captain Harry with a stack of AAF Form 5s to verify his flight time qualification. Captain Harry bristled at this presentation and informed John to 'go home', bring his flight time records up to the required status, and then return for his interview. John, in a perplexed and anxiety filled statement said, "Captain Campbell, TWA maximum age for pilot employment is 26 years of age. I'll be 27 the day after tomorrow, and if you do not hire me now, I will be too old later."

Relenting, Captain Harry continued the interview, picked up the stack of AAF Form 5s and paged through them. Concentrating on one of the Form 5s he said, "This 5 indicates you were assigned to AAF Base Stead Field, Reno, Nevada. Who was your commanding officer?"

Running his hand through his hair and trying to recall the answer, John finally replied, "I'm sorry sir, I do not recall."

Red in the face, AAF Colonel Campbell replied, "You idiot, I was!"

After much consternation and hopeless apologies, John figured he'd had it. Recognizing John's dilemma, Captain Harry moderated his antagonism and hired him. Captain Harry did not err; John was a good pilot, and a personable individual.

Flying in the same crew, we discovered a mutual interest which was game bird hunting. We became members of a 'duck club,' and in the migratory wild fowl season, we hunted ducks. As any duck hunter knows, duck hunting requires arising in the middle of the night to drive to the area of duck blinds, and to be in place well before sunrise. Shooting time is set according to sunrise, the time when ducks begin to move about in flight.

The Ode to the Duck Hunter:

'For mighty are his preparations;
Early in the morning he arriseth,
Disturbing the whole household.
When the day is well spent,
He returnith, smelling strong of drink,
And the truth not in him.'

The last sentence may or may not be true; the ode is, at times, referring to the "fisherman."

With the gear packed in the station wagon the night before, arising at 02:00 on the morning of a duck hunt, and off to pick up John at his residence, the result would often be a sleepy John coming to the car, gun in hand, dressed in his old military fatigues, without a coat in the cold morning air. After being reminded how cold it was, John would disappear back into the house to return wearing his hunting coat, along with his Brittany spaniel bird dog. The male Brittany spaniel was a wiry, well conformed dog of his breed. The Brit, an aggressive hunter and a joy to have on any hunt, would hop into the back of the wagon and go to sleep.

When we arrived at the duck club, it was necessary to walk through knee high water to get to the duck blind. We would arrive at the water's edge in darkness, and on occasion, would find out John had forgotten to don his hip boots. The matter was dealt with by carrying John piggy back to the duck blind, while he held the shotguns. Once there, the Brit would hop into the blind and then lie down to wait for sunrise. On cloudy mornings we usually had a good shoot. Then there are days when the sun rises bright and shining, a so called, "blue bird day." On those clear days, the Brit could stand inactivity for only about thirty minutes. Bored, he then would hop out of the blind and disappear. In a few minutes, the Brit would reappear with a duck in his mouth. He would scour the area for "'cripples," ducks shot on a previous day that had not been retrieved. The Brit would hop into the blind with his retrieve, as if to say, "If you can't shoot 'em, I'll find 'em."

The Brit was a determined hunter and on his lone forays, it was not always a crippled duck he would retrieve. On one clear morning, he returned with a mature mink, still in the trap which had caught it. Still alive, the mink was not a happy prisoner. With his sharp teeth, the mink is a dangerous animal. The Brit was fortunate not to have been bitten. With great caution, we freed the mink to give him another chance at life. Nonetheless, the Brit did not allow boredom to set in on a clear day.

The duck hunting season often occurred in the same time frame as the upland bird hunting season. One clear 'bird-less' morning we were returning to the wagon without firing a shot, much to the Brits disgust. As we approached the wagon, a ring-neck cock pheasant rose from the brush with the usual cackle and whirr of wings. John dropped the pheasant with one shot. Still alive, the Brit retrieved the bird, as the shot had only broken a wing. The pheasant's neck was rung with the usual rotation of the wrist, and then thrown into the back of the station wagon. The Brit hopped into back of the wagon and we drove out on our way home, with the Brit asleep in the rear. It is a well known fact the Ring Neck pheasant is a tough old bird. About thirty minutes later, while we were driving along the highway, the cock pheasant recovered enough to attempt flight. It was a cold day with all the windows fully up. When the pheasant began his attempt at flight, the Brit awoke from his nap. The result was a cock pheasant flying inside the perimeter of the station wagon with a Brittany spaniel in close pursuit. This is an exciting sight to behold, but not to be desired while driving. We pulled off the highway and stopped as soon as possible. The Brit finally caught up with the wounded pheasant, retrieved the bird for John, who dispatched it properly this time.

To the last hunt, John's Brittany spaniel was always a remarkable companion. John went on to become a captain and flew for TWA until the FAR 91:353 Age 60 Rule ended his career. He retired to the country where one could hunt game birds and a bird dog could roam free in pursuit of them.

Lockheed

The development of turbine powered aircraft had been in progress for several years. Lockheed began the development of the turbine powered Lockheed Electra. My past involvement in the Constellation projects led to an invitation to be part of the Electra development program.

The Constellation series aircraft had been the major part of the TWA fleet. The military C-69 aircraft became the commercial version, the L-049. There were many models to follow until the final designated L-1649A, which TWA registered as trademark, Jetstream®. The L-1649A, powered by Wright 3350 Turbo Compound engines, was originally designated the L-1249 and L-1449. Both of the configurations were proposed to be powered by Pratt & Whitney turbine propeller engines. The Pratt & Whitney Turbine engine did not attain satisfactory specifics to be used in airline operation. The specific fuel consumption was too high for the engine to be commercially viable. Consequently, neither model was built.

Note: "Specifics" are defined as the fuel consumption in pounds per horsepower per hour. The L-1649A was built using the Wright 3350 compound engines, after the turbine P&W proved unsatisfactory.

For a long period of time aircraft wing design and construction had been similar. The aircraft wing was comprised of a center section, with outer panels attached to the center section. The wing center section was, as the word implies, attached below the fuselage at the midpoint. The outer wingtip sections were attached to the main outer panels. In the four multi-engine aircraft, the inboard wing panels carried the engine mounts.

The problem inherent in this design was the engine and propeller vibration, or 'resonance,' which caused a harmonic at the spar caps. The propellers at the tip of the circumference attain very high tip speeds. The high tip speeds create a harmonic with other parts of the aircraft structure. The spar caps are the attach points of the center section and the outboard wing panels. The harmonics created at the spar cap fittings were severe enough to cause cracking, or failure of the metal at these points. This is commonly called 'metal fatigue.'

In order to eliminate these fatigue points, the wings were redesigned to a configuration of two main wing panels with outer tips. The two main panels would be joined at the center of the fuselage. The design eliminated the spar caps and the associated fatigue point. This wing design was successful in the flight operation of the Constellation L-1649A.

Lockheed had obtained a large milling machine. It was fascinating to watch the milling of the main wing spars in the Lockheed facility. These longer than usual main wing spars were milled from a long, solid aluminum forging. The process was lengthy, as the spars were fully shaped for assembly. The wing span of the L-1649A was 150 ft including the wing tips. This spar extended from the center of the fuselage to the wing tip portion. This newer type of wing design, perhaps, used the longest main spar to this time.

In the 1950s, the requirement for a turbine powered propeller aircraft was met with the Lockheed Electra. The development of the Electra was the prime program at this time; it had the complete attention of President and CEO Robert Gross.

Having experience over a long period of flying Lockheed aircraft, the Lodestar and all models of the Constellation, led to the invitation by Bob Gross to participate in the Electra program. Bob would appear in his Aston Martin. His long lasting affection for these vehicles was a bit difficult to comprehend. Possibly, it was the association with the British image that attracted him. The Aston Martin was noisy, uncomfortably hard to ride in, but image was everything. After all, image was the important thing about the car, wasn't it? There were three major U.S. air carrier purchasers of the Electra before the actual production began. Perhaps, the invitation to participate in the Electra program was due to the fact that Howard Hughes had not been involved in prior production purchases of the Electra, as he had been in the early stages of the Constellation development. It was quite natural to believe Bob Gross hoped to sell the Electra to Hughes. This wish, along with the feeling the sale would occur, resulted in Lockheed setting aside production line spots for Electras to be built for a Hughes purchase. Every fourth aircraft on the production line was reserved for the sale to TWA. This amount of reserved production positioning was highly unusual for a commercial aircraft manufacturer. Upon sale confirmation to TWA, these production line spots would assure timely delivery.

"TONY" LeVier

"TONY" LeVier and "FISH" Salmon were synonymous with flight test at Lockheed. As part of the Super Sonic airliner program, Lockheed had constructed a 'mock-up' of the proposed Lockheed Super Sonic Aircraft. The 'mock-up' was large and in order to save space, it was built with just the left wing. One afternoon following lunch, Tony suggested, "Let's go take a look at the SST mock-up."

We inspected the projected passenger cabin, then made our way up to the flight deck. The flight deck had the projected instrumentation set up. The long, streamlined, pointed nose was to drop to a lowered position for landing in order for it not to interfere with the pilot's vision. The mock-up had a fully functioning nose, which when activated by a control, lowered the nose from its normal 'up' position to 'down' position for landing, after which it could be returned to the normal 'up' position. Following Tony's turn in the left seat, we switched positions and a repeat operation was performed. It was an entertaining period of time, after which we departed to the ground level via boarding stairs. While again inspecting the large mock-up at floor level, Tony's question was, "Well, what do you think of her?"

"Tony, have 'em put on the other wing and we'll fly it." This comment brought the usual LeVier grin and we departed.

From personal collection - photo signed by Tony LeVier.

CAA Evolves Into FAA – Enter Age 60 Rule

On June 30, 1956, a TWA Super Constellation and a United Airlines DC-7 were involved in a fatal midair collision above the Grand Canyon. The TWA L-1049 Super Constellation had taken off from Los Angeles International Airport bound for Kansas City, Missouri. Shortly thereafter, the United Airlines DC-7 took off for Chicago, Illinois. The TWA Super Constellation was overtaken by the faster United Airlines DC-7, as they both flew over the Grand Canyon. The DC-7 propellers made contact with the tail section of the Constellation, causing both aircraft to plunge into the Grand Canyon. The magnitude of this tragedy with the great loss of life shocked the aviation community.

The tragedy resulted in congressional action to reorganize the existing Civil Aeronautics Authority, the CAA to the current Federal Aviation Administration, the FAA. This change made it mandatory all pilots bring up-to-date flight log books to FAA offices for examination by a FAA inspector. A new certificate was then issued in the changed format of the FAA. In many cases, there was a long retrieval effort to update flight log books to conform to the new agency requirement. The reorganization brought about many changes in the regulations governing air carrier operation. One of the changes, FAR 91:353 which terminated all commercial airline pilots flying upon reaching age 60, was to prove highly contentious in the industry.

In the late 1950s and early 1960s, many points of disagreement existed. At age 39, while serving in the position of Legislative Relations Chairman of Air Line Pilots Association (ALPA) Master Executive Council, many personal flights were made to Washington, D.C. to confer with those on Capitol Hill. The purpose of these trips was to voice opposition to the age 60 rule. The reward for this effort was to have the additional crew member (ACM) position permanently occupied by the FAA on all flights under my command. This apparently was one method of retaliation for my opposition to the age 60 regulation. Respect for the older pilots flying for TWA had been reality for years. Consequently, there was widespread opposition within the pilot ranks to this rule. In later years, this would to change when the regulation was seen as a method of personal promotion by eliminating those at the top of the seniority list.

There was a 'tongue in cheek effort' by the ALPA to assist in the case of the three American Airlines pilots, who were resisting leaving at age 60. Due to their age, the three AA pilots were the first ones to be affected by the regulation. There were admissions by ALPA that their retirement benefits were minimal. This created a financial hardship for them, as the pilots in question were not involved in any long standing retirement program.

ALPA statement: It was not until 1980 ALPA endorsed the age 60 rule.

This statement is incorrect. In 1978, at age 60, personal unemployment became reality. It is easily recalled that ALPA supported the age 60 rule well prior to my departure. It is perhaps more logical; the statements by ALPA are a vain attempt to absolve the union from a position not to be admired. Under the stewardship of ALPA, the age 60 rule is no longer a problem, as many pilots are seeking to depart the industry long before they reach age 60.

It is interesting to note in an article published in Consumer Reports on Health, March 2008; "Early retirement boosts risk of premature death, according to a study of about 17,000 men and women. Retirees of any age were about 50% more likely to die over the study's 12 year follow-up period than people of a similar age who continued working. Each 5-year increase in the age of the retirement was linked to a 10% decrease in the risk of death. Considerable research documents the health benefits of remaining active—either through work, volunteering, or social activities—as you age. So when you do retire, try to remain engaged in meaningful activities."

Now, as matter of record on December 31, 2007, Congress revised the age 60 regulations, extending the retirement age to 65. When the rule was initially enacted, there was no credible data presented to justify the arbitrary age 60 rule. As with the age 60 rule the change to age 65 was not backed by any medical evidence.

Chairman of the Civil Aeronautics Board, Alan S. Boyd proposed a requirement that all international air carriers be required to file capacity agreements. This agreement would require before initiating increased flight schedules to and from the United States, the foreign air carriers would set forth their proposed operations.

As an international carrier, TWA had recently been restricted from flying local passengers between the principal cities of Europe. This restriction had prevented TWA from carrying a large amount of the air traffic which originated in Europe.

Mr. Boyd requested ALPA approval, support and backing for this capacity agreement. In Washington, D.C. at this time and meeting with president of ALPA, Mr. Clancy N. Sayen, a letter to Mr. Boyd stating 'complete ALPA approval of the capacity agreement,' over my signature, was presented to Mr. Sayen. After reading the proposed correspondence, Clancy stated, "I cannot possibly agree with this as I am also president of the International Air Line Pilots Association."

"Clancy, that's where we have a strong divergence of opinion. As chairman of the Legislative Relations Committee, it is my position to represent all United States airline pilots. The recent restriction applied by foreign governments has reduced the United States air carrier revenue. Therefore, it is required we give Alan S. Boyd complete support for his proposal."

There would be no concurrence on this subject. After departing Clancy's office with the letter in hand, it occurred to me, if the letter was left to be mailed by ALPA, it would probably wind up in the 'circular file.' With this in mind, my letter was placed in an addressed, stamped envelope and personally mailed. When Clancy became aware of my action, he removed me from the position of Legislative Relations Chairman and quickly filled the position with someone else. The required dues for ALPA membership were paid until my last flight, May 8, 1978. The dues 'check-off' provision had not been part of ALPA's contract with TWA at this time. Dues payment had always been voluntary.

In June 1957, the Lockheed 1649A went into service in the TWA system as the Jetstream®, a TWA registered trademark. The original development of the airplane called for Pratt & Whitney turbine-propelled engines. In the late development stages, the turbine-propelled engine did not reach satisfactory fuel consumption standards. In addition, it faced possible resonance difficulties. Consequently, the Wright 3350 turbo-compound engine was adopted. This engine was currently in use on the Lockheed Super G Constellation. The 1649A was the last of the Constellation series. Within a year of its development, the Comet 4 and the Boeing 707 were introduced—the "Jet Age" had arrived.

When the decision was made not to use the turbine-propelled engine on the 1649, there were those in TWA who recommended the airplane not be purchased. However, Howard Hughes went ahead with the purchase. The useful lifespan of the 1649A turned out to be short, as had been anticipated by those of the negative opinion. There were only 44 aircraft built, and they were operated by three other airlines. As Hughes had hoped, TWA operated non-stop flights between Paris and Los Angeles. The westbound flights were 24 hours in length. The new wing on the 1649A was of a different design and a longer span of 150 ft which made it possible to carry more fuel internally. The wing tip tanks of the Super G were not necessary. The aircraft met with good pilot acceptance, but it came too late in the industry evolution of aircraft development. When Boeing 707s went into service, the 1649s were converted to cargo carriers.

'Maestro' Arthur Fiedler

It was fortunate Arthur Fiedler was fond of airplanes and flew in them often. Reported to be Viennese in origin, it was a matter of heritage Arthur Fiedler would be a connoisseur of wine, women, and song. Perhaps Arthur changed the order of preference to; song, women, and wine. A profound belief he often expressed: "There is not any poor music, just poor arrangements."

A Fiedler arrangement of "Thirteen Tons of Number Nine Coal©" could turn the song into a symphonic presentation. A vibrant person, Arthur had two passions other than music; fire engines and airplanes. Perhaps in time the order changed to airplanes and fire engines. The fact airplanes were his great interest is providential, as it was for this reason we met. As soon as Arthur became aware of my great fondness for music, he desired to make it possible for me to attend the Boston Pops. The Pops in Boston on the East Coast, and my residence on the West Coast required some coordination. After flying a TWA Jetstream® Constellation all night non-stop from Los Angeles to Boston, an early morning telephone call was made from my hotel to Boston Symphony Hall. The call was pleasantly answered by Mary, the symphony secretary. After Mary identified me, she promptly replied Mr. Fiedler had made my name known to her, and my attendance was expected that evening at the concert.

Fortunately, the assumption was ahead of my request to attend, and certainly eased the situation.

Mary assured me Mr. Fiedler wished me to be his guest that evening at the Pops, and at my convenience stop by her office at Symphony Hall to pick up the ticket. Since the flight had taken all night and a short nap requirement was explained, the question proffered was, "Could the ticket be picked up late afternoon?"

Mary said she fully understood and, "Yes, the ticket could be obtained late afternoon."

The Boston Symphony Hall was a short walk from the hotel. Mary, who was briefly filling in at the ticket window, called my name and asked me to join her there. After pleasantries, Mary asked if there had been time for breakfast. Without waiting for a reply, she quickly passed a paper cup through the ticket window. The paper cup contained four fingers of Scotch. The only proper response was, "How can anyone not love Boston?"

During the conversation which followed, the lobby clock had quickly moved to 5:30 p.m. Mary stated it was time for her to go home for dinner before returning for the evening performance. It was highly in order we have some proper form of food other than the cup of Scotch. Perhaps it would be a better choice if we dined together. If we did so, Mary would avoid the quick trip home and return. And after all, it was a small token for all her kindness. Mary concurred, and we departed for a restaurant just down the street from Symphony Hall. After dinner, we returned to the hall and were joined by the assistant to Mr. Fiedler, and the secretary to the Boston Pops, which made for a table of four. After the evening performance, it was the custom of Mr. Fiedler to host a buffet for invited guests. The buffet was located on the balcony above the stage.

In times to come, it was my good fortune to attend Boston Pops concerts when they were on the road outside Boston. Being greeted by Arthur Fiedler was always a pleasant addition to the concert. The Arthur Fiedler arrangements presented by the Boston Pops showcased music at its very best. Regardless of the instrument of the soloist or the vocalist, the Fiedler arrangement would always enhance the guest presentation. Mr. Fiedler was truly modest in manner, a talent in a world of musical mediocrity. A delightful woman in charge of RCA sales once reminded us Mr. Arthur Fiedler's Red Label recordings were the top sellers at RCA. Arthur Fiedler's music will be with us forever. The performance of the Boston Pops remains a pleasant memory.

From personal collection – Boston Pops Mr. Arthur Fiedler - 1959

The Jet Age

The airlines "Jet Age" began in the late 1950s. The first jet had been the Comet 4, which had met with a fatal crash. The fuselage had been built with a window at the top of the fuselage. The frame had been held in place by several rivets around the perimeter. The large number of holes that were drilled for the frame resulted in a metal fatigue point in the aluminum skin. Thus, a fatigue point under cabin pressurization resulted in an extended area of metal skin failure, culminating with the complete failure of the aircraft. After redesign, the Comet 4 returned to service. However, the reputation was severely damaged; the aircraft was not widely accepted.

The Boeing 707 was the first American-built jet aircraft to go into service. The aircraft rapidly won world-wide acceptance, and the production rate was not adequate to satisfy initial orders. The Douglas DC-8 followed in production.

We were invited to attend the initial flight of the Douglas DC-8, which took place at the Long Beach, California International Airport. The DC-8 had been built at the Long Beach facility. Previous commercial aircraft had been built at the Douglas facility at Santa Monica, California. The longer runway requirement for jet aircraft resulted in moving production to the Long Beach facility.

The actual aircraft demonstration was short, as the DC-8 was flown to Edwards Air Force Base immediately after takeoff. This had been planned as further flight-testing was to be done at Edwards AFB. After the departure of the DC-8, the dedication and presentation was held at the Long Beach terminal area. Mr. Donald Douglas, Jr. conducted the festivities and cocktail hour to follow. In his dedication address, he remarked, "It was heart stopping to witness the 'total net worth of Douglas' rolling down the runway." Such was the amount of money required to develop the new DC-8. To date it had been the most expensive commercial aircraft development cost for Douglas Aircraft.

The introduction of the jet aircraft initiated a completely new training program for pilot qualification to fly the aircraft. The stress levels were higher than at any previous time in airline history. The results were not pleasant. Under the stress of the program, many pilots suffered health problems, some of which resulted in the termination of their careers.

The flight simulator made its appearance early in the training program. The simulator was not advanced enough in its development to qualify for all required maneuvers. As a result, many of the engine failure situations had to be performed in actual aircraft. In fact in many cases, simulated situations were executed at low altitude when control was lost. There was not adequate altitude to recover control before contact with the ground. In the early stages of the program, several jet aircraft were destroyed along with the loss of the lives of many crew members. This also added to the pressure on all pilots involved in the training program.

The simulated emergency procedure required by the FAA was the simulation of the failure of two engines on the same side of the wing. This was referred to as 'simulating the failure of two engines on a side.' The throttles on two engines were retarded to simulate the engine failures. In this flight situation, considerable rudder control, and in some cases, full or maximum rudder control, was necessary to maintain directional straight and level flight. The airspeed required for this flight condition was much higher than normal. In several cases, control was lost during this simulation, resulting in a fatal accident. The condition was exacerbated by the design of the original 707. The tail section was modified to a larger vertical stabilizer and larger surface rudder. A hydraulic control system was added to the rudder, and this added to the effective control of the rudder. The hydraulic boost reduced the amount of physical rudder pressure forces. Fortunately, these later modifications brought an end to this type of training accident.

Final Connie Flight

The Lockheed 1649A Constellation, the latest and the last of the Constellation series, was powered by the troublesome Curtiss Wright turbo compound 3350 engine. The reliability of the 3350 had been hampered by the installation of the power recovery turbines that increased the amount of heat in the engine nacelle area. The PRTs, as they were called, had increased the required maintenance.

The Boeing 707 had gone into service on TWA flight schedules and notice to attend the Boeing 707 ground school and flight training had been received. The last Constellation flight was a scheduled coast-to-coast round-trip flight sequence.

We were flying a Lockheed 1649A Jetstream® Constellation on the final westbound flight bound for Los Angeles. The weather was clear for most of the flight which had been routine. Sun had set, as the flight proceeded in a clear evening sky. The course to Los Angeles had taken us above the state of Oklahoma and we were approaching the Texas panhandle.

The flight engineer had been directing his attention to the number three engine, studying the cathode ray screen now directed to that engine. Charlie, the F/E said, "Lyle, there is a PRT on number three overheating."

"Charlie, please. This is my last flight on these Connies. Please, no problems." It had been a uneventful flight thus far, and it was hoped it would remain that way.

A few moments later a more urgent voice said, "Lyle, that PRT is about to fail and if it does, it will probably come right through the engine cowling."

"All right, Charlie, have it your way, feather number three."

This means shutting down the number three engine; feather the propeller, which stops the engine rotation; then perform the after engine shut down check list, read by the first officer, completing the engine shut down procedure.

It was a beautiful, clear night with the great weather extending all the way west to Los Angeles. We were now approaching Amarillo, Texas. (Amarillo—yellow in Spanish: Yellow, Texas; wonder why the Texans haven't changed this? Six Gun, Texas or Panhandle, Texas as it is in the Texas Panhandle.) The hostesses had been busy serving dinner to the passengers. Our change in the engine operation was done smoothly so no one would be disturbed. The FAA-FAR reads to something like; 'If power is lost or an engine is no longer developing power, a landing will be made at the nearest satisfactory airport facility.' Weather was not a factor; it was more logical to continue on to Los Angeles rather than subject everyone to the hassle of an unscheduled landing.

The meal service now completed, the number one hostess of the first class section came forward through the door to the flight deck. Prim and attractive, the hostess leaned on the back of the captain's seat;

"Well, Lyle, I noticed you have feathered number three and were still going to Los Angeles."

"Yes, we did not wish to disturb you while providing the passengers with your usual excellent service."

"Yes, Lyle, we are now flying on three engines and we are <u>still</u> going to LAX."

"That's correct. There isn't a cloud anywhere to be seen. At our weight, this bird will easily fly on three."

"Well, Captain, we forgot to tell you two FAA guys got onboard in Oklahoma City. They are both sitting there looking at the number three engine with a feathered propeller." With her beaming, 'white-teeth' smile she turned saying, "Is there anything ELSE I can do to help?" and then left the flight deck.

Albuquerque, New Mexico, was the next major city along the route and an airport ahead on our flight. We landed there and taxied to the TWA gate at the terminal building. We discussed the PRT failure with the TWA mechanics who informed us there was a spare PRT in stock. It would take a considerable amount of time to remove the failed PRT and replace it. The staff of mechanics was minimal; there were only two on duty to perform the required R&R change.

After entering the terminal building, a stop was necessary in the men's room. Standing at the essential plumbing equipment, the vacant stalls on either side were suddenly occupied by two unknown males.

"Captain, what were those lights back there when you feathered number three engine?"

It was obvious who these two gents were, and the lights they were referring to were those of Amarillo. They were suggesting a regulation had been violated.

"Those lights were those of Tucumcari, New Mexico." This was not quite correct, but we had flown above Tucumcari before we arrived in Albuquerque. With a flaring look of sarcasm, they both departed.

The two mechanics were doing their best to remove and replace the PRT, but they were interrupted from time to time to service a regularly scheduled TWA flight. The PRT change completed, we departed for Los Angeles to arrive well after midnight, in the early hours of the morning. The last flight on the Constellation had not been routine thanks to the Curtis Wright turbo compound 3350 engine that had proven to be a nemesis since we began flying them. Resisting the urge to relieve my bladder on the nose wheel of the Connie, we walked to the nearby TWA operations office to turn in the engine failure report before departing for home. Over a decade had been devoted to flying all the commercial models of the Lockheed Constellation.

Conventional reciprocating engines had become larger to develop more horsepower, in order to fly larger aircraft faster and farther. As a result of the larger engines developing more horsepower, they also produced more heat. The efficient dissipation of heat was efficient cooling. However, it was not possible to dissipate the heat in this engine. The result: excessive heat centered in a relatively small area broke down engine components, causing engine failures.

The jet turbine engine, using the laws of motion to develop thrust, in essence, thrived on heat. And while excessive heat caused engine failures in the reciprocating engine, it had the opposite positive effect on a jet turbine engine. Heat and the expansion of gases developed thrust—the principle of the jet turbine engine.

The Boeing 707 and 747 would be the aircraft flown for the remainder of my career in commercial aviation. The reliability of the jet turbine engine ushered in a new age of airline transportation.

BOOK FIVE

THE SIXTIES

The Jet Age Comes of Age

TWA had begun flying the Boeing 707 aircraft in the late 1950s. In the 1960s, the TWA fleet of 707 aircraft would become one of the largest fleets in the world. The International Division became an all Boeing 707 fleet. The around the world flight operation was inaugurated when landing rights were finally obtained from the British at the Crown Colony at Hong Kong, China, a British colony or protectorate. With the Hong Kong authority, TWA flew to Taipei (Formosa); Okinawa; Guam; Hawaii; and to Los Angeles. This route structure completed the around the world operation envisioned by Jack Frye and Paul Richter years before.

The pilots of TWA were very well satisfied with the 707 airplane and enjoyed flying it. The higher altitudes involved a new group of airways to be established for jet level operation. A major change in the flight operation was all jet flights were flown strictly on instrument flight rules. This required all jet flights to file an instrument flight plan, be in contact with Airway Traffic Control (ATC) throughout the flight where these airway traffic control centers existed. Other aircraft, including military aircraft, were still allowed to fly on visual flight rules (VFR) after clearing flight controlled areas.

Airoligation: flying a pattern of flight relative to the high and low pressure areas had been a plan devised by TWA pilots in the early 1940s. This method had been in practice on the North Atlantic Ocean flights. The success of this application led to the practice of establishing that the eastbound flights be flown on southerly tracks, and the westbound flights on northerly tracks across the North Atlantic. The amount of flights had increased greatly from the 1940s, and more routes were required for traffic separation by ATC. In using this procedure, more favorable air mass movements were utilized. The jet aircraft made wider use of airoligation possible; the greater distances of the flights made wider use of this method feasible.

Long distance flights, which had been highly traveled, were non-stop flights connecting the West Coast of the United States and Europe. There were several flights flown on these routes with the reciprocating engine aircraft. However, any great amount of non-stop flight operation had been limited. The Lockheed 1649A Constellation flown by TWA had made a few westbound flights from Paris to Los Angeles. The number of flights had been limited as the flights were 24 hours in length, and fuel loads reduced the available payload.

The greater speed of the jet aircraft and the longer range made the desired flights possible. Due to the prevailing air mass movement, the eastbound flights were more easily planned and flown, as had been the case earlier in the piston powered aircraft era. Planning the westbound flights on the TWA route–London to Los Angeles required more study. The Great Circle Route had been accepted as the shortest and fastest. The application of the principle of airoligation refuted this practice. The air mass movements, if properly flown, offered more effective components and reduced flying time. The Great Circle Route was a northerly course of flight. If this course was altered slightly, better flight times could be accomplished.

The study of this Great Circle Route produced thought about the application to the principles of air movement. In any area, the greater the difference in temperature gradients, the greater is the velocity or movement of the air mass. The winter temperatures in the Arctic Circle area are extremely cold; there is little temperature difference over a wide area. The application of this principle to the westbound flights from London to Los Angeles would make a more northerly course more favorable. The farther north of the Arctic Circle the flight was flown, the more constant air temperatures were found. As a result, the velocity of the air mass movement would be less. Therefore, the negative component would be less.

At this time, reports of air mass components at high altitudes north of 70 degrees north latitude were not available to verify this principle. The Distant Early Warning Line (DEW Line) was established at 70 degrees north latitude. Radar stations had been established along this latitude for constant monitoring of the airspace for any intrusion by Russian aircraft. As a matter of security, if there were any high altitude weather observations available, security did not allow for their transmission. There was an objection to flying a course north of 70 degrees north latitude as the DEW line radar stations had to accurately be advised of flight times and position of the flight at all times to conform to the security. In flying these flights north of 70 degrees north latitude, we found this communication requirement did not pose a problem. All the radar stations maintained a constant listening watch on the same frequencies. Our constant communication was easily established. The military personnel manning the radar stations welcomed the conversation with the commercial flights to break up their long periods of boredom as there was not much other radio communication. At the present time, flight clearances on these far north tracks were easily obtained due to the limited air traffic.

Accordingly, the westbound course from London was above England, Scotland, Iceland, Greenland north of Sondestrom Fiord, north of Baffin Island, the Northwest Terrorities and Lake Athabasca, above Alberta, Province of Canada, Edmonton, Calgary, Spokane, Washington, to Los Angeles.

The north latitudes resulted in the mild air mass movements above the Arctic Circle. When the flights arrived above southern Canada and the northern United States, the high velocity air mass movement was most often a westerly movement. This high velocity air mass movement is commonly referred to as the "jet stream." At this point, flights were flying a southerly course resulting in a positive component, which is desired for shorter flight times. The procedure of flying a course as far as 73 degrees north was successful. On one occasion flying a 707 flight from London, we arrived in Los Angeles one hour ahead of schedule. There are set tracks along this route of flight which make air traffic separation a fact of flight operation. Currently, this procedure is widely flown.

Elizabeth Taylor

The arrival of the Boeing 707 airline flight service caught the interest of the motion picture industry. Coast-to-coast non-stop and international flights now were flown with shorter and more reasonable en route flight times.

Mr. and Mrs. Eddie Fisher (Mrs. Fisher, more popularly known as Elizabeth Taylor) were to visit Moscow, Russia. TWA was chosen as the airline to fly. There was the usual amount of publicity before departure from Los Angeles International Airport. After the photographers had exhausted their film and flash equipment, we departed for New York City. Eddie and Elizabeth were delightful passengers, accepting the amenities and attention of the flight hostesses with appreciation. Elizabeth Taylor, dressed in an electric blue silk shift, wearing a mink coat, was a show-stopper. We arrived at Idlewild Airport, New York where we met good friend of many years, Captain Lyle R. Hincks, who flew the New York to Moscow potion of the flight.

The attention of the motion picture industry was no accident. Principal stock holder of TWA, Howard Hughes, was also the owner of RKO Studios. The publicity worked both ways; great for TWA and RKO.

Very Close Call

On June 9, 1960, at 09:00 EDT flying TWA Flight 5 we departed from Idyllwild Airport, New York. Our destination was non-stop to Los Angeles. The weather was typical for a June day, generally clear skies all the way across the U.S. The navigation was done using the network of Visual Omni Range stations across the U.S. The flight was one of the enjoyable ones—clear for sightseeing with smooth air all the way. To add to the passenger's enjoyment, we had flown over the Grand Canyon, always an enjoyable experience.

Before arriving over the Los Angeles area, the route to be flown was over the Boulder City, Nevada, Omni radio range; then direct to the Hector, CA radio Omni, to overhead the Ontario, CA radio Omni; to the outer marker beacon at Downey, CA; thence, via the Los Angeles Instrument Landing System (ILS) to landing. The route visually was overhead Boulder City, NV; the high desert at Hector, CA; above Cajon Pass, Ontario; to Los Angeles International Airport.

Even though the weather was clear, the entire flight was conducted on instrument flight rules. We were in radio contact with airway traffic control at all times. The flight had been flown at flight level 350, (35,000 ft). We had flown over the Boulder City Omni and were cleared by ATC to descend to flight level 280, via the cleared route to LAX. It had always been a personal policy to discontinue flying on the auto-pilot after beginning the decent for landing. This was the one day this practice would pay off. It was standard procedure for ATC to issue decent clearances from the cruising altitude down to the final approach for landing in accordance with other aircraft traffic. We had reported over the Hector Omni, then we were cleared to descend to flight level 200 (20,000 ft) to report leaving flight levels 280, and 260. We had descended from flight level 280, had reported same, and had reported out of flight level 260. We were proceeding on course to Ontario Omni. As we descended from flight level 260 and were approaching flight level 250, a small speck appeared on the horizon and rapidly gained in size. It was an aircraft headed directly at us, flying on a course exactly opposite to ours. As soon as the aircraft increased in size, our decent was broken off and a roll executed to the left, at which time the other aircraft passed directly below our right wing. The pilots of the other aircraft had not seen us until they were passing directly beneath our right wing. We could see the horrified looks on their faces as they flashed below, so close all of us thought they would make contact with our inboard jet engine, which fortunately they narrowly missed. The split second view of the aircraft identified it as an Air Force T-33 jet trainer. The Lockheed F-80 jet fighter had evolved to become the U.S. Air Force T-33 jet trainer.

The entire near disaster had occurred in split seconds; the favorable outcome was a result of the practice of hand flying the aircraft from cruising altitude to landing. If the aircraft had been on the auto-pilot, there would not have been sufficient time to push the auto-pilot disconnect button and resume flying to execute the avoidance maneuver. A God-given gift of

20-15 vision played a major role in favorably resolving the incident. The flight continued on to land at Los Angeles International Airport. The near miss was quickly circulated through communications channels, and before leaving the flight deck, there was the radio request to contact the FAA office ASAP.

As soon as we deplaned, we went immediately to inspect the right wing. We had felt no contact, nor had any instrumentation indicated contact had occurred. Nevertheless, we examined the right wing and the engine nacelles. There was no indication of any damage, though the aircraft was to undergo further inspection by the TWA maintenance personnel.

The flight crew then proceeded to the offices of the West Coast Manager of Flying, Captain Fred Austin. A complete report was made; copies of the reports were signed and filed. The TWA office had been advised of the FAA investigation and hearing to be conducted at 09:00 the following morning at the Los Angeles Airport. Our presence was mandatory, not requested.

The FAA hearing was conducted the following day as scheduled by the FAA chief inspector, air carrier division, Los Angeles. There were numerous inspectors from the FAA present. In fact, so many inspectors the hearing officer did not take the time to introduce anyone. We were called upon by name. There was no further information to give; our written letters from the previous day thoroughly covered all testimony. The letters were formally entered into the record as evidence.

The two U.S. Air Force pilots were in attendance. The command pilot of the Lockheed T-33 was Major

Beauregard. The major stated he and his student pilot had departed Norton Air Force Base on a flight to the USAF Edwards Air Base area. The major also stated they were flying visually at flight level 250, and they did not see the TWA Boeing until they were about to pass beneath the wing of the 707. He also commented he thought they were going to strike the engine nacelle of the right wing. The major had little else to add to the testimony. At the end of his testimony, he groused he would be passed over for future promotions as a result of this incident. The other pilot testified to much the same information. He added he also thought they would strike the engine nacelle of the 707.

There was some discussion by the FAA inspectors present relative to being alert when flying in the most heavily flown air corridor on the West Coast. This statement could not include us, as we had executed the avoidance maneuver. Discussion concerning the T-33 flying Visual Flight Rules was not introduced. At that time, military pilots could fly VFR without restriction. The Air Force pilot could not be charged with a violation for his VFR flight. On the other hand, if we had not been under Instrument Flight Rules, we would have been held in violation. When flying on an IFR flight clearance, the flight crew is mandated to observe all possible air traffic, weather conditions permitting. We had been in full compliance.

There was some internal conversation, and then comment was made by the chief inspector. He was glad we were all there to talk about the incident because the outcome could have been entirely different. No one objected to his statement. At the beginning, of the hearing, it was evident all the FAA participants were former military pilots. Therefore, there would be the minimum of negatives regarding the T-33 pilots.

After the discussion or hearing was complete, the chief inspector said to me, "I guess the charge against you could be under Part 91; 'flying in the close proximity of another aircraft.' " Smiling as he made this statement, he thought this comment humorous. We did not smile, chuckle, or otherwise acknowledge his feeble attempt at humor. We just departed.

There was a considerable amount of written correspondence to follow with the Air Line Pilots Assn., and others. There was nothing further from the FAA, not even a final report.

Note: The Lockheed T-33 was cruising at Mach number .80 at flight level 250. The airspeed would have been approximately 495 knots per hour. The T-33 was on a heading of 180 degrees from that of the Boeing 707. At the point of near impact, the T-33 was quartering slightly to the right of the 707. This was the reason for the pull up and simultaneous left roll of the 707. The speed of the 707 was descending at Mach number .88 or approximately 535 knots per hour. Therefore, the 'closing speed' was approximately 1030 knot per hour. In miles per hour, the closing speed is even higher at 1185 miles per hour. The reaction time was minimal. There would be small corrections for temperature and other variables not calculated here.

The first officer went on to checkout as captain. The flight engineer was very angry and disgusted by the conduct of the investigation, and he made his feelings well-known to me. All three flight deck crew members had seen the T-33 at close range and the near termination of our lives was to become an indelible memory. The flight engineer bought a farm in Arkansas and was not heard from again.

Captain "Eddie" Rickenbacker

While flying a TWA DC-3 as captain in the 1940s, a gentleman stopped me in the airport terminal building and introduced himself, which was not necessary because he was immediately recognized. Captain Eddie had been in a life-threatening experience in the Pacific. Also involved in the mission was a Captain Cherry from American Airlines, who had been recalled to the Army Air Force. The lengthy ordeal in the Pacific had been widely covered by the news media. Captain Eddie was returning home and explained that during his recent trial, he had injured his leg badly and was suffering from recurring pain. He asked me if it would be possible to arrange for him to occupy the most forward, single seat on the DC-3. That seat had a majority of the leg room between the seat and the forward bulkhead. The DC-3 had seven rows of two seats on the left side of the aircraft and seven rows of single seats on the right. His request was granted. It was a night flight and Captain Eddie and the other passengers slept throughout the duration of the flight. When leaving the flight deck, Captain Eddie stopped and thanked me profusely for granting his request and for a pleasant flight.

Years passed and the Boeing 707 was in service. Upon arrival at Miami International Airport to fly a flight to Los Angeles, the station manager greeted us and informed us Captain Eddie, now president of Eastern Airlines, Mr. Carl Froesh, VP of engineering for Eastern,

came under fire as the reason for the poor performance. Justified or not, the Eastern board of directors made the decision to replace Captain Eddie. Their selection was the VP of Operations of TWA. Possible dissent among top management of Trans World Airlines led this vice-president to be readily available to accept the offer to become the president and CEO of Eastern. The new president and CEO of Eastern, while initially exuberant, fared no better than his predecessor. There would be another change at the top to a different, well-known person, when former astronaut Frank Borman took over the helm. Route structure, plus the 'Ahab philosophy' unionism prevailed with some union members openly calling for the bankruptcy of Eastern. After a long period of financial uncertainty, and an encounter with one of the 'corporate raiders,' this philosophy was finally realized when Eastern Airlines filed bankruptcy and ceased operation.

Dr. Theodore Von Karman

On February 17, 1963, after checking in at TWA flight operations at Los Angeles International Airport to fly Flight 18 non-stop to Dulles Airport, Washington, D.C., the dispatcher handed me a note from the TWA director of passenger service. It read, "Please contact me at the TWA Ambassador Club before your departure." The Ambassador Club was located on the second floor of the departure terminal. The Passenger Service Director came to the desk to advise me Dr. Theodore von Karman was flying to Washington to receive the initial award of The Medal of Science from President John F. Kennedy the following day. He introduced me to Dr. von Karman, who was seated in the lounge. As a courtesy after the introductions, Dr. von Karman was asked if he would like to enjoy a drink of his preference. A smiling Dr. von Karman advised he preferred Slivovitz, but would have a whiskey while we chatted. Dr. von Karman was a pleasant, relaxed conversationalist with a great sense of humor. After several minutes, it was time for me to board the Boeing 707 at the departure gate. Advising Dr. von Karman of this, he was asked if he would like to accompany me onboard the flight at the same time. He answered in the affirmative and we departed the Ambassador Club for the aircraft. TWA served a generous drink and after consuming it, Dr. von Karman became more relaxed and was in good spirits. We boarded the aircraft and after escorting Dr. von Karman to his seat in the first class cabin, continued on to the flight deck. We departed from Los Angeles on schedule.

After takeoff and climb to cruising altitude and the flight was established in normal cruise flight, the flight deck door opened and a smiling, attractive, impeccably groomed hostess in charge of the first class cabin appeared. With the same 'toothpaste-white' smile she inquired, "Who is that aging rouge you escorted aboard? After you left, he pinched me as I was walked by."

"He, lovely one, is Dr. Theodore von Karman who is flying to Washington, D.C. to receive the very first Medal of Science award from the president."

"After his uncouth pinch of my posterior, I thought he was a friend of yours," she replied.

"Well, dear, look at it this way. It isn't every day you are pinched by someone receiving a Medal of Science award from the president. The same thought relative to your anatomy has occurred to me, a non-recipient of any presidential award."

With the same brilliant smile she departed, closing the door gently behind her.

Dr. Theodore von Karman's great accomplishments in aeronautics, including the design of jet supersonic aircraft, were renowned. It was truly a gratifying experience to meet him. Dr. von Karman was well-known for his great sense of humor relative to the usual, somewhat dull, engineer personality. He often told stories about himself and enjoyed relating self-deprecating humor.

Dr. von Karman told of his early residence in Aachen, Germany, where he was employed in 1919. He lived in a small apartment to which he had returned after a long, hard day at work. Shortly after falling asleep, he was awakened by loud noises emanating from a party taking place in the apartment directly above. He arose, bathed, shaved, groomed, and dressed in his best clothing. He then climbed the stairs to the apartment above. After knocking on the door, it was opened by an attractive girl. He politely stated the noise was keeping him awake and since sleep was not possible, could he join the party? The pretty girl promptly invited him in to join the party. Later, this girl became Mrs. von Karman and remained so for a lifelong marriage. This story has been told by other people, though perhaps his version of 1919 was the original.

The jet age was in full operation. Threats of the old world became reality when piracy became a hazard to airline operation; skyjacking and monetary ransom became prevalent. A Boeing 707 was involved in a skyjacking attempt at El Paso, Texas Airport. The attempt was thwarted, but not before considerable damage was done to the aircraft.

Piracy in the Sky: A Dilemma in High Policy

"This is piracy." snapped the tanned, rugged-looking airline pilot. "The government has to take a stand. This isn't just a felony against the airlines. It's a crime against the government."

Relaxing between flights in the wide gray corridors of New York's Idlewild airport, TWA Capt. Lyle D. Bobzin summed up the reaction of most U.S. pilots to the latest airliner hijacking attempt at El Paso. Other airline personnel at the big metropolitan air terminal, especially younger clerks and stewardesses, found a wry humor in the situation. They called out to each other: *"Buenos dias, amigos."*

But responsible airline and government officials saw nothing to laugh at: The El Paso "skyjacking" came just ten days after the commandeering of an Eastern Air Lines Electra by one of Fidel Castro's supporters—the threat had become a grave problem, not only of aerial safety, but of high national policy.

The Kennedy Administration responded to the air-age version of the old Prohibition crime by asking Congress to make the hijacking of planes, like piracy on the high seas, punishable by life imprisonment. The requested legislation, furthermore, would make it a Federal offense to assault, intimidate, threaten, or interfere with airline crews; or to

August 14, 1961

carry a deadly weapon aboard a plane.

Congressional reaction was equally immediate: Hardly had the first reports of the El Paso hijacking chattered off the press-service tickers than the more volatile legislators began filling the air with angry (and in this case, misdirected) statements against Castro. Later, in an almost unprecedented show of wrath, they rained into the legislative hoppers bills designed to discourage the seizure of airplanes, aloft or on the ground.

Conscious of the helplessness of crew members—surrounded as they are by the delicate instruments of a jet transport flight deck—the Federal Aviation Agency's new administrator, Najeeb E. Halaby, advised pilots to lock cockpit doors from the inside. He also authorized airlines to arm their crews, or, if they chose, hire guards to ride shotgun (which at least one line was doing).

Pilots' View: Gun-toting, however, met with unenthusiastic response from pilots. As Captain Bobzin put it: "The pressurized cabin of an airplane is no place for a shooting. We don't want firearms aboard." Capt. Byron D. Rickards, pilot of the hijacked Continental 707, added: "Guns are not the answer."

Any answer will be difficult to find. For a pilot's dilemma is this: To a desperate man with a gun, a locked cockpit door poses no great problem. One shot could shatter the lock. Furthermore, stewardesses are required to carry a key to the flight-deck door and, obviously, could be forced to open it. Hence, many pilots say that, confronted with such a situation, they would "play it cool." As one captain explained: "In a case where you have a man with a gun loose in your plane, our instructions are: 'Don't jeopardize the lives of your passengers or your own. Do as you are told'."

Newsweek

Newsweek interview August 14, 1961.

Higgins of Petticoat Junction

TWA attracted canine performers of note. Provisions were made for the proper attention to these well adapted air travelers. All of these canine passengers were well behaved and a pleasure to meet. One TWA flight drew the attention of Higgins, the canine star of "Petticoat Junction," a popular television 'situation comedy' program. Higgins was a charming Terrier, accompanied by his most attractive feminine handler. During our ground time, we had a pleasant get acquainted meeting with photographs taken aboard the Boeing 707.

As usual, we are belated in our thanks to you and the TWA staff for helping us get the photos of the dog from "Petticoat Junction" aboard a 707. I thought you might be interested in seeing the result, so I am enclosing prints of the occasion. I have sent prints to Capt. Bobzin, too, and hope that we can do something exciting again.

Meantime, thanks for all the cooperation you always give all of us at KD.

Ray

KDKA-TV 2 W

Thanks for being so nice to us the other day when we took the photos of "Higgins" in your 707. Here are copies for your personal use.

Sincerely,

Ray Hoffman
Public Relations Mgr.

KDKA-TV 2 W

Personal note of thanks from KDKA TV for 'doggie' photos.

The author and special 'co-pilot' Higgins of Petticoat Junction fame

Owning pointers and retrievers had created a lasting affection for all of the canine species. This fondness for animals became well-known to the TWA personnel. All passengers shared a mutual interest in the safe transportation of their pets when they were flying. It became commonplace to have TWA ground personnel request additional consideration be given to the pets accompanying the passengers. It was always a pleasure to give the pet owners peace of mind regarding the handling of their 'best friend'.

The yellow 3"X5" buck slip was an informal, widely used TWA instrument of the communication. Before a flight departure, one of the buck slips was in my mail box requesting my appearance in the chief pilot's office. Entering the office, the greeting was amicable. "Lyle, a gentleman and his wife traveling in first class are members of the TWA Ambassador Club and are on your flight. They would like to have their two Golden Retrievers accompany them in first class."

My answer, "There isn't any problem with that."

"Thanks, Lyle. You know the TWA Operations Manual states, 'There will be a maximum of one animal in each compartment.' "

While leaving and giving him the smile of a cynic, my parting shot was, "That's your penalty for reading it."

Mr. Floyd B. & Jacqueline Cochran-Odlum

There are few married couples who can encompass the legendary accomplishments equal to those of Jackie Cochran and Floyd Odlum. "Jackie," as she was known world-wide, had become famous in her own right prior to meeting and later marrying Floyd Odlum. Floyd did not have any objection to Jackie retaining her own identity. It included a career as the most famous aviatrix in the world, along with Jacqueline Cochran Cosmetics Co., and other numerous accomplishments. At one time or the other, Jackie won perhaps all of the major air race competitions in the United States. The speed record for women aviatrix is held by Jackie, flying a Lockheed F-104 jet fighter. Mr. Floyd B. Odlum became CEO of Convair, one of the principal aircraft manufacturers in the world, among his many other accomplishments.

The Cochran-Odlum Ranch of Indio, CA served as the full-time residence for Floyd and Jackie. The Cochran-Odlum Ranch was a showplace, adorned with many date palm groves. Dates from these groves were packaged and high on the list of desired gifts to be received from the Odlums. A citrus orchard produced some of the most delicious oranges and grapefruit. An invitation to be a guest at the Odlum Ranch was a delightful experience. Floyd had fallen victim to advanced arthritis. As treatment for his pain, a large

Olympic size swimming pool had been built, and the water was always heated to a high temperature for the relief from the arthritis pain. The Thermal Airport, which also served as the site for Jackie's aircraft hangar, was located a few miles south of the Cochran-Odlum Ranch. A nine-hole golf course on the ranch also served as a heliport.

Their hospitality was boundless. As a result, the ranch was constantly hosting top participants in the field of aviation, scientific research and development. The large ranch-style residence was the center of the activities, with condominiums and guest houses grouped around the main house. Next door was a large two-story building, which housed several condominiums and offices. A well-kept secret in this building was a large office, complete with an array of telephone equipment, and a large, walnut executive desk. This office was used by President Dwight D. Eisenhower when the president was vacationing at the Eisenhower residence in the nearby Palm Desert area.

During one visit to the ranch, Jackie expressed an interest in establishing a flight school, whose principal purpose would be to train pilots for future employment in the airline industry. While flying for TWA was my principal aviation pursuit, flight and ground instruction had been pursued prior to joining TWA. The idea of this project appealed to me. Consequently, we began the planning, or development of this venture. As part of the plan, we envisioned the possible acquisition of all the aviation facilities at nearby Thermal Airport, which at the time, were in an underutilized state of operation. The plan included a proposal for acquisition of training aircraft, ground school equipment, hiring of personnel, and other requirements.

We made several visits to the Thermal Airport, and discussed the planned use with the local management involved. Jackie became quite enthusiastic about the proposal, and enlisted the support of her many friends. There were numerous meetings at the ranch. Each meeting gathered more input from future participants in the pilot training program. Proposals for the acquisition of additional flight training aircraft at every meeting inflated the budget figures to an extreme. The flight training program had begun as a plan for a modest fleet of aircraft. The additional proposed aircraft were not only higher in performance, but also much higher in cost. The costs related to these additional expenditures had not been included in the initial business plan.

Jackie was a night person who rarely showed up before noon. One morning at breakfast, Floyd had been reviewing the increased investment capital require-ments. He stated his concern about the probable difficulty in securing sufficient capital from the investment group involved. We shared a mutual concern for the proposal in the present form. The income from the student training program was not adequate to sustain the increased cost of the proposed aircraft. During the breakfast meeting, we made an objective analysis of the program. We knew Jackie had been an enthusiastic supporter of the program from the outset. Anything less than a positive consensus would disappoint her.

We continued the evaluation. After examining all the items in detail, my suggestion to Floyd followed. We had devoted a great deal of time and effort into planning for the flight school. However, if he concurred it was not a viable program and wished to terminate it, there would be no objection on my part. Floyd was startled by this statement. After a few moments of silence followed by a slow, broad smile, Floyd agreed. Perhaps it would be well to terminate the flight school program. One qualification was added to our agreement. It was not a good idea for me to break the unwelcome news. Therefore, it would be up to Floyd to advise Jackie her program was to be terminated. Also, it was obvious by Floyd's attitude this discussion had enhanced his opinion of me.

COCHRAN-ODLUM RANCH
INDIO, CALIFORNIA

June 29, 1966

Mr. Lyle D. Bobzin
510 De Anza
Corona del Mar
California

Dear Mr. Bobzin,

I am enclosing herewith a revision of the estimated expenses for the pilot training school.

Jackie has sent out a letter to various of the airlines, along with a brief prospectus. I am enclosing herewith a copy of the letter she sent out, and of the prospectus.

In connection with the estimates, I think you should now check them very carefully for omissions and errors. If each student is to get two hours per day for six days a week in the air and four hours per day in classwork on the ground, then you have got to figure out how many flight instructors and how many ground instructors it takes. Also there is one point that troubles me a bit - if there are to be two ground classes a day with twenty students in each class and flying goes on for the entire day, how will it be worked out that any particular student can still attend all his classes and get in his flight time?

Sincerely,

Floyd B. Odlum

Letter re: Pilot Training School - Floyd Odlum, 1966.

July 25, 1966

Mr. Robert E. Johnson
Manager of Personnel
Southwest Region
United Air Lines
Los Angeles International Airport
Los Angeles, California 90009

Dear Mr. Johnson,

     My wife, Jacqueline Cochran, is in the Far East
at the present time but is expected back sometime
around the 8th or 10th August. In the meantime, I
have read your letter to her of July 13th about the
pilot training program. She will get in touch with
you as soon as she returns and can see you either in
Los Angeles or here at the ranch.

     Captain Lyle Bobzin, who has been with TWA for
many years and at present, during the strike, is
flying to and from Saigon for the military, has been
one of the partners of Miss Cochran in developing
the ideas for this pilot training program. Captain
Bobzin lives here on the West Coast a little south of
Los Angeles and gets back to his home occasionally
between runs. He is thoroughly familiar with the
plans for the school and, if you need to discuss them
before Miss Cochran's return, he could probably meet
you at your office. I am sending a copy of your
letter to him against such a possibility.

       Sincerely,

       Floyd B. Odlum

c.c. Lyle Bobzin

Photo of Jackie Cochran and letter from personal collection.

We had departed Los Angeles International Airport flying a TWA Boeing 707 flight non-stop to Washington, DC. Upon reaching our cruising flight level, the hostess from the first class cabin entered the flight deck to inform us, "There is a woman in the first class cabin who is highly upset."

To personally ascertain the reason for the difficulty, it was necessary to leave the flight deck and enter the first class cabin. The lady in the area turned to greet me. We were both taken aback, as we had met in the past.

"Jackie, what is the problem?"

Astounded, Jackie replied, "Lyle, I am supposed to be on a flight to New York. One of your passenger representatives escorted me out to my airplane and put me on the wrong flight. I am due in New York this evening for a board of directors meeting of Northeast Airlines."

Surprised to see Jackie in such a dilemma, there was not much that could be said or done. It seemed unlikely a person, as well traveled as Jackie, could be on the wrong flight. TWA did have three non-stop flights departing for the East Coast, in the same time frame, and in the same terminal area. Jackie had relied on the TWA passenger representative to escort her to the correct flight.

"Jackie, we'll advise TWA by radio communication of the mishandling of your flight, and advise a connection from Washington Dulles Airport to New York be made for you, as soon as possible, upon our arrival at Dulles. Any diversion to New York on my part would put me in the unemployment line."

The TWA employee error was a difficult one to cope with. Jackie made the connecting flight from Dulles to New York; however, she was late for the Northeast Airlines board meeting. The board had been advised of her late arrival for the meeting.

Another unplanned meeting occurred several years later. Flying a TWA International Division around the world Boeing 707 flight, we had flown Bombay, India, to Colombo, Ceylon. We saw Jackie in the airline terminal where she announced she was flying with us to Bangkok, Thailand. We were pleased to see her once again. Jackie and her secretary were on the flight to Bangkok as part of an around the world flight. We landed at Bangkok, where she deplaned, and we continued on to Hong Kong.

General J.W. "Jimmy" Doolittle

It would be difficult, if not impossible, to accomplish in one lifetime the feats of General James "Jimmy" Doolittle. Early in his career, the General devised a fabric hood for a De Havilland DH-4 to accomplish instrument flight across the United States. In the same time period, he flew, raced, and won air races with aircraft which had proven fatal to other pilots of his generation. Jimmy Doolittle won the Bendix Trophy Race, a flight from Burbank, California, to Cleveland, Ohio, flying a Laird Super Solution. He won the Thompson Trophy at the Cleveland Air Races flying the Gee Bee, one of the first, fast, low-wing aircraft. The ability to diagnose the critical characteristics of racing aircraft made his flights a success. His accomplishments while serving in the U.S. Air Force are numerous; the most well-known, "Thirty Seconds over Tokyo," General Doolittle commanded the flight of North American B-25s from a Naval carrier in the Pacific.

Thompson Ramo Woolridge (TRW) established a space technology laboratory in El Segundo, California. General Doolittle was in charge of this operation. The position made it necessary for the General to make many flights from Los Angeles to New York. The TRW multi-storied headquarters was easily reached from Los Angeles International Airport. In command on many of these flights, it was always a great pleasure to see General Doolittle. The General always flew first class. From there, he was visible when we boarded the

It was 27th day of John's climb on the bald face. He had reached a rock outcropping, which was made more dangerous by an accumulation of ice and snow. It was in this area John's climbing rope became entangled in a sharp combination of ice and rocks, which tragically severed the climbing rope. John fell to his death some 4,000 ft. below.

As soon as the tragic occurrence became known, a wire of condolence was sent to his father in the Congo. At that moment, Sue's location was unknown. This tragic accident claimed the life of their only child. As we had become very fond of John Jr., and his family, it was a heart wrenching experience.

Sometime later, a chance meeting with John Sr. occurred. This was not unusual, as pilots frequently met friends while flying the line. In relating to John our intended visit Montreux, Switzerland, John stated, "Leysin is a short distance from Montreux. We have contracted for markers to be placed on John's grave at the cemetery in Leysin. Would you please make a visit there to see if the grave markers have been installed?"

My assurance was quickly and sincerely promised. John Jr. had been interred at a cemetery near the mountain climbing school. After our arrival in Montreux, we took the train to a small village below Leysin. From there, we rode a funicular train to Leysin and, without delay, proceeded to the Leysin cemetery. Upon locating John's grave, we stood above it. While standing there, we felt an overwhelming presence for several moments. This invisible, but overpowering presence was discussed later; we had not previously experienced a feeling like this. John Jr. had left this world at the age of 30. Did he return for a few moments to be with us, to reward us for visiting his final resting place? We believe John did. The unmistakable presence was too intense not to be real. John Sr. had been correct in his doubts; the contract for placing the markers on John Jr.'s grave had not been completed.

Hilton Hotels-International

A merger between TWA International Division and Hilton International Hotels was made. There were many factors which made this a most favorable combination. A large number of the Hilton International Hotels were located in the major cities of the world, which were the terminals served by TWA.

The Hilton family controlled the Hilton International Corporation. There had been a TWA relationship with Hilton Hotels going back to the early days of Conrad Hilton, the founder of the hotel empire. During the time of Transcontinental & Western Air DC-3 operation, TWA flight crews had stayed at the Albuquerque, New Mexico Hilton. The Albuquerque Hilton was one of the first; if memory serves correctly, one of the first two hotels of the early Hilton Empire. The Hilton family had a lifelong interest in aviation. The founder's son and president of the corporation, Baron, had a personal interest in aviation, was a pilot, and owned his own airplane.

The merger was greeted with enthusiasm by the employees of both organizations. International flight crews were billeted at the Hilton Hotels on regular layovers. Relationships between employees of both organizations were excellent. The merged organizations complimented one another. Both represented standards of excellence, and were service industries, needing to attract and accommodate the traveling public. The business plan was, to offer bookings for flights, and the required hotel reservations on the TWA International Division reservation system. Combined flight and hotel accommodations were offered as a complete travel package. The program was a natural, as many of the new TWA international travelers were not familiar with the foreign cities, and welcomed the complete booking service. Initially, complete bookings were well received, and in many cases, sold out. The initial pricing had been under estimated. Consequently, what had been a 'sold out' program was a 'revenue losing' program. The entire promotion should have been better planned, and priced to make a profit. The market was there, but it was not fully exploited. Unfortunately, the all-inclusive bookings were dropped, instead of being reviewed and priced accordingly.

The employees recognized the favorable prospects of the two services together. Apparently, senior management did not. From the outset, there were, clearly, cultural differences between top management of both organizations, which could not be reconciled. Although the entire concept was correct, the successful execution did not occur. The CEO of Hilton International and the CEO of TWA were never on the same page, let alone part of the same book.

Bombay, India

Bombay had been the eastern terminus for TWA since 1946. The flight crews had a layover in Bombay until the next TWA flight arrived, which would provide an aircraft to originate the westbound flight.

The Taj Mahal Palace Tower Hotel was the hotel used for the flight crews. Layovers could be for several days, as the service to Bombay was not a daily occurrence. The "Taj," as it was affectionately called, was a delightful hotel. The interior décor was in conformity to India's elegant standards; lavish, and brightly decorated. Principal rooms had high ceilings, and impressive wood beams, as part of the construction. Time spent there was most enjoyable.

There are different versions of stories as to the origin of the Taj Mahal Hotel and, perhaps depending on the travel guides involved, the stories differ. The print version states, "The hotel was built by the founder of the Tata Empire, Mr. Janstiee Tata, and was officially opened in 1903." The luxury hotel took its name from the original Taj Mahal Palace located near New Delhi, India. The magnificent structures had been constructed by Mughal Emperor Shah Jahan in memory of his wife. The beautiful, white, marble edifice is referred to as the "Monument of Love." The Arch, or Gateway to India located in Bombay, was constructed later. King George V of England visited India in 1924. The Gateway to India is mentioned in connection with his visit. There is no mention as to why the palatial entrance of the Taj

Mahal Hotel does not face the harbor, as it then faced the heart of the south Bombay slums. The entrance would have been more elegant facing the harbor, the Indian Ocean. The Arch or Gateway stands alone across the street from the rear of the hotel. Had Mr. Tata been active in this decision, it seems unlikely this great error would have been made.

The location for this great hotel was selected for its proximity to the coast and harbor. The very shallow harbor was not deep enough for ships that require a large draft. It was necessary for those ships to anchor off shore; passengers were taken ashore by "lighters," small boats with a shallow draft. The location was in the heart of a highly impoverished and undesirable part of Bombay; however, the desirability to be close to the gateway to the Harbor overrode this negative. When staying at the Taj Mahal, one could not help but notice how the impressive entrance faced the heart of the depressed area. The back of the hotel faced the harbor. This was a strange and puzzling fact. Why did the lavish entry not face the Harbor and the Indian Ocean?

The story: a Scottish architect was engaged to design and supervise the complete construction of the Taj Mahal Hotel. The Scot had designed and supervised the plans up to the point where the construction was to begin. Unfortunately, a critical situation, involving a close family member, required him to return to Scotland. During his extended absence, construction began. The journey by ship was long, and by the time the Scot returned, the hotel was nearly complete. Upon his arrival, and much to his horror, he observed the austere rear of the Taj Mahal Palace Hotel faced the

Harbor and Indian Ocean, while the lavish façade, towers, and the magnificent entry of the Taj Mahal Palace Hotel faced the slums of south Bombay. In his absence, the hotel had been constructed backwards from the initial plan; he was devastated by this terrible error. So grief stricken, he tragically took his own life. It was later noted; a sizable portion of the impoverished area was cleared, resulting in a large square at the entrance to the Taj Mahal Palace Hotel.

As the memory and the experiences of the Taj Mahal Palace Hotel are written at this moment, November 30, 2008, the historic Taj Mahal Palace Hotel has been in flames for more than three days. A terrorist attack in Mumbai, formerly Bombay, has taken a heavy toll with loss of life. Fear and destruction have been rampant. The extent of the damage is unknown at this time. The magnificent, wood timber beams, and the beautiful, wood parquet floors have been a source of the long burning fire. The hope of restoration will be present in the days ahead. If the Taj Mahal Palace Hotel cannot be restored, it will tragically join two other great and historic hotels built by the British at the height of the British Empire; the Sheppard's Hotel in Cairo, Egypt; and the New Stanley Hotel in Nairobi, Kenya.

The prestigious Sheppard's Hotel in Cairo was sacked and burned by a mob in a violent demonstration against the British influence. During the reign of King Farouk, this terrorist action took many lives in Cairo, to include personnel at the airport.

The fame of The New Stanley of Nairobi, East Africa, was worldwide. The abode of the great 'White Hunters,' especially the famous 'Men's Bar,' used in many films and stories over time, was a part of the atmosphere the institution offered. The New Stanley was the only hotel of mention in the early fame of Nairobi, and the famous huts in East Africa. The New Stanley was bombed and burned to the ground by terrorist mobs, thereby ending a wonderful age of East Africa. The fatal ends of all three hotels were brought about by the malcontent, liberal intelligencia. The planners of these horrific deeds used mob violence as their tools, since they could not execute these destructive movements themselves.

The three marvelous hotels were located in cities served by TWA. The hotels became part of the services there. Fortunately flying, as captain, led to a personal relationship with all three. The Taj Mahal Palace, the Sheppard's Hotel, and the New Stanley are distant fond memories.

Recalling Bombay in the series of events leads to more memories; in particular, one very humorous occurrence is fondly remembered. The airlines with long distance operations had to set up schedules for passenger convenience. The passenger load factor was the lowest for the flights transiting Bombay. The time of day was important to passenger convenience, and their health requirements. Therefore, some cities schedules were part of the early hours of the clock. Bombay schedules, both eastbound and westbound, were in the early morning hours between midnight and 06:00 local time. As a result, our flights, both eastbound and westbound, were at 02:00 to 04:00.

All flight crews arriving at these times would be delayed in customs. The fact they had been on duty for extended periods did not enter into Indian customs agent's consideration. When they did finally appear for duty, the customs people were usually unpleasant, and took great effort to make it difficult to clear the possessions of the flight crews. The flight crews were aware of this problem, did their best to tolerate the unreasonable searches of their baggage, and in some cases, personal searches by the Indian customs authorities.

We arrived in Bombay in the early hours of the morning for a scheduled layover. Prior to our arrival, a flight of Australian origin had arrived. The crew was sitting on uncomfortable wood benches, awaiting the arrival of Indian customs personnel. The flight purser was sitting with a rather comical look on his face, with what appeared to be a new garden hose wound around his shoulders. When approached and asked if he did gardening on his layover, his reply was, "Certainly." Thinking no more about it, and after a lengthy process, we cleared customs and proceeded to the area for transportation pickup. Meeting again in this area, and before boarding his transportation to the hotel, the captain stated, "We are having a little get together this evening. Please join us."

As the same hotel was used by both airline crews, his invitation was easily accepted. After a short nap, we proceeded to the captain's room to join the gathering. On top of a large dresser cabinet was the purser's new garden hose, full of gin. This was his method of outsmarting Bombay customs. After being converted to martinis, the contents were now being dispensed. This is only one of many 'we will find a way' stories, and ranks fairly high on the list. The ingenuity of the flight purser had outwitted the unpopular customs agents.

Hong Kong-British Crown Colony

In the spring of 1967, the long wait ended as TWA finally was granted approval to fly schedules in and out of Hong Kong. The necessity for a major traffic source in the Asian Market was essential for TWA to complete the Around the World network. Finally, TWA flight operation was inaugurated into Kai Tak International Airport, Hong Kong.

Kai Tak was named for the two business men, Kai and Tak, who started the airport in the 1920s. Throughout the years, the airport had gone through many construction and enlargement programs, to exist in its present state in 1967. Kai Tak consisted of one runway 13 and 31, for use in each direction. The entire area had been reclaimed by filling in the Kowloon Bay part of Victoria Harbor; hence, associated required structures were spaced close together. The terrain arose abruptly to the north and north east. The city of Kowloon had expanded, to extend beneath the flight approach pattern to runway 13. The pattern altitude was below the tall buildings, immediately to north and east. Passengers were given a sight-seeing tour of Kowloon and Hong Kong on every approach to runway 13.

Kai Tak Airport was well-known for the approaches to land on runway 13 to the south east. The approach to landing on runway 13 was called the "checkerboard approach." The flight path below was marked with checker boards, painted on the buildings below, to serve as check points for an approach pattern, which began at 180 degrees to the final landing runway. There were the usual, non-directional radio beacons to begin the approach.

Landing at Kai Tak during marginal weather conditions was a challenge to remain in the close-in pattern, and to make the safe altitude letdowns required. If visibility was marginal, it was far safer to make the landing approach to runway 31. This approach was made over Victoria Harbor, directly to runway 31. It was more acceptable to land with a slight down runway component. In most weather conditions, low ceilings, and low visibility were not usually accompanied by strong wind velocities. Typhoons were the exception. Ty Fung, as the Chinese termed them, brought gale easterly components.

Kowloon and the associated hotels made for a short ride to the city of Kowloon and the amenities. However, Victoria Island required the use of constantly operating ferry boats, plied over Victoria Harbor in a constant pattern.

From the beginning of commercial flight operations, there were numerous accidents at, or in the vicinity of, Kai Tak. A new airport was constructed using three islands west of Kai Tak. In 1998, flight operations were moved to the new airport and Kai Tak closed. The challenges it presented to pilots flying into Kai Tak were only a memory.

Dirk Brink

The TWA International Route flight operation had extended from Bombay, India; to Bangkok, Thailand; and Hong Kong. The eastbound flight had reached Bombay. We were preparing for our departure for Hong Kong. A first class cabin hostess came forward to the flight deck and reported there was a slight disturbance in the first class section. Her concern was a first class passenger bound for Hong Kong was being questioned by an Indian authority. She further stated she knew the passenger, and he had flown on TWA in the past. Known to many TWA flight crews, the gentleman appeared to be of excellent character. To address the situation, my presence was required immediately in the first class cabin, where the passenger and the Indian authority were standing in the middle of the aisle. The ensuing conversation divulged the Indian authority wished the passenger to deplane for further discussion. The flight attendant had given what she believed to be a great opinion of this gentleman's character. Our past experience with Indian customs authorities had left a negative impression. This particular situation appeared to be more of the Indian customs bureaucracy, with whom we all had difficulties in the past. This knowledge utmost in mind, my presence was made known to the two people involved. These opinions were quickly expressed to the Indian authority suggesting he kindly cease his action, and allow the passenger to proceed without further delay. The Indian authority was highly provoked by my interjection, but he deplaned without further action.

From the outset, there was a personal awareness the Indian authority had priority in the decision-making while the aircraft was still on the ground in Bombay. However, as is often the case, a man must attempt to do whatever is required to correct a problem. In this instance, the outcome was a positive one, and we departed for Bangkok and Hong Kong.

After arriving in Hong Kong and deplaning first class, the passenger was waiting for us. With a great smile he introduced himself saying, "I am Dirk Brink. Can you be my guest for this evening? And this invitation is to include the entire flight crew."

He had flown TWA to Hong Kong in the past, and was aware TWA flight crews made a layover in Hong Kong. We accepted this invitation, and so began a friendship with Dirk.

Dirk was born in Batavia, Indonesia, now called Jakarta. His parents were Hollanders living in the Dutch colony at the time. In his youth, Dirk served in the military, and was in the Hollander Forces at the outset of WWII. While in military service, in the early stages of the war, Indonesia was overrun by the Japanese. Captured by the Japanese, Dirk was taken prisoner-of-war, and incarcerated in the infamous Thailand prison camps. Those who survived this forced labor imprisonment suffered some of the most iniquitous torture of World War II. As a survivor of this ordeal, it is not necessary to comment on Dirk's resolve. Quite the character, he was very personable and enjoyable to be around. Thus, we would get together many times on future flights to Hong Kong.

Dirk was the head of a Hong Kong financial institution, which engaged in far flung operations; the most worthy of note, the transfer of substantial amounts of funds. This operation was successful in moving large denominations of currency from country to country. As many of these countries had currency restrictions, normal transactions were not possible.

There were many methods involved in the transfer of sizable amounts of currency from these countries, which did not permit their currency to be moved out of the country in any substantial amount. The most widely used method was to prove decidedly out of the ordinary. The operation involved using the services of diplomats. International law exempts people with diplomatic passports from search and disclosure by customs agents. This clandestine operation involved using these qualified individuals to physically carry the currency under the veil of diplomatic immunity. Dirk would often jokingly remark how newly appointed diplomats would contact him immediately upon receiving their credentials, to advise Dirk their services were available.

In the laws of human nature, it is only natural that on occasion, some of the carriers would go 'south', as the saying goes, and disappear with the funds. It then became Dirk's personal responsibility to recover these large 'missing' sums. This made it necessary for Dirk to board an aircraft for nearly any part of the world, at a moment's notice. There were not many points, or countries in the world, which were off-limits to Hong

Kong residents. During this time of the Cold War, there were many countries including Russia, which were off-limits to United States citizens. Such was not the case for subjects of Hong Kong.

When we met in Bombay, Dirk had been returning from a recovery venture. The operation of the underground is wide-ranging. The Indian authorities obviously knew of an alleged, large amount of money in his possession. At the time, perhaps Dirk was in possession of a considerable amount currency. He was transiting Bombay, and had not deplaned in India. If the Indian authority had been successful in getting him to deplane, the currency could, or perhaps would, have been confiscated.

Dirk was truly a nice person. His life style and pursuits were accepted in Hong Kong, although the authorities apparently did not accept all representatives of governments as totally legitimate. His main business office was located in Shell House, a prestigious location on Victoria Island, which also housed the TWA sales office.

Early one evening unannounced, Dirk appeared at the hotel. He extended an invitation to the entire flight crew to join him on a 'get-acquainted' trip of Hong Kong. We engaged two taxi cabs, and Dirk directed the entourage to an old section of the city. We arrived in an old, but densely built up area of stores. Our destination was a store at the end of the street, which had a corner entrance. The doors were steel roll-ups, with the entire corner of the building opening up. Stacked inside, head high, were woven steel boxes. The entire store was filled with these woven steel boxes, with aisles between the stacks, to allow access to them. The shop was unattended when we arrived, save for an elderly Chinese man, who appeared shortly thereafter.

Dirk greeted him in Cantonese, and told him the purpose of our visit. The man clapped his hands, and a young Chinese chap appeared. He took down one of the basket woven, steel containers, which contained many snakes, obviously of the venomous variety. The older man spread a white cloth on the floor, placing a single, large tea cup to the side. He then took one snake from the container, and holding it behind the head, placed it on its back. He then produced a small, very sharp blade, and deftly slit open the snake's belly. As he then squeezed the snake to make the gallbladder pop out, it was evident he knew exactly where to make the incision. Next, he carefully twisted the thin skin of the gallbladder until he could separate it from the snake, without spilling its contents. Upon separating the gallbladder, he gently placed it on the inside rim of the tea cup. The assistant then returned the snake to a basket.   The process was repeated two more times. Each time after the procedure, the young assistant placed the snake back into the steel container. After three snakes had been separated from their gallbladders, the young assistant closed the lid, replaced the box on a shelf. He then obtained another container, which we observed held a different species of snake. The process of removing the gallbladders continued for another group of three snakes. After each procedure was performed, the snakes were returned in their box. A third container was brought, opened, and the same procedure repeated, until the tea cup was lined with nine gallbladders from nine venomous snakes, the Viper, and two others.

When we arrived at the location, there was no one in attendance, other than the two men. Now, looking above the man's shoulders, the entire corner opening was filled with Chinese, all standing, watching the proceedings. For the first time after noticing the audience, Dirk said, "Whatever you do, do not laugh at what is going on."

The older man rose from his knees. Holding the cup and its contents, he walked to a small bar at the end of the room. He then squeezed the contents of each gall-bladder into the tea cup. When finished with his extractions, he took a bottle of Chinese rice wine from the shelf, and poured wine into the tea cup, stirring the contents of nine gallbladders from the venomous snakes with about two ounces of Chinese rice wine. When he finished, the tea cup was handed to Dirk. Standing next to him throughout this ritual, Dirk turned and handed the tea cup to me. After giving Dirk a 'drop-dead' look, he then offered the cup to the first officer, who looking quite green refused it. The same offer was made to all the men in the group. All declined. That left Dirk still holding the cup. Throughout the proceedings, the crowd of Chinese observers in the gallery had grown in size to cover the entire store entrance.

After everyone had refused the cup, Dirk then turned once more to me, extending his hand with the cup. It was obvious this had now become a game of "chicken." Observing the Chinese gallery, integrity or 'face' was on the line. Taking the cup from Dirk, the contents were drained in one 'bottom's up.' It was a hot, steaming evening in Hong Kong. Perspiration was on everyone's brow, and began appearing on their shirts. It was not a time for consuming snake gallbladders, or anything else of a revolting taste. The nine gallbladder wine mixture hit the bottom of my stomach, to bounce several times, before being choked back down. We then departed through the audience, back to the cab and once inside, my statement to Dirk was, "Let's get to the source of a cold beer to remove this horrible taste from my mouth."

After we drank a beverage to restore our digestive systems to normal, we asked Dirk, "Just what was all that?"

Laughing, Dirk replied, "That mix is a Chinese aphrodisiac; a potion of the contents of the nine gallbladders will insure immediate sexual potency."

He was advised the only reason that goop was consumed was due to the gallery of Chinese, who had been observed. It was a matter of intestinal fortitude for me to drink it. Still laughing, Dirk told of entertaining a Russian delegation. He had taken three Russians to the Chinese snake farm. Rather than admit defeat, the three Russians had drunk the potion, and immediately all three had thrown up on the spot. Still in a jovial mood, Dirk commented on the strength of my stomach.

"Well, Dirk, before we move on to the ground rhinoceros horn, perhaps another cold beer will remove this pungent aftertaste. Or did you have some other kind of Chinese aphrodisiacs you would like us to sample?"

The whole incident was cataloged as part of flying around the world. Most countries customs laws were respected. We were subject to immediate dismissal for proven violations. Dirk never asked, nor would he, for any of us to do anything for him of this nature.

Our friendship continued for many years. Later Dirk moved to South Africa with his family. The original colony of South Africa, the first colonial settlement of the Dutch, had become almost an obsession with him. Dirk loved it above all other countries of the world. Unfortunately, Dirk succumbed to a stroke at a relatively young age, ending a most respected relationship.

General Wong Bor

Just how the relationship with General Wong Bor came about is not clear to my mind. There are unlimited persons of interest in Hong Kong. Perhaps, as a lifelong bird shooter, it was this interest that led me to the business of the General, the owner of apparently the only licensed gun shop in Hong Kong. After entering his place of business, the General was quick to observe an American. Thus, he began to proudly show many of his personal shotguns. A return visit resulted in my invitation for the General to accompany me to lunch.

Hong Kong is a fascinating place to pursue almost any appetite. The General suggested a restaurant he favored, where we enjoyed a truly palatable cuisine. During lunch, General Wong Bor related he had been a general in the Nationalist Chinese army under the command of General Chiang Kai-shek. The General had been a devoted subject of Nationalist China. His service had been a result of his love for China, and his high respect for General Chiang Kai-shek.

After the end of a WWII, General Chiang Kai-shek and his followers faced a difficult transition. Quite naturally, they expected the Chinese Nationalist government would prevail. As history tells us, the communist movement began in the north of China under Mao Zedong and Chou En-Lai. The advance of the communist forces was rapid and largely unopposed, resulting in the communist takeover of the country. The communist Chinese forces were armed and supported by Russia.

As a former ally of the United States during WWII, General Chiang Kai-shek had appealed to the United States for assistance to resist the communist takeover of China. His appeals were unsuccessful, and General Chiang Kai-shek and his army retreated to the island of Formosa, to establish the Nationalist government of Taiwan.

General Wong Bor had opinions relative to the abandonment of support for Chiang Kai-shek by the United States government. The opinions, quite naturally, involved a long standing negative opinion of President Harry S. Truman. It was only natural this long-standing feeling on the part of the General would be venomous and unforgiving. The loss of his native China to the communists, and the result of his exile along with General Chiang Kai-shek to Taiwan, was a lifelong, bitter disappointment. The General related the facts, which were known at the time. There were tremendous amounts of military equipment located all over the Pacific, due to the planned invasion of Japan, which did not occur. This equipment became military surplus. Without further expenditure, this military ordnance could have been transported, and put at the disposal of General Chiang Kai-shek. So equipped, it would have been possible for the General and his forces to resist the communist military takeover. The General was of the opinion the amount of military surplus possessed by the United States military would easily have offset the military commitment made by Russia. The military surplus was disposed of at pennies on the dollar; some brought nothing at all.

This luncheon and others with the General were remarkable and mind searching for the possibility of an earth shattering result, from what was had become reality. With the end of WWII, there were political stories and efforts to discredit General Chiang Kai-shek, and his wife Madame Chiang Kai-shek. There is no doubt as history indicated, this negative move was successful. General Chiang Kai-shek and the Nationalist government were not supported in their efforts to resist the communist takeover.

If Nationalist China had been supported and prevailed, the around the world operation of TWA would have begun in 1946, instead of being delayed until 1969. The operation could have been inaugurated to the Chinese cities in the original route award, which would have allowed flight operations throughout China, and the Pacific. The delay until 1969 was due to the English control of Hong Kong. The rights and operations had to be approved by the Hong Kong authorities; therefore, the resultant delay. If Nationalist China had prevailed, there would not have been a communist China to deal with. Nationalist China was a WWII ally. There would not have been a communist North Korea to deal with, as a communist North Korea would not have come into existence. The partitioning of Korea was a result of the communist North invading the South, resulting in an extensive war and tragic loss of life.

The General was a colorful, dignified, and sincere person to respect. General Wong Bor became part of another fond memory of Hong Kong. The Crown Colony of Hong Kong would later return to the Chinese under communist rule. Did it have to end this way?

The flight operation into Hong Kong made closing the gap in the Pacific a reality. August 1, 1969, marked the beginning of the TWA around the world operation with the addition of Taipei, Taiwan; Guam; and Honolulu, Hawaii; to Los Angeles air service. Later, Okinawa was added, and became a staging point as part of the Viet Nam operation; the military flight operation in the Pacific while the Viet Nam conflict was taking place. As a part of the international operation, TWA setup flight operations from Travis Air Force Base, CA to Saigon, Viet Nam. As a captain flying the International Division, this had taken me into the beginning part of this operation.

The TWA around the world flight operation was now complete. The vision of Captain Jack Frye, the first president of TWA, and Captain Paul Richter, executive VP had become reality. Tragically, they had not lived to see their dream become reality. The threesome of Standard Airlines, to become Transcontinental & Western Airlines; Jack Frye, Paul Richter, and Walter Hamilton had departed this earth.

The around the world fights were a daily service. Every day, a flight departed New York eastbound around the world, and every day, a flight departed New York westbound. TWA flight crews completed the around the world flight and returned to New York upon completion. The layover points were determined both geographically, and as close as possible to flight duty times. Geographic distances often made for long flights, and long duty periods; e.g., Los Angeles to London, and London to Los Angeles non-stop. TWA flight crews were the only U.S. flight crews to complete around the world flights from origin to completion.

The metabolic clock was difficult to cope with. The eastbound operations were the most difficult. Some flights traversed eight time zones during one flight. Flying eastbound, against the clock, was more difficult than flying westbound with the clock. There are many terms given; metabolic clock, circadian rhythm, and others. Nevertheless, it was a challenge. Each layover point was approximately twenty-four hours, as each day the next flight arrived and departed.

The Boeing 707-331; the basic type was the TWA 331 series, the aircraft flown in this operation. The reliability of the aircraft made the operation what it was, a success. This series 707 was the largest of the Boeing 707 aircraft design, had the longest range, and the greatest fuel capacity.

'ROUND THE WORLD/TRANS PACIFIC SERVICES
EFFECTIVE SEPTEMBER 1, 1970 (ALL TIMES LOCAL) INTERCONTINENTAL STARSTREAM

WESTBOUND	1	741-743 Daily	745
	DAILY	EXCEPT TUE SAT / TUE SAT	DAILY
NEW YORK Lv	D17 45		
SAN FRANCISCO Lv	747	19 30 / 19 30	08 40
LOS ANGELES .... Ar / Lv	20 30	20 46 U21 45 S / 20 46 U21 45 S	09 57 L11 00
		K / K	K
HONOLULU .... Ar / Lv		00 05 S01 45 B / 00 05 S01 45 B	13 20 014 15
		Ex We Su ExTh Mo / We Su Th Mo	Next day
@ INTERNATIONAL DATELINE			
GUAM ISLAND .... Ar / Lv		06 20 B07 15 / 06 20 B07 15	18 50 019 45
OKINAWA .... Ar / Lv		08 15 M09 15 / 08 15 M09 15	
TAIPEI - h .... Ar / Lv		09 30 L10 30 / 09 30 L10 30	
HONG KONG - h .... Ar / Lv		12 55 D20 30 / 12 55 18 45	22 10 23 00
BANGKOK .... Ar / Lv		21 05 U22 30 / 19 20 D20 20	23 35
		741 / 741	
COLOMBO .... Ar / Lv		21 50 U22 45	
		Tu Fr / Ex Tu Fr	
BOMBAY .... Ar / Lv		00 50 01 50 / 00 50 01 50	
TEL AVIV-YAFO .... Ar / Lv		04 55 B06 00 / 04 55 B06 00	
ATHENS .... Ar / Lv		07 50 08 45 / 07 50 08 45	
FRANKFURT .... Ar / Lv		10 30 L11 30 / 10 30 L11 30	
NEW YORK .... Ar		15 05 / 15 05	

CONVERT LOCAL TIME TO GMT	EASTBOUND	740-742 Daily	744
		EXCEPT MON THU / MON THU	DAILY
+7	LOS ANGELES Lv		
+4	NEW YORK .... Ar / Lv	D19 00 / D19 00	
		Ex Tu Fr / Tu Fr	
—1	FRANKFURT .... Ar / Lv	07 30 B08 45 / 07 30 B08 45	
—2	ATHENS .... Ar / Lv	12 25 L13 25 / 12 25 L13 25	
—2	TEL AVIV-YAFO .... Ar / Lv	15 05 D16 10 /	
		Ex We Sa	
—5½	BOMBAY .... Ar / Lv	02 00 B03 00 / 23 10 00 30	
			We Sa
—5½	COLOMBO .... Ar / Lv		02 35 B03 40
—7	BANGKOK .... Ar / Lv	08 30 09 30 / 08 25 09 30	07 45
		742 / 742	
—9	HONG KONG - h .... Ar / Lv	14 00 S15 30 / 14 00 S15 30	12 15 L13 10
—8	TAIPEI - h .... Ar / Lv	15 50 16 45 / 15 50 16 45	
—9	OKINAWA .... Ar / Lv	18 50 D19 40 / 18 50 D19 40	
—11	GUAM ISLAND .... Ar / Lv	00 40 S01 30 B / 00 40 S01 30 B	19 30 D20 20
		Ex Th Su ExWe Sa / Th Su We Sa	
® INTERNATIONAL DATELINE			
+10	HONOLULU .... Ar / Lv	11 40 L13 20 / 11 40 L13 20	06 30 B08 00
		K / K	K
+7	LOS ANGELES .... Ar / Lv	21 25 22 35 / 21 25 22 35	16 05 17 20
+7	SAN FRANCISCO .... Ar	23 38 / 23 38	18 24

SERVICES

All flights offer *Royal Ambassador* service with superb cuisine and fine wines in First Class section. All flights also offer Economy Service

Indicates flights on which eight audio channels and wide screen movies by Inflight Motion Pictures, Inc. are shown in First Class and Economy sections. Eight audio channels are also available Westbound Honolulu/Tel Aviv and Eastbound Bombay/Honolulu. The charge on International flights is $2.50 per person

h—No local traffic between Taipei and Hong Kong
Ⓔ 743-741 is a thru plane
740-742 is a thru plane
K Economy Thrift service
Ⓐ When crossing Int'l Dateline Westbound add aday
Ⓑ When crossing Int'l Dateline Eastbound subtract a day
Ⓒ No local sales permitted from Colombo for final destination Bangkok Flt. 740 thru Colombo Wed. and from Colombo for final destination Bombay Flt. 741 thru Colombo Thur.

MEAL SERVICE AND BAR SERVICE
Complimentary meals served aloft
Complimentary liquor available for First Class Passengers, or for purchase by Economy Passengers
B Breakfast   L Lunch
D Dinner   M Meal for Boarding Passengers
E Brunch
S Snack
U Deluxe Supper Club for First Class Passengers
J Breakfast for First Class Passengers
T Dinner for Economy Passengers
Food service not available on Economy Coach

'AGE 30

Example of TWA Around the World Flight Schedules Timetable Eff. 9/1/1970

As a part of the TWA International Division, the military operation was flown from military installations on the East Coast to the USAF bases in the British Isles and Western Europe. This flight operation was on a separate schedule from the regular commercial flight schedules. The aircraft flown were Boeing 707-331 aircraft, with high density seating.

On July 1, 1966, a military contract operation was extended to United States Air Force operations from Travis Air Force Base over the Pacific to Saigon, Vietnam.

Saigon, Viet Nam

The telephone rang with the chief pilot of the International Division on the phone, "Lyle, this is short notice and is the reason I am calling. We have been requested to operate the military flight contract from U.S. Air Force Base Travis Field, California, to Saigon, Viet Nam. The flight operation is to begin tomorrow. Can you be there at Travis AFB to fly this operation?"

Of course, the answer was, "Yes."

It was the beginning of a large military flight operation in the Pacific. In order to carry a maximum payload on the Boeing 707-331 freighters, it would be necessary to set up fuel stops at Hickam AFB, Honolulu, Hawaii; USAF Base at Guam; Kadena AFB at Okinawa; and Tan Son Nhat Airport, Saigon, Viet Nam. The trip would be one operation. Upon arrival at Tan Son Nhat, Saigon, it was necessary for the aircraft to be offloaded and depart for a return flight to Kadena with a minimum amount of ground time due to security, and extremely limited ramp space. This flight operation for the U.S. Air Force would become extensive. The operation first began with the TWA 707-331 air freighters; but later was extended to include the high density passenger models for transportation of military personnel.

There were many unusual variations and challenges during this flight operation. In the preflight preparations at Travis Air Force Base, California, the aircraft for the proposed flight could not be located in the normal departure area. After acquiring transportation of a military jeep, the 707 freighter was found. It was parked in the same area with the black, military Boeing B-52s flown by the Strategic Air Force Command. This area was reserved for the loading of strategic ordinance. The fact the aircraft was parked in this area gave an indication as to the type of cargo to be loaded aboard. After dismissing the jeep driver, easily observed below the aircraft were 13 pallets to be loaded aboard the 707 freighter. On all four sides of each pallet were large orange and black signs, which completely covered the cargo. These large orange signs with huge black letters stated—'HIGH EXPLOSIVE.' This quickly explained why the aircraft had been parked in a remote, restricted area. The pallets of high explosives were armed missiles, ready to be used. In Viet Nam, the TET offensive was not going well. This was the initial shipment of armed missiles to be flown to Tan Son Nhat, Saigon, Vietnam, and was a 'high priority shipment.'

The first scheduled landing was a refueling stop at Hickam Field, Hawaii. We had arrived overhead Oahu, the island on which Hickam Field is located, only to be given a delay in our arrival, due to low clouds in the area. We entered the flight holding pattern to wait for our clearance to make an approach and landing, which would take us to Hickam Field. The holding pattern is an oval-shaped flight pattern, comprised of time elements, which keep the aircraft in a desired airspace and altitude, until the clearance is received. While flying in this holding pattern, the weather changed markedly. An area of thunderstorms developed, with associated lightning and turbulence enveloping the sky around our aircraft. The highly explosive cargo we were flying, now with the insertion of thunderstorm conditions, was not conducive to peace of mind. The cargo we carried was of a substance we did not wish to expose to thunderstorm activity. We advised airway traffic control of our cargo, and the thunderstorm conditions, asking for our landing approach time as soon as possible, as our cargo was not the usual. ATC quickly grasped our dilemma, and issued an approach clearance. We landed and taxied to the arrival dock at Hickam Field. As we gathered our flight gear on the flight deck before deplaning, we discussed the possible negative outcome of the previous situation.

There were many similar flights to follow. These flights were flown without incident, but not without great concern by the flight crews involved. Flight operations in Viet Nam would be extended to fly to the strategic points of the conflict; Cam Rah Bay, Da Nang, and others. This flight operation continued until the end of the Viet Nam conflict.

Saigon, Viet Nam, was an operation worth noting. At that time, the ramp area space was limited. The available area would accommodate two aircraft the size of jet cargo aircraft. This was the reason for expediting arrivals and departures. The area surrounding the Saigon Airport was not entirely secure from the Viet Cong. The flight operations office was a small shack, just off the cargo ramp area. The sole occupant was the flight plan clerk, a small Vietnamese girl. This attractive Vietnamese girl was dressed in a black silk, close-fitting shift. The black, silk shift was slit on both sides, from the bottom well up above the knees, exposing an eye-catching bit of flesh. The whole setting was right out of "Terry and the Pirates" of comic strip fame. Clearly, this operations shack had to be the imagination of the flight duty officer in charge. The scene had been envisioned by someone smitten with "The Dragon Lady," updated to the attractive, young version thereof. The welcome environment made the dull task of filing a departure flight plan much more appealing.

On a visit to the young 'Dragon Lady' to file a return flight plan to Kadena, Okinawa, a USAF colonel came into the office. The colonel asked, "Captain, are you departing for Clark?" (Clark Air Force Base was in the Philippines). I would appreciate a lift to Clark, if you are going that way."

"No, Colonel, we are going to Kadena. You are welcome to join us."

"No, Captain, it has got to be Clark."

My reply, "Colonel, the captain of the C-133 parked on the ramp just walked out of here. He filed a flight plan for Clark. The aircraft hasn't started up yet. You could fly to Clark with them."

His reply was quick and to the point. "Before I'll fly in that turkey, I'll swim to Clark, sharks and all." And with that statement, the colonel called for a jeep to pick him up.

The C-133 was not popular. In fact, in his opinion, as the colonel expressed it, those aircraft were to be avoided at all cost. The C-133 was a turbo-prop powered aircraft. Some had just disappeared on flights over the Pacific, without any trace or recovery. It was assumed, it was a resonance or vibration problem, called a harmonic, which can be set up between two, or more parts of the structure. Over time, a harmonic caused by the high tip speed of the turbo propellers, can cause metal fatigue of a critical part of the aircraft structure, and when failure occurs, destroy the aircraft.

Terminal 5 JFK – A Chance Encounter

In the late 1950s, TWA commissioned the world renowned architect, Eero Saarinen to design a flight center for the future. Unfortunately, he died prior to completion of the project. On May 28, 1962, TWA opened the Trans World Flight Center at John F. Kennedy International Airport, New York, which became known as Terminal 5, or simply T-5.

Trans World Center at JFK International Airport May 1962. TWA promotional photo.

Aerial view of Terminal 5, TWA JFK International Airport, New York.

Terminal Five had become the prominent landmark of the New York Air Terminal. The classic, swooping, building design, often described as suggesting a giant bird in flight, had captured the attention of the flying public. An International arrivals terminal had been constructed next to Terminal Five, as it was necessary to incorporate the United States customs facility in the passenger arrivals terminal. The aircraft parking area for both terminals was a large common area serving both facilities. The large ramp area allowed the ground servicing for both, international and domestic, flight arrivals and departures. The International arrivals building was also the point of international flight crew clearance, prior to the flight crews leaving the airport. The flight crews deplaned after the passengers had adequate time to clear U.S. customs. Therefore, the flight crews were cleared by the customs agents without delay. It had become practice to open my personal baggage, while waiting for the customs agents. During this time, my uniform coat, cap, and tie were placed inside the open luggage; a blue jacket was removed, and replaced the uniform coat. A non-uniform tie was donned. After customs clearance, the baggage was repacked, closed, and ready for my commuting flight to the West Coast. Upon clearing customs, the exit door to the aircraft ramp was used to return to the flight departure terminal. My arrival in New York completed a long flight assignment to Europe, the Middle East, British Crown Colony of Hong Kong, and return to New York.

Once U.S. customs was cleared, and with bags in hand, the walk across the aircraft ramp had taken me to a Boeing 707 bound for the West Coast, with all four-engines running. The TWA passenger agent, in charge of boarding the flight, had observed me crossing the ramp, and knew commuting to and from New York was a part of my schedule. The passenger agent opened the ramp service door on the Jetway® and signaled me to hurry. Running up the service ramp and through the aircraft entrance, the door immediately slammed closed behind me. Thanks to alert co-workers, this commuter made his flight!

The passenger entrance door served the first class compartment. The hostesses were busy securing the aircraft, for the taxi to the takeoff runway. The flight was full. There was only one passenger seat available, which was in the lounge area directly opposite the first class galley. This seat was immediately taken, as the Boeing 707 was taxiing for takeoff.

First class service began as soon as the passengers were seated. Prior to takeoff, all first class passengers were offered champagne for their enjoyment. While still fastening my seat belt, glasses of champagne were being served to the occupants of the first class cabin. Glancing up, my eyes looked directly into those of the serving hostess, whose green eyes and face bore a striking resemblance to the lovely Gene Tierney, a film actress of the 1940s-1960s, later a television actress. Since my uniform jacket had been exchanged for the blue jacket, the acceptance of a delightful glass of champagne was permitted, served by the beautiful image of the movie star, long admired. The excellent TWA first class service continued throughout the flight to the West Coast. The greater portion of this service was performed by the green-eyed lovely, and all the fatigue from a long flight assignment slowly melted away.

During the flight, my offer to take the hostess out for dinner was politely turned down with, "It's my personal policy not to date passengers." When my status was confirmed as that of a crew member, the lovely vision stated emphatically, "That goes **<u>DOUBLE</u>** for flight crew members!"

However, as the flight had a full passenger count, service to the passengers had not allowed extra time for the hostesses to have any food service. After the passengers had deplaned, my invitation, to 'Hostess of the Year' to go out to dinner, was offered one last time.

As hunger overcame 'personal policy', the hostess named Rita decided to join me for dinner.

During the dinner, our conversation centered on pursuits, which were of mutual interests, such as sailing. Before departing on my last flight assignment, a plan had been put in place for a major sailing event. A good friend was in command of a new 'CAL 48' sailboat, which he was 'shaking down' for the new owner. This process involved making several trial sailing sorties; to make adjustments to the rigging, and other pertinent parts of the sailboat. The Queen Mary was on her final voyage, to be berthed in Long Beach Harbor, California; to be used as a hotel and tourist attraction. The plan was to sail the new CAL 48 out to meet the Queen Mary, as she approached the harbor. Our departure time was scheduled for 06:30, in order to meet the Queen as she arrived. An invitation was extended to Rita to join us for the event. The early hour was discussed briefly. However, no set commitment had been made.

On the day of the planned sailing, we had arrived at the marina at about 05:00 to make ready for our departure. During this time, there was no appearance by Rita. At 06:30 just after castoff, a loud shout of, "Hey, wait for me!" was heard coming from Rita, who was running all out as she approached the end of the dock. We returned to the dock long enough to retrieve our late arrival.

A large, high pressure area had moved in to center over the high desert, north of Los Angeles. This weather phenomenon is termed a "Santa Ana." The resulting high velocity, northerly air mass movement brought high air mass velocity to the entire region, to include the Pacific Ocean off shore. This blow was in motion when we departed the harbor. The CAL 48 rode the swells quite well; however, sea spray was prevalent. The entire crew donned foul weather gear, and the rendezvous with the Queen Mary was made, as planned. The sail continued until the Queen made her last entry into the harbor. The Santa Ana, with the associated blow, made the voyage rough, and not the best for new sailors. Nevertheless, Rita withstood the rough voyage well, and actually seemed to enjoy it. We returned to the mooring and enjoyed the usual after sailing festivities. One year later on September 28, 1968, we were married.

Rita Ann Bobzin *nee* Bond - TWA Hostess 1966-1970

Palestine

Tel Aviv had become a termination point for some flights originating in the United States. Westbound flights to the United States originated there. Cairo and Bombay flights operated on a separate schedule. The termination and origination of flights in Tel Aviv made it a layover point for TWA flight crews.

In years past, Palestine had been a British Colony. The English devotion to bird hunting made great changes in the game bird habitat in Palestine. The British had found Chucker partridge fared well in Palestine; as a result, brought the species to Palestine from India. The climate and habitat were favorable, and the Chucker numbers increased greatly. After the governing of Palestine was turned over to Israel, most of the English departed. This left the coveys of Chucker partridge unhunted, causing their numbers to greatly increase.

Some of the flight crew layovers were long enough to take advantage of the excellent bird shooting, which was readily available. Great coveys of these partridges consuming vast amounts of grain forced the farmers into an all out effort to reduce the bird population. The farmers welcomed our hunting the Chucker. Another one of the methods used to reduce the bird population was poisoned grain. When followed anywhere in the world, this procedure is highly dangerous. Once poison has been put out, where it will travel, and what it will kill is too uncontrolled to be considered. The United

States Ambassador Barbour became aware of this lethal program. The Ambassador and United States Attaché Cliff English were often visited while on Tel Aviv layovers. During one of our visits, the ambassador broached the subject of the poisoning of the birds, and stated his objection to the lethal program. Attaché English made an appointment to meet with the Israeli farmers who were involved in the poisoning program, and invited us to attend. We stated that the danger of indiscriminately placing poison anywhere was a great danger to all, and pleaded with them to cease the practice immediately. The farmers in attendance were cordial, and we felt we had made definite progress to stop this practice.

The meeting produced one facet which had not been anticipated; one of the farmers brought a German Shorthair pointer puppy to the meeting. This indicated an interest in bird shooting by at least one of the farmers. This chap could fully appreciate the danger poison presented to his puppy. We had a pleasant chat as we discussed the GSPs, which had always been part of our household in the United States. If there was to be more interest in bird hunting by the farmers, the practice of putting out poison would likely stop. The TWA maintenance personnel were of European and American nationalities. Consequently, there was a considerable amount of Chucker hunting done in the countryside.

East Africa

TWA flights to East Africa were added to international flight operations. The cities of Entebbe, Uganda; Dar es Salaam, Tanzania; and Nairobi, Kenya; were the principal cities of East Africa. Entebbe, on the shores of Lake Victoria; Dar es Salaam, on the Indian Ocean; and Nairobi offered access to the famous Rift Valley.

As mentioned in an earlier discussion, Nairobi was the site of the legendary New Stanley Hotel; the hangout and meeting place for the famous white hunters. There are many favorable memories of stays here. The 'men-only' bar was the favorite of the white hunters, and all the dignitaries visiting East Africa. The New Stanly Hotel, with everything expected of East Africa, was later destroyed, and burned by terrorists.

When visiting Nairobi, we were invited for cocktails at the Italian Embassy residence. While enjoying their hospitality, we were told of the origin of the building. As an interesting point of aviation history, the structure was built for Walter Beech of the Beech Aircraft Company, Wichita, Kansas. Walter Beech had become fond of East Africa, and had constructed the attractive, comfortable, masonry home there. After he died, the Italian government acquired this striking home for their residence embassy, which was what the name indicated. In addition to being the residence of the Italian Ambassador to Kenya, it also was used to host all official embassy functions. We found this information of particular interest as we had admired the aircraft built by Walter Beech, had flown many of the different Beechcraft models, and currently owned a Beechcraft Bonanza.

During our discussion with our host, Ambassador Rividen, we found he was attracted to our interest in bird shooting. The sport was one of his major interests, and he owned a German Shorthair pointer, 'Simba', which he graciously loaned us for our bird hunting. This was more than coincidence; we owned and loved our own German Shorthair pointers in the U.S. The Ambassador decided to overcome any difficulties we might encounter while hunting. He gave us the use of his Land Rover that had embassy license plates, providing us with diplomatic immunity. At his suggestion, we left our rented Land Rover at the embassy for his use. Kenya had been a British Colony for years. The British, longtime devotees of bird shooting, had imported game birds from other British possessions to Kenya. Part of British policy was to bring an ornithologist to each colony to determine which bird species would do well there. Species appropriate to each region were then imported from other British colonies.

The Rift Valley was one of the most wonderful places to hunt game birds in my lifetime of enjoying the sport. Early one morning, we had driven to the site of a former cattle ranch, located just outside Nairobi in the Rift Valley, for a bird hunt. Most of the foursome was slow to get with it. In humorous disgust along with the German shorthair "Simba," we departed to find and direct a covey of birds back to the slow moving shooters at the Land Rover.

It was just after daybreak with sunlight reflecting on the open field. Waist-high tall grass was normal for this time of year. Enthusiastic Simba was working back and forth, raising his head at times to make sure of my presence. Coming to a sudden stop, Simba had frozen on a beautiful point. We were still within shouting distance of the others if the birds flushed in their direction. Simba was slowly and quietly advancing, taking one step, then stopping, before slowly taking another. Between steps, while on point, he would remain rigid. While standing by Simbas' tail, there was a sudden burst of sound. The burst was not the whirr of game birds wings. The burst was a mature leopard springing straight up, then racing off in a sprint at high speed. There, with the bright morning sun reflecting on his gold and black coat was a mature, healthy leopard. Asleep in the waist-high grass, Simba had interrupted his snooze. Fortunately, during his departure the leopard ran within a short distance of the Land Rover for all to see. My double was loaded with number 7½ and number 8 shot, not much of a deterrent against an aggressive game animal. We joked about it later. Certainly, the leopard must have been aware we were bird shooters and had no interest in shooting him.

In a more realistic review of the incident, had the leopard taken aggressive action, perhaps he would have attacked Simba first, since Simba was on his point and within striking distance. It was always customary for me to carry a handful of heavy load double O buckshot in the right pocket of my shooting vest, readily accessible for loading. If the leopard had attacked Simba, there would have been time to rapidly reload the over and under shotgun to the heavier shot. The difficulty then would have been not to shoot Simba. If the leopard had directed his charge at me, he would have taken two barrels of shot at very close range. Hopefully, this would have destroyed his vision, which would have given me time to reload to the more lethal shotgun load. We enjoyed the remainder of the day hunting partridge and quail. Simba was tireless; as the sun was setting he was still eager to hunt.

<u>Note</u>: There are warnings about hunting in tall grass, and we take these seriously. As stated earlier, this area was a former cattle ranch; an area not considered habitat for dangerous game animals. They obviously neglected to tell the leopard that, as he perhaps had been hunting cattle, whose strong scent still lingered. The beautiful October morning with the bright sunlight shining on a leopard in full stride will always be fondly remembered.

We returned Simba and the ambassador's Land Rover late afternoon and were invited to join him for the usual five o'clock libation. The ambassador was an outgoing person with a great sense of humor. He related that when we had made our first visit, we mentioned the difficulty we had encountered at the hunting license office. When we had entered the office, a well-dressed woman was alone at the counter talking to the official in charge. The lady became hysterical when her effort to communicate with him was not producing any results.

Prior to our going to this office, we had seen the headlines in the local newspaper. The story related: On the previous day, a longtime Dutch settler had been told to leave Nairobi, Kenya on the midnight flight. He had complied. This woman was his wife. They had operated a ranch in Kenya that was now being taken by the government of Kenya. The ranch was located in what was now designated as a game area. In her attempt to sell their ranch to the government, the lady had been told that before she could sell the ranch, since the ranch was in a game area, she would have to obtain a release from the Office of Game Licenses. This was her reason for being at the office. Her appeals continued unabated over a long period of time. The distraught woman did not receive any satisfaction for her appeals and finally departed in a state of complete frustration. This entire scene had been extremely unpleasant to witness. She had been told what she needed to do by the new Kenyan officials, who were in reality seizing the land, and was not able to comply.

After the woman left, we spent most of the afternoon sitting in the same office only to discover the lone person now in charge could not read. He had placed our applications on his desk. He then sat there, staring at them, not saying a word. After we had been in the office for quite some time, we finally gave up and returned to the New Stanley Hotel.

A few days before our arrival, the British officials had left Kenya and British government ceased. The Office of Game Licenses, once staffed by the Brits, was now staffed by Kenyans. Result: No organization. The ambassador heard our story and he quickly offered us the use of his Land Rover with the diplomatic license plates. The cattle ranch on which we hunted had belonged to an Italian settler, who was a friend of the ambassador and had also been confiscated by the Kenyan government. Before we departed the residence embassy, the ambassador related his tenure as ambassador to Kenya had expired. The Italian Diplomatic Legation Headquarters in Italy had financial difficulties and lacked the funds to send the replacement ambassador to Kenya. As a result, his tenure was extended until such time sufficient funds became available. With a broad smile, the ambassador related he was not upset about the delay in his replacement; he enjoyed Kenya and would stay as long as possible.

Picture taken at Treetops compound, north of Nairobi, Kenya

The Boeing 747 entered airline service in the late 1960s. TWA purchased twenty Boeing 747s and the aircraft received enthusiastic acceptance by the world-wide flying community.

Terrorism had increased in the Middle East. As a result, several aircraft were skyjacked to countries in the Middle East that were not the original points of landings. On September 29, 1969, TWA Flight 840 was skyjacked on a flight that had departed from Rome, Italy. The Popular Front for the Liberation of Palestine (PFLP), a Palestinian terrorist organization, was involved in the skyjacking. After the terrorists directed the TWA captain to fly a circuitous route over Palestine, the flight landed in Damascus, Syria. The passengers and crew were removed from the aircraft, after which explosives and hand grenades were thrown into the flight deck of the Boeing 707, causing extensive damage to the aircraft.

Senegal passengers were held by the PFLP, which demanded the release of Palestinian prisoners held in Israel. The long drawn out detention of all the passengers, who were held hostage in turn for the release of Palestinian prisoners, was an extremely difficult time for TWA. During this period of imprisonment, there was no political action TWA could perform to help obtain their release.

After lengthy negotiations, the passengers were finally released in exchange for the prisoners held. The captivity of passengers and crew was a terrifying ordeal for those concerned. After their release, the TWA flight crew returned to New York. Boeing Aircraft Co. personnel were flown to Damascus, Syria, to perform the necessary temporary repairs, after which the TWA Boeing 707 was flown as a ferry flight to Seattle, Washington, where permanent repairs were made to the aircraft before it could be returned to commercial service.

Missed Opportunity???

Floyd Odlum and Howard Hughes owned the controlling interest of Atlas Corporation, which as one of the interests held the majority stake of Northeast Airlines. A New England flight service, Northeast Airlines had most of the flights originating and terminating in New England. One exception was a flight from Boston to Miami, and another was from Boston to Nassau, Bahamas. Profit relative to the investment was low, and the airline was in need of newer aircraft. It appeared that Floyd and Howard were seeking a possible buyer for Northeast. Howard Hughes held the controlling ownership stake in TWA, which was in the process of buying a large fleet of jet aircraft. The capital required for the purchase of this fleet had put tremendous financial strain on Hughes, and all sources of possible capital had been exhausted.

A TWA around the world flight had been flown, and the commuting flight from New York to the West Coast had just been completed. A few moments after arriving home, the telephone rang and it was Jackie stating, "We are entertaining some guests from Boston and would like for you to join us for dinner."

"Jackie, please allow me to beg off. Rita has just picked me up at the airport after an around the world flight."

Jackie replied, "Drive over now and you can take a rest in one of the condos before dinner. They have sold

Northeast Airlines and Floyd would like you to meet the new owners."

It was with a great deal of apprehension we complied. Rita drove the trip to Indio. As soon as we arrived at the Cochran Odlum Ranch, we both retired for a quick nap in one of the condominiums as Jackie had suggested. The dinner party had been planned to honor the new principal owners of Northeast Airlines. The new owners were very well-known in New England society. Unbeknown to me, Floyd had discussed the possibility of a senior executive position for me with the newly reorganized Northeast Airlines. This was the opportunity for us to meet with the new owners. The desirability or possibility of me leaving TWA had never been discussed in any of our previous conversations. In a state of fatigue, we did not arise on schedule and as a result, we were very late for the cocktail hour, which in turn delayed dinner. Jackie was displeased and did not keep it a secret. Our apology and explanation for our tardiness was accepted by all, except our hostess. We met the new owners and their families. Jackie remained irritated, and to avoid further embarrassment, we excused ourselves and departed before dinner. On the return drive home to Newport Beach, my relieved statement, "Rita, guess we blew the opportunity to be in the executive suite at Northeast." We both laughed. At this time, flying a Boeing 707-331 around the world was sufficient reward, and we were happy with the way things were.

Ultimately, Jackie did forgive us and we were able to enjoy the hospitality of the Cochran-Odlum Ranch many times. We always enjoyed our stay there. Time was to prove our decision to be the correct one. The ownership of Northeast Airlines was later sold to Delta Airlines with the usual resulting loss of management positions.

TWA Corporate Officers

The 1960s brought an end to the Hughes controlling interest in TWA. The new stock owners changed all top management and the board of directors.

TWA Flight 8 was a Los Angeles to New York non-stop departing at 16:00. The flight departure made it possible for business travelers to spend most of the day conducting business, then late afternoon depart for a return flight to New York.

After arriving at LAX for departure, a TWA lead passenger agent, an old friend and a person of past high caliber working relationships, greeted me. The agent related TWA officers from the New York headquarters at 605 Third Avenue, New York, had conducted a business meeting in Los Angeles, and the group was returning to New York on Flight 8. The entire first class cabin had been sold out to our regular TWA first class passengers. The TWA president and chief executive officer, along with the other officers, "bumped" or removed all of the first class passengers to tourist class so they could occupy the first class cabin for their own transportation. The TWA officers' flight passes qualified them to do this; however, the result was one of questionable judgment.

Those removed from the first class section were highly incensed when they arrived at the terminal for their flight and were informed of this situation. In anger, most cancelled their TWA ticket, walked across the street to the American Airlines terminal and purchased a ticket on an American Airlines flight to New York. It was highly unlikely any of these passengers would choose to fly TWA anytime in the future.

TWA Flight 8 departed for New York on schedule. The few passengers who had accepted the tourist accommodations would observe, through the curtain separating the two cabins on board the aircraft, the entire first class cabin filled with TWA officers. After arrival in New York, the displaced passengers deplaned through the first class cabin to witness the TWA VP of Marketing on his hands and knees under a row of seats, attempting to find his shoes.

As a matter of policy, the former TWA officers from the Hughes era had checked the flight status before removing local TWA passengers from their reservations. Was this the new management team now directing TWA?

BOOK SIX

THE SEVENTIES

THE CAREER ENDS

Skyjacking and the Terrorism Continues

TWA around the world flights involved many different segments of political and historical interest. The flight from Athens, Greece; non-stop to Bombay, India; over flew the capital of Turkey, Ankara; above the Turkish border with Iran; above Teheran; the Iranian border with Afghanistan; the capital Kabul; above the historic Khyber Pass; Karachi, Pakistan; to Bombay.

The areas and cities have a long and historic past. Afghanistan was invaded by Russia, in what was a military effort to take over Afghanistan, which became an all out war. The purpose of the Russian invasion to take control of Afghanistan was never fully explained. Observing the geographical area from the flight deck, the most logical reason appears to be to establish a direct ground route and, or an oil pipeline to the Indian Ocean. Russia has one access to the seas from the south of their great landmass, which is the Black Sea, through the Bosporus to the Mediterranean Sea. There is no other ocean access until the Port of Vladivostok on the north Pacific.

The importance of a successful takeover of Afghanistan was great. Russia was defeated in its effort to conquer a country right on its own border, even though the logistics of the war were minimal. Russia was defeated by the oldest form of warfare known to man; that of guerrilla warfare. The internal resistance overcame the invader with substantial assistance from the United States. The same principle defeated the legions of Rome in what were the forests of Germany.

Afghanistan is largely a mountainous country with the Himalayas having their western origin there. The western portion of Afghanistan is a plateau, sloping up rapidly to the mountains and the Khyber Pass, east of Kabul. The western plateau of Afghanistan would make possible unobstructed access to the border of Pakistan, then south to the Indian Ocean. Surface transportation was not the prime reason; an oil pipeline is the most logical. Russia, just north of the border of Afghanistan, has a large area of oil reserves, which to this day have not been fully developed, due to the lack of a pipeline to the sea that would deliver the oil for world-wide shipping. A pipeline could be constructed across the western plateau of Afghanistan to the border with Pakistan. A treaty or agreement could be made with Pakistan for the pipeline to cross western Pakistan to the Indian Ocean.

As the political takeover and war were unsuccessful, this plan was thwarted. Then and now, the possible plan faces great difficulty. Iran has resisted efforts to build a pipeline across its territory which would provide access to the seas for foreign oil. A major oil producer, Iran would not wish to aid competitors in the oil business.

The existence of five to seven warlords who are active in Afghanistan has been known for some time. Separated geographically, the war lords control the country. Their participation in heroin drug trafficking is well documented. The warlord in power in the west of Afghanistan, the area which borders Iran, enjoys unlimited support from the Iranian government. The supply of ordinance is abundant. Any major pipeline development in the area would face great difficulty with this opposition. The entire western border of Afghanistan from north to south is a common border with Iran, spanning a vast distance. Iran's interest in the oil business was a major factor in the warlords' opposition to Russia. Perhaps it is still a major opposition to those who might desire to construct this infrastructure at any time in the future.

The critical location of Iran, relative to Middle East oil, was well recognized in the 1940s. A coup supported by the United States and Britain was successful in placing the Shah of Iran on the throne. The stability of the region was dependant on the stability of the government of Iran. The Arab states were in the process of emerging to their present position of importance. In the 1970s under the Carter administration, the United States chose not to continue supporting the Shah of Iran, resulting in the failure of the Shah's government. Chaos ensued; the U.S. Embassy was sacked, and U.S. citizens were held hostage. American influence in Iran ceased, and a key geographic country of the Middle East was no longer an ally. United States international flag carriers had free access to all Iranian airspace and the Iranian Central Intelligence Agency had been a source of accurate, daily, terrorist information. After the fall of the Shah, this information ceased. Aircraft skyjacking has been supported from within this area. All forms of terrorism and negative actions targeted the United States airline industry. The future of Afghanistan will largely depend upon the relationship with Iran, pro or con. Iran was the key nation in the Middle East in the 1940s, and there has been little change to alter that position. The acrimonious regime change resulted in the loss of influence by the United States of America.

The Boeing 747 entered airline service late in the 1960s. In the early 1970s, as the airlines took delivery of the projected fleets, the aircraft was in service over all world routes. The 747 changed the operation of the route structure on TWA international flights. The 707 had been highly successful flying the TWA around the world operation, both eastbound and westbound. The 747 was placed into service on the Los Angeles to London non-stop flights, both eastbound and westbound. This change made the 747 part of the around the world flights, which had been flown solely with the 707.

FAA regulations, which did not allow pilots to fly two types of jet aircraft in the same time period, made a great change in the schedules on the around the world flights. Pilots could no longer fly the complete around the world operation. As a result, in the 707 operation, flight crews flew westbound flights from Los Angeles. Eastbound flights were flown from New York. In both cases, flight operations had layover, or rest points and turnaround of flight operations, at midpoints in Asia.

The political situation had worsened in many parts of the world, notably in the Middle East. The armed conflicts had resulted in more threatened and actual terrorism to TWA flight operation. The Iranian Secret Service had been our sole source of critical information in the Middle East. This important security information

why the shipment was divided, one device was placed aboard an Austrian Airlines Caravelle flight bound for Tel Aviv, Israel with an intermediate stop in Vienna, Austria. The other device was placed aboard a Swissair Convair 990 flight, also bound for Tel Aviv with an intermediate stop in Zurich, Switzerland.

Encased in a radio-like disguise, the first bomb was placed aboard the Austrian Airlines Caravelle jet. The distance between Frankfurt and Vienna is a rather short flight. Therefore, the aircraft was flown at a relatively low altitude. Fortunately, the projectile package was placed in the aft compartment. The low flight altitude did cause a pressure differential that was enough to discharge the explosives. However, the low flight altitude did not provide a great enough overall pressure differential between inside and outside pressure of the aircraft to cause a large explosion. The resultant explosion blew off the aft compartment door, without further damage to the aircraft. At the time the flight was flying over the Munich, Germany area and landed at Munich without further difficulty.

The second of the two bombs was placed aboard a Swissair Convair 990 Jet scheduled to fly from Frankfurt to Zurich, then on to Tel Aviv, Israel. The flight from Frankfurt to Zurich is very short, approximately thirty-five minutes. The short flight resulted in a low altitude flight between the two cities. The low cruising altitude allowed the cabin pressure to be maintained at ground level throughout the flight. Consequently, the barometric explosive was not detonated. However, the next flight segment was to be flown at a jet flight level. The explosive package had been placed in the forward lower compartment for shipment to Tel Aviv. After departing Zurich, the Swissair Convair 990 began its climb to 37,000 ft for the flight to Tel Aviv. As the cabin altitude increased, the barometric pressure decreased which activated the explosive unit with a fatal result. The change or drop in barometric pressure which had detonated the explosive bomb occurred while the flight was still in Swiss airspace. The bomb instantly destroyed all the flight instrument gyros located in the lower forward compartment. The flight had entered instrument flight conditions during the climb and was flying on reference to flight instruments. The loss of the gyros immediately caused instrument failure, making flight by instruments impossible. The aircraft lost control, plunging to the ground in Switzerland with the loss of all life on board. These were the detailed facts of the disaster related to me by the Swissair captain. Our thoughts then focused on how to plan for the westbound flights, as both of us were destined to fly next to the Middle East.

There was neither personal baggage inspection, as presently known, nor was there individual inspection of passengers or their carryon baggage prior to boarding the flights. No one inspected cargo prior to being loaded aboard the aircraft. Our lengthy study of the possible negatives led to a long discussion. Our concern; we did not wish to join the three jet aircraft currently held hostage at Dawson Field, Jordan, or become part of any other terrorist activity.

The passengers were observed as thoroughly as possible before departure. However, this was only a shot in the dark. In the early hours of the morning, we departed Bombay for Tel Aviv with the skyjackings still in progress and relative information still at a minimum. The negatives were only known in theory. As a result, one threat could be coped with. If we flew at an altitude which was no higher than the cabin pressurization system could maintain at sea level pressure, we eliminated the possibility of a pressurized explosive device detonating. After departure from Bombay, the cabin pressure was held at the elevation of the Bombay Airport which is only a few feet above sea level. During climb to cruising altitude, this cabin pressure was maintained. As soon as the aircraft reached an altitude at which sea level pressure could no longer maintained, the aircraft was leveled off. This cruising altitude was maintained throughout the entire flight. The Boeing 707 pressurization system was adequate to provide a high cruising altitude and still maintain cabin pressure at sea level. This cruising altitude was high enough to be well above any terrain along the route from Bombay to Tel Aviv.

The decree by most Arab states to TWA was, if our flights originated or were destined to arrive in Israel, the TWA flights could not over fly any Arab state. The Shah of Iran was on the throne at the time or TWA could not have flown to or from Israel to points east. Our flights from Bombay flew over the Indian Ocean to the south coast of Iran, flew over Teheran, then west crossing above the Turkish border, over flying Turkey south above Incirlik, Turkey, the Mediterranean Sea until offshore from Israel, then to Tel Aviv. The eastbound flights were flown on the same route in reverse of the westbound direction. The seven hour flight from Bombay to Tel Aviv was flown with cabin pressure at sea level eliminating any possible threat.

Tel Aviv Airport is only a short distance across the border from Dawson Field, Jordan. When we arrived in Tel Aviv, information was still very limited as to the multiple skyjackings in progress only a few miles away. The procedure of our inbound flight and the cargo on board was discussed with the outgoing captain. It would be his decision to plan for the continuation of the flight. There were interesting side lights from time to time which were thought provoking. The Middle East remained in a state of conflict. Renewed in 1948, this state of unrest would continue, and remains in conflict today.

Later, flying a Boeing 747 flight to Tel Aviv, we had checked into the Tel Aviv Hilton for our layover rest period. The hotel baggage handler brought my luggage to the room. Tall, muscular in build, the Palestinian chap had deposited my baggage on the stand and turned to me saying, "Captain, I used to carry your baggage in the Heliopolis Hotel in Cairo. I remember you from there."

The incident of which he spoke had taken place over twenty years earlier so his recollection was quite remarkable. When checking into hotels, we rarely had time to exchange our U.S. currency for local currency. In order to leave the baggage handlers with a reward, it had been personal policy to carry a carton of cigarettes in the flight kit. This supply could be replenished easily before each departure at the 'in bond' or duty free stores. Being a non-smoker always left me with an adequate amount of cigarettes for gifts. As cigarettes have always been very expensive, these gifts were well received. If they did not smoke, the value on the black market gave them a good return, far more than any monetary tip. The fact this Palestinian chap had a memory going back at least twenty years, and apparently a favorable one, was noteworthy. After thanking him with the usual two packs, he departed. The incident was one for further contemplation.

The ongoing conflict had begun in 1948. It was now post-1967 war time; over two decades since this chap had been employed in Cairo at the Heliopolis Palace Hotel, and now he was employed in the country of opposition, Israel. The question: 'Did he leave Egypt for a better paying job in Israel? Or was he part of an infiltration move? Or was it both?'

The conflict had spawned espionage actions on both sides. Hotel baggage handlers had access to all parties and their belongings at least twice during every hotel stay. On the surface, the chap in question was amicable, and not aggressive in attitude. However, it might have been due to what had been a favorable relationship in Cairo. Other cases might have had an entirely different association.

There had been a long standing individual doubt relative to the baggage handling in our operation. After checking into the hotel, all crew members had their baggage brought to their respective rooms. After the layover rest period was over, luggage was retrieved from the rooms and taken to the transportation for the return trip to the airport. During crew briefings, it had been my personal policy to request all crew members thoroughly examine their own baggage. Some had thought it an unnecessary request and chose to ignore it. The pleasant meeting with the chap and the reminder of the Cairo relationship was worthy of note, though it did renew worry about the exposure of baggage to possible contamination with explosives. Unfortunately, the concern would become reality.

In the 1970s TWA had two arrivals and departures daily into Tel Aviv; two were Boeing 707s, two were Boeing 747s. The 707 flight departed for New York, with an intermediate landing in Paris. The flight was flying over the Adriatic Sea when an onboard explosion occurred. A Pan American Airways flight eastbound in the same area witnessed the explosion and the breakup of the TWA 707 as it plunged into the Adriatic Sea. It was an extraordinarily unusual fact for one aircraft to witness the destruction of another, and thus be able to provide valuable information. The Pan American crew had seen the aircraft explosion that caused the tail section to fail before breakup, and the subsequent plunge into the sea. The eye witness account made it possible for the Pan American crew to provide the exact location for the recovery of the wreckage.

When the wreckage of the TWA 707 was located, a large portion of the aircraft was recovered, allowing for an investigation into the accident. With the knowledge that the tail section had suffered failure prior to the fatal breakup, it was possible to direct the initial investigation to that area. An examination revealed that an explosion had taken place in the aft compartment where the cabin crew baggage, as well as passenger baggage, and cargo were carried. Further analysis revealed an explosive had been placed in a crew case, the type TWA issued to flight attendants. All flight attendants were required to carry identical cases for their luggage requirements.

Subsequent investigation in Tel Aviv revealed more pertinent information; one of the flight attendants had been given a portable radio as a gift. A plastic high explosive had been placed inside the radio, with a timer set to detonate the firing mechanism. The flight attendant had placed the radio in her personal baggage for the flight to Paris, where the cabin flight attendants were based. This flight attendant had been an unwitting pawn in this fatal terrorist action.

Great tragedies are not without irony. The flight attendant, who had been given the deadly present, was flying her last flight prior to her marriage. The flight attendants had gathered the previous evening for dinner, and to extend best wishes to their fellow employee. It is possible this celebration was observed by those involved in the terrorist plot, and used the opportunity to present the future bride with this gift.

There was no indication this particular TWA flight was specifically chosen or targeted for the terrorist action. It is possible the terrorists involved did not single out any one person to perish as a result of the action. The news of the disaster made headlines in the local Israeli newspaper. Before recovery of the wreckage, the news immediately reported the farewell party on the evening before the flight departed. The inference was there was no doubt a relationship of the party to the accident the following day. The news inferred the entire flight crew had taken part in the festivities, and were no doubt worse for wear the following day. The captain, first officer, and flight engineer had not taken part in the farewell festivity, so there was no possible relationship to the cause of the tragedy. Wreckage of the Boeing 707 established the aircraft had been a target of terrorists, and an explosive device had been in the flight attendants baggage. The rush to judgment by the newspaper with their insidious accusation was never retracted by the newspaper, as is too often the policy of the news media.

Flying a TWA 747 into Tel Aviv in the same time frame with the westbound departures involved, provided possible exposure to the same fatal action. All flights were subject to potential terrorist acts by placing explosives in items carried by passengers or crew. With no examination equipment at the time, inspection of gifts, presents, and personal purchases was difficult. Is it possible an unknown favorable action influenced one of the persons involved, perhaps a baggage handler, to eliminate one flight as the target over another for the fatal deed?

All countries with ports of call have their own attractive domestic products that many people desire to take home for enjoyment or souvenirs. One of the cities in this category was Madrid with beautiful porcelains, clothing, and all sorts of decorative items. Madrid offered the opportunity to purchase models of the ships, which Columbus had used on his famous voyage in discovery of the New World; wooden models of the Santa Maria, the Pinta, and the Nina. TWA flew thousands of Columbus' model ships to the United States. There were occurrences when small trucks and taxis could be seen driving up to the departure area with outgoing shipments. These wooden models were large and hollow, an ideal place to conceal items of destruction. In addition to passengers, TWA flight crew members acquired a fondness for these model ships, and in turn, took them home as gifts. My efforts to impress on those concerned this danger existed fell on deaf ears, with some showing obvious resentment. On one occurrence when some control was attempted, a caustic remark was heard, "Oh, he's the captain who is trying to sink the Columbus fleet."

Security in a 'non-sexist' security period was a challenge. For example; we departed Madrid flying a 747 flight, with an intermediate landing in Lisbon, Portugal. Approximately three hours after our departure from Lisbon, TWA New York dispatch called on the radio with an urgent message, "Lyle, we have just received a telephone call stating there is a bomb on your flight."

This particular terrorist organization had been in operation for several months, and was extremely efficient to the degree they did not use printed time tables to determine when to make a call relative to a specific TWA flight. In their operation, they would have observed and noted the actual takeoff time of the flight at the point of departure. They would next make the calculation in time which would place the flight at a point in mid-ocean, and then place the threatening phone call. These calculations for the threats to be received at mid-ocean left all flights concerned with the same dilemma. They were at a mid-point over the ocean with land the same distance in any direction. When this call came in, we were equidistant from any point of feasible landing. One possible action was to descend to a low altitude to lessen the explosive effect. The difficulty with this procedure; to fly at the low level would result in fuel consumption higher than acceptable, with fuel being exhausted before reaching a point over land. The terrorist bomb threat was now in full operation. Frankly, there was not much that could be done. Our onboard examination was put into motion. We had departed Madrid with a landing in Lisbon. The terrorist call was traced to a Lisbon location. This would indicate someone had observed our actual time of departure. Lisbon had been contacted to evaluate all cargo placed aboard. An interim questioning of the flight crew revealed a female purser, without authorization, had three cases of Portuguese wine put aboard at Lisbon for her personal use. When she was confronted with her action, it was perhaps then obvious to her what the possibility could be.

The course the flight, and the actual route the flight was on, made the destination New York as close as any other diversion point. As a result, the flight continued on to New York and landed without incident. Not until the aircraft was on the ground could it be thoroughly searched for explosives. None were found. The whole telephone call had been a hoax. There were many terrorist bomb threats which turned out to be hoaxes. However, a threat of any nature could not be ignored during the time of the flight.

The loss of the Pan American 747 in Cairo, Egypt; later, the time-actuated explosive bomb that destroyed a Pan American 747 above Lockerbie, Scotland, resulting in the complete loss of all life onboard, including many fatalities on the ground, cannot emphasize enough the threat to U.S. air carriers. The aircraft that were destroyed by terrorists in Europe and the Middle East; the TWA 707 lost over the Adriatic Sea with a loss of all onboard were adequate warnings the same terrorist action could take place in the United States. The repetitive tragedies all occurred well in advance of the infamous 9-11-2001. There are those who state there was not adequate warning, the misstatement of the century.

Boeing 747

The widespread acceptability of the Boeing 747 aircraft was the reliable operation it provided. The airliner brought a further advancement to the flying public. The jumbo jet entered service in the late 1960s, offered a first spacious interior for passenger comfort, and the associated cabin service. The aircraft airframe and the turbine engine, the Pratt & Whitney JT-9, were to go into service together. A new aircraft and a new engine; this had not often occurred in the past. Once in operation, the combination presented fewer operational problems than had been anticipated. However, inauguration of the new aircraft was not to become reality without some malfunctions.

In past aircraft design and construction, the wing flap and the wing leading edge flaps had been controlled and synchronized by the functioning associated mechanical devices in the wing structure. The 747 utilized a similar system controlled, as before, by the wing flap handle on the center console. The major change was the utilization of the wing flap position indicator, located on the pilot's instrument panel, to signal and control all wing flap operation. The flap position indicator was a rectangular shaped instrument mounted vertically, with white tape indicators moving to indicate the wing flap position. The instrument was new in design, and as such, had its own developmental problems. The major problem; the instrument was prone to overheating, causing operational difficulties.

Originating in Rome, Italy, TWA Flight 841 operated daily, flying non-stop to New York. The long-range flight was extremely popular and the passenger load was always full. Each time the required fuel for the flight and the passenger load resulted in the aircraft being at maximum takeoff weight for departure.

On a beautiful, sunny day with the ground temperature in Rome over 100 degrees Fahrenheit, we departed Rome for New York. The takeoff was normal. However, at the takeoff flap retraction sequences, the wing flap position did not respond to the positioning of the wing flap control handle, which clearly indicated the flaps did not retract. The flight was continued according to our flight plan clearance. While in climb attitude, we began to trouble shoot the difficulty. With the wing flaps still in their takeoff position, a reduced airspeed was maintained accordingly.

We were aware of prior difficulties which had been experienced with the flap position indicator. The tendency to overheat had been exacerbated by the high ground temperature in Rome. The aircraft had arrived from New York in the early morning and remained on the ramp in considerable heat until our departure. The sensitivity to the high ground temperature caused the wing flap position indicator to overheat.

We continued climbing on course, which took us above the west coast of Italy, to over fly the island of Elba, off shore from Pisa, and Genoa to northern Italy, and Switzerland. The deviation most acceptable to me was to continue this flight plan, flying at the speed allowable for the flap position, and to fly at 20,000 ft, the maximum structural altitude for the 747 with flaps extended.

Attention to the wing flap indicator immediately proved what we expected. A finger placed on the glass panel was quickly removed from the overheated instrument. In some manner, the instrument had to be cooled in order to retract the extended wing flaps, both the trailing and leading edge flaps. Using a Phillips head screwdriver, the four mounting screws were removed. With gloves and caution, the instrument was pulled out from the instrument panel. When completely out of the panel, the instrument was held in position by the connector bundle of wires which transmitted the signals. The instrument, approximately eight inches in height, was resting outside the instrument panel. It was obvious that to cool of the instrument by normal means was going to take some time. Somehow, we had to cool the instrument faster. We knew there were ice cubes in the galley for passenger drink service. Ice cubes in a pillow case could withstand the heat, whereas a plastic bag containing the ice would melt. The purser was summoned to the flight deck and a request for ice cubes in a pillow case was made. Quickly grasping the situation, the purser suggested using dry ice from the first class galley which he could quickly bring to the flight deck. The purser returned with two slabs of dry ice, wrapped in a large TWA first class napkin to prevent burned fingers. The napkin package was placed on top of the exposed wing flap indicator. Within a few minutes, the dry ice rapidly cooled the instrument case and the interior mechanism, allowing the mechanism to function normally. The wing flaps slowly began to retract to the desired 'up' position.

With the wing flaps retracted, we continued our climb to cruising altitude. Our plan had been to fly at reduced speed at 20,000 ft, and if we could not retract the wing flaps, we would land in Paris or London for mechanical correction. After being 'dry ice' cooled, the flap indicator was placed back in the instrument panel and secured by the four screws. TWA Flight 841 flew on to New York as planned and arrived on schedule.

Patience, ingenuity, and twenty cents worth of dry ice had avoided a flight interruption, a return to Rome, and the dumping of thousands of gallons of aviation kerosene. After takeoff with the 747 at maximum takeoff weight, the high temperature on the ground at Rome would have dictated fuel is dumped until the maximum landing weight was achieved. Also, the high ground temperature would have added to the heat of braking after landing. A full passenger load would have experienced an undesirable delay and late arrival in New York. The aircraft utilization would have been seriously altered when the scheduled flight was delayed. An unknown number of frayed tempers were avoided.

Yes, patience, ingenuity, and twenty cents worth of dry ice can go a long way. Later, the flap position indicator was re-engineered to eliminate the over-heating problem.

On another flight schedule, we had departed from Rome flying TWA Flight 841, a 747 non-stop flight to New York. The flight had over flown France and was flying above the North Atlantic Ocean. At a point of thirty degrees west longitude, which is mid-Atlantic, the number three turbine engine stopped, for no reason indicated on the instrument panel. The main check to be made immediately was the oil pressure, which remained normal for the decreased revolutions per minute. The flight was flying at 39,000 ft, an altitude which could not be maintained with three performing engines. The fight descended to 31,000 ft, an altitude at which safe operating airspeed could be maintained.

In the interim, close monitoring of engine instruments did not indicate any further damage to the failed engine that could pose a problem. The flight continued on to land in New York without further difficulty. The aircraft air speed was reduced as three engines were maintaining flight. However, the flight arrived in New York within fifteen minutes of scheduled arrival. After the flight terminated, a ground inspection revealed a failure of the accessory section drive shaft. Immediately, this failure removed the engine driven fuel pumps from operation. Therefore, the engine had shut down. The power available, above minimum requirements for flight, made the operation possible. Boeing 747 power plants now provided a greater margin of safety than had been available previously. The flight had successfully flown 5 hours 41 minutes on three engines.

We departed Los Angeles on TWA Flight 760 flying non-stop from Los Angeles to London. The length of the flight, combined with passenger popularity, always made the takeoff gross weight the maximum for the airplane. We had begun the takeoff roll, and just at the point of rotation, a large flock of pigeons arose in flight immediately to the left of the aircraft. The entire flock of pigeons flew directly beneath the aircraft and was ingested by the number three engine. The ingestion of the increased mass was noted momentarily on the number three engine instruments. The entire incident involved only a few seconds. All engines continued to function normally and the takeoff was continued. Any attempt to stop the aircraft at this speed would have had serious consequences. During the departure climb, all engine instruments continued to indicate normal operation. Therefore, the flight continued as planned to London. The flight of approximately 10 hours was flown without incident.

After arriving at London Heathrow Airport, an external examination of the number three engine revealed 10 of the blades had been bent by the impact of the flock of pigeons. The ingestion of a large flock of pigeons had momentarily increased the mass flowing through the engine. This increased mass had been very briefly indicated on the number three engine instruments. The P&W JT-9 engine incorporated mechanical surge bleed valves. The surge bleed valves were not electronically controlled. As a result, engine function remained normal throughout. As stated, the increased mass of the flock of birds could have been incorrectly diagnosed by an electronic system. The result could have signaled the fuel controller to reduce the amount of fuel flowing into the engine. In the greatest amount of correction, the entire fuel flow could have been interrupted, thereby shutting down the engine. In summary, the mechanical controls designed by P&W were to function properly under the most adverse condition.

Final Flights

The required 'six-month instrument check' had been part of airline flying. During the check, a pilot's ability to fly the aircraft on instruments, perform instrument approaches to airports, react to simulated engine failures during the flight, and other operational procedures, was evaluated. With jet age changes, the six-month instrument check became known as the 'recurrent six-month proficiency check,' as many more functions were added. The flight simulator had become an operational part of the training review program. Also included was a classroom ground school to review and incorporate new procedures. Successful completion of the proficiency check was mandatory to continue flying the airline.

The staff and equipment requirement for this mandatory program was extensive. Consequently, there was a degree of flexibility involved. One of the two required recurrent training periods could be deferred to the following month. The FAA age 60 regulation was to terminate my career in the spring of 1978. In the fall of 1977, personal examination of the recurrent training requirement made it very apparent, if the current schedule remained in effect, there would be a recurrent training requirement in the month of forced retirement.

A visit to the International Division manager of flying, i.e., chief pilot was made to discuss the situation. After explaining the coming recurrent training schedule, a slight change was suggested. By rescheduling the upcoming recurrent training period one month later, the last recurrent session could be avoided, as age 60 would occur before it was required.

The 35 years which had passed in the employment of this company had conditioned me for surprises. The one to follow was high on the list. With the great smile and hand gestures, "Lyle, the last month you probably won't fly. You have all the vacation credit, unused sick leave, and other time, so we won't have to change the training schedule."

This clearly indicated a current lack of understanding as to why pilots flew; at least, why some pilots had flown to begin with. This marked the last visit to the office in question.

Flying the airline had been a chosen career. The Boeing 747 had brought flying the finest transport aircraft in history into my career and there was not any possible desire to leave it. When talking with good friend, Captain Dick Colburn, Dick would often remark, "I would fly these airplanes for nothing, just to be flying them."

My reply was, "Know how you feel, Dick. Just do not let management hear it." This was just one example of the dedication of the pilots involved.

The retirement month approached during which only eight days could be flown. The FAA regulation mandated immediate incapacitation upon reaching the 60th birthday.

At the end of the previous month, the required recurrent training period was scheduled. In order to fly the eight days in the following month, the recurrent training program was attended and completed as required. The time spent attending required; payment of expenses, use of an expensive flight simulator, and the personnel involved. This could have been avoided had my previous suggestion been accepted. Flying the last flight on a Boeing 747, knowing it would not occur again, is an emotional travesty to those who were there because they wished to be.

Employment had begun while Captain Jack Frye was president of Transcontinental & Western Airlines (TWA), which became Trans World Airlines in 1950. Jack Frye had been the first president. Currently, TWA was directed by its eighth president, and there had been many changes. Some pilots with TWA were still there because they loved to fly. Flying up to the last flight possible was done because they detested the thought it was the last flight. For some, flying was only for the financial reimbursement. While financial reimbursement is a requirement of life, the reason most pilots were there had been forgotten. The reality of retirement is not the same for all people. If a person has gone through life with work not enjoyed, retirement is a welcome elimination of all the marginally pleasant workdays. On the other hand, if a person is fortunate enough to be in a chosen work that is fully enjoyable, with each assigned task looked forward to and enjoyed, then acceptance of retirement is highly questionable. Both examples assume good health is present.

Retirement which occurs by directive, not by the wish of the person, has a great unknown factor, or at the very least, not a previously discussed factor: the subconscious mind. The greatest possible harassment of pilot retirement is the subconscious mind. A pilot, by directive, stops flying. In some cases, the subconscious mind does not stop flying. During many nights of sound sleep, the subconscious mind continues to fly. New, not previously flown flights are flown with great reality. These dreams are not violent or unpleasant. They are not reliving some past unpleasantness, or a hair-raising, life threatening experience. These functions of the subconscious have great appearance of reality. Some are relative to what was past routine. For a long period, there were the same retired persons gathering for lunch. The question often asked in humor was, "How many flight pay cards did you have to fill out this morning?"

In these nocturnal functions of the subconscious, the occurrences are very real. Aircraft are boarded for flight; crew members say, "We thought you had retired."

The answer is, "No. There is one more flight."

There is always 'one more flight'. It seems the subconscious is stating its request. On some of these nocturnal expeditions, another flight crew member will answer the question as to why you are there with, "He doesn't let regulations bother him. He never did."

The Dream Ends

The dream of Jack Frye and Howard Hughes of an around the world airline was not to survive. An around the world airline, which is flying a single flight around the world, must at each point of landing, enplane passengers to replace those who have deplaned. This is an economic factor to provide a stable load factor throughout the entire flight. The governments of the major world market cities involved, to protect their own airlines, passed regulations that forbid TWA from flying local passengers between other cities on the around the world route, unless the passengers had originated on a TWA flight departing from the United States. It wasn't possible for any airline to schedule around the world passengers in such a manner that would have the same number of passengers arriving as departing. Passenger convenience, and the reason for their around the world flight, would not permit this. Conflicting regulations did not allow citizens of the respective countries to purchase tickets on TWA, if the same destination was served by the carrier of their country, or there was a mutual agreement with another carrier. Then, this carrier would be their choice. The gateway system evolved with each flag carrier flying non-stop to the major city of another country. This still prevails today. Passengers connecting to other points are booked on authorized carriers.

The airline industry has always been cyclical. There are periods of good financial return followed by periods of down revenue. The corporate tax payments make it difficult to maintain cash reserves. Lines of credit are mandatory in order to assure payment of obligations, wages and salaries, employment taxes, and other. The revolving door of TWA top management had taken a toll. By their own admissions, the 'fast learners' had a serious overall lack of judgment.

In one of the most favorable business cycles, when profits and additional capital were accumulated, a decision was made to become a conglomerate; to acquire businesses unrelated to the airline operation. The move resulted in the acquisition of Century Twenty One, a real estate brokerage company, Denny's Restaurant Chain, Canteen Corporation, a food vending machine company, and other companies outside the airline industry. This decision was really difficult to understand as the earlier merger with Hilton Hotel International had been a dismal failure, in spite of the fact the two service organizations should have been a success. Both organizations were international in scope and should have been successful offering the traveling public a combined booking for each international traveler. The conglomerate venture was inappropriate, as funds from the prosperous period should have been directed to aircraft fleet upgrades, and the elimination of high cost operation aircraft. The conglomerate venture failed, and left the aircraft fleet upgrade unaccomplished. Aircraft not suited to the route structure were purchased. Some of these were high cost operating aircraft with related high cost maintenance. Airline competitors took take advantage of this error in judgment.

Perhaps one of the most damaging miscalculations was the decision to change the entire computer system. The computer programs recorded all passenger reservations, passenger and business contacts, future bookings, all personnel functions to include payrolls; in general, all operational procedures covering the operation of TWA. The complete computer changeover required the construction of a new facility in New Jersey, to serve as the computer nerve center for the entire company operation. When the new system was implemented, it failed causing the passenger reservations system to collapse, throwing all operations into turmoil. The passenger ill-will and loss of business was monumental. The whole program was discarded and TWA returned to the original system– IBM. The long standing loss of passenger goodwill and patronage was perhaps never to return. The New Jersey facility, which had cost over one-million dollars to build, was closed and abandoned. The revolving door of management was taking a severe toll on the competitive position of TWA in an aggressive industry.

The conglomerate debacle removed capital the airline needed. TWA was spun off from the other entities. As a result, the airline was left vulnerable. In the 1980s, the corporate 'raiders' began to focus on the airline industry. Eastern Air Lines fell victim to one of these raiders and failed. This same raider attempted a takeover of TWA. In a desperate move, employees of company joined forces with another raider, who unfortunately was not any more interested in the future of TWA than the original possible raider. In a short period of time, the takeover organization had put TWA in debt for over 600 million dollars, only in the end to walk away from TWA. All operating equipment and real property had been sold, and now had to be leased. These costs, combined with the cost of servicing the debt, were too great for TWA to survive.

Forced to file bankruptcy in 1992, again in 1995, and with the TWA 800 accident on July 17, 1996, financial problems persisted. In April, 2001 Trans World Airlines was acquired by AMR Corp. As part of the deal, TWA declared Chapter 11 bankruptcy (for the third time) the day after agreeing to be purchased. Trans World Airlines failed and cease to exist. The dedicated employees lost the thing they cherished most.

When living by your wits, do not lose them, even for a moment. Until later.

Addendum

AIR MASS MOVEMENT
AND THE LAWS OF MOTION -
A technical discussion

AIR: Defined as a noun: Mixture of gases, nitrogen, oxygen, hydrogen, carbon dioxide, argon, neon, helium, and other inert gases. Air: Standard air temperature is 59 degrees Fahrenheit, Pressure 14.7 pounds per square inch (the weight of dry air at sea level is approx 2.5 pounds per cubic yard),. Standard: 29:92 inches, or 1013 millibars in a column of mercury. All of this accurate analysis is later referenced with relation to a word "wind." The application of the word wind to the movement of "air" is a dirty four letter word. Air, while not visible, has weight, volume, and exerts atmospheric pressure. As Air moves it is not wind, it is "AIR MASS MOVEMENT."

AIR MASS MOVEMENT, "AMM"

The weather forecasts, weather maps, and air movements are projected as air masses and the movement over geographical areas. The terminal areas and airports are subject to the effects of the air mass movement.

There is an inconsistent relationship in the use of the word "wind" in regard to the operation of aircraft, and other vehicles in the atmosphere.

The use of the word "wind" in the operation of aircraft is perhaps the use of a questionable "four letter word."

It is the "concept" of the reality of air mass movement, and flight in the air mass environment, that should preclude any reference to the use of the term "wind." The concept of the word "wind," and applications, is singular in dimension. The airplane operates in an all dimensional air mass.

The correct application or terminology is Air Mass Movement or Air Mass Velocity. The term "Air Mass Velocity," AMV, is more descriptive of what occurs in air mass movement. The word wind does not properly convey the forces involved.
In teaching, we recognize the use of the proper words, terminology, or phrases by definition, is of the utmost importance. This factor is axiomatic in teaching flight. Use of terminology that can be interpreted with the result of two or more actions has proven to have negative results.

The word "wind" defined, from Webster's Unabridged Dictionary: Air in motion, a strong current of air, air bearing a scent as in hunting, air regarded as bearing information, etc., a rumor, breath or the power of breathing, empty talk, gas in the intestines, the wind instruments in an orchestra, to get the scent of, to be out of breath, to hear, to get wind of, in the wind: happening or about to happen, to break wind: flatulence, windy, poetic wind, three sheets to the wind: intoxicated, out of wind : breathless.   The definitions continue, none of which have correlation to the operation of aircraft.

We recognize we live in the atmosphere, which is composed of air masses that encircle the world. The air masses are in constant motion. The air masses move: "air mass movement," the air in motion we feel is air mass movement, not wind. The air in which vehicles to include aircraft operate, is an air mass. The movement of the air mass has a direct effect upon the operation of an aircraft at all times. The air masses exist in all dimensions, not singular as interpreted by the reference to wind. The air mass has pressure as measured in inches, or millibars of mercury. This is a factor we all recognize, but if the word wind is used, the proper forces involved are not defined.

It is important to understand the laws of physics, in the effect of these forces on air masses, Newton's Three Laws of Motion.

Newton's First Law of Motion:

Every object in a state of uniform motion tends to remain in that state of motion unless an external force is applied to it.

Newton's Second Law of Motion:

The relationship between an object's mass m, its acceleration a, and the applied force F, in $F = ma$. Acceleration and force are vectors (as indicated by their symbols being displayed in slant bold font). In the law the direction of the force vector is the same as the direction of the acceleration vector.

Newton's Third Law of Motion:

For every action there is an equal and opposite reaction.

In the century after Sir Isaac Newton another physicist elaborated further on Newton's Second Law of Motion, $F = ma$. This Law of Motion was $F = ma^2$, which greatly increases the value of F, or resultant force. This equation applies to the circular motion of M. This equation explains the violent high velocity air mass movement in tornadoes, hurricanes, typhoons, and other associated storms so described by the area of the world in which they occur.

The application of $F = ma^2$, the circular forces involved in vertical motion of an air mass accounts for the tremendous vertical forces in both directions, up and down. In the equations there has been a change of a, acceleration, to v, velocity. The equations have been revised to $F=mv$ and $F=mv^2$

This vertical movement of the air mass is often termed ascending or descending currents. The reality or proper result is an air mass weight causing forces not desirable in flight.

The equation $F=ma$, 'a' is a variable, the equation $F=mv$, 'v' is a constant.

Air Masses have weight and are subject to the laws of physics. The law of gravity retains the air masses in the atmosphere.

The weight of Air Masses is subject to the laws of motion: The weather conditions which evolve are caused by the reaction, or result of movement of the air masses to the laws of motion.

TEMPERATURE: The changes of, or difference in temperature, are the elements which set air masses in motion. The change in temperature of an air mass causes a change in density of the air mass, which changes the weight of the air mass. The change in the weight of the air mass causes the motion of the air mass. The air mass when set in motion conforms to the laws of motion: Newton's Laws. A colder, denser air mass by weight moves to displace a warmer less dense air mass. A warm air mass with the characteristic to physically retain more moisture expands with the absorption of the moisture. The expansion sets the air mass in motion in accordance with Newton's law of motion. The area, at which the cooler air mass and the warmer air mass meet, is defined as a "frontal area" or "convergence area," Air Mass Convergence Zone (AMCZ).

The operation of aircraft involves the low level or surface air mass. Airports are in this category. The high level air mass or the jet level air mass involves the en route portion of the flight.
In preflight planning we recognize the aircraft while motionless, is in an air mass. We then consider all factors: The air mass condition or existing weather:

the air mass movement for direction of takeoff: the air mass temperature or air density: the field elevation relative to temperature, or density altitude. The application of pre-planning considers the air mass results in automatic examination of all performance factors.

If the air mass movement, AMM, is not directly "down the runway," there is a correction to be made to fly the aircraft directly down the runway centerline. If we observe the AMM to be moving at an angle to our desired flight path during takeoff or landing, we must make a control correction equal to the AMM for desired directional flight. The air mass is moving all along the desired flight path and must be considered. The use of cross wind, while an accepted terminology, has not resulted in the complete understanding of what occurs during takeoff and landing. The air mass exists in all dimensions, is not just singular in effect.

The observation of air mass convergence in the immediate area of takeoff and landing is important. Air mass convergence: AMC, the movement of the two different air masses to create areas of convergence along a line at which they converge. It is necessary to consider that these areas of convergence are all dimensional; they occur not only horizontally, but vertically. It is in this area that present day reference is called "wind shear." While the adverse effect upon flight is evident, the more accurate terminology is air mass convergence shear; AMCS.
The forces involved here are an application of F = ma, can result in the cause and effect of the air mass movement.

This phenomenon exists not only at low levels of flight, but at all levels up to those exceeded by most turbojet powered aircraft. Air mass convergence: the convergence of two air masses of temperature difference, and movement, are often of the overrunning type of air mass convergence. One air mass overruns the other at the point of convergence. This occurrence, when in the flight path of takeoff or landing, is the cause of most incidents and accidents associated with the air mass convergence shear phenomenon. The radical change in direction of the air mass movement induces aircraft attitude and air speed changes. In the takeoff or landing approach stage of flight this can cause a difficult situation as the aircraft is close to the ground. Recovery from an unusual attitude is mandatory. This overrunning air mass convergence is frequently encountered on approaches under instrument flight conditions where all corrections must be made entirely by reference to and by flight instruments. The changes in indicated airspeed during these corrections are often great, as the actual aircraft attitude changes are often abrupt. The occurrence of this type of air mass convergence shear is perhaps the most contributing cause for aircraft accidents. In the landing approach, and the takeoff phase of flight, it is quite easily recognized the condition is more threatening under instrument flight conditions than visual flight conditions. However, neither can be ignored.

The final approach to landing, either visually or an electronic instrument approach, (Instrument Landing System) is made at a predetermined indicated airspeed. The rate of descent to maintain on glide slope position, either visually or on an instrument approach is governed by the ground speed. The rate of descent, in feet per minute, necessary to maintain the glide slope is often referred to as the "sink rate." If the landing approach is begun in an overrunning air mass, the ground speed will often be higher than the indicated airspeed. The result is a high rate of descent necessary to maintain flight on the glide slope for landing. This phenomenon can exist with an air mass movement entirely proper for the landing runway on the surface. It is at the shear, or convergence point of these two air masses, while on approach, that the problems occur. A higher than normal rate of descent has been established to maintain the glide slope. At the convergence point the direction of the air mass changes to what was reported on the surface, the ground speed decreases, and the rate of descent to remain on the glide slope decreases. At this point the attitude change will require additional power as the change in attitude has increased the angle of attack. The changes in aircraft attitude and engine power must be coordinated throughout all segments of the approach to the landing. This air mass phenomenon is perhaps the greatest contributor to accidents while operating an aircraft in close ground proximity. Again the difficulty of successful flight through this condition is greater under instrument flight conditions, than visual flight conditions. Associated convergence shear is the major cause of landing short of the runway resulting in severe aircraft damage and personal injury. Flying in this air mass movement requires the performance of exceptional airmanship.

The knowledge of the application of the laws of motion is most important in this phase of flight, as in all others. The weight of the air masses develops high loads, $V=ma$, or in the case of vertical movement striking the ground, $V=ma^2$. The downward forces are in accordance with the latter when striking the ground. This force then becomes upward, maintaining the force of motion. This phenomenon accounts for the changes of attitude and airspeed imposed upon the aircraft. It is in these situations that extreme caution must be observed, and the most proficient airmanship must be executed.

The negative incidents or accidents, which occur in some downwind landings, are perhaps a result of the use of the term "down wind." In reality the aircraft is always flying in an air mass. In this case the air mass effect is moving the aircraft with a down or adverse relationship to the ground. The effect of which is increasing the ground speed at a time when deceleration to zero ground speed is required. If the word "down" must be used, it should be down component, or down air mass.

In flight, the reference is made to head wind, tail wind, cross wind, etc. In reality, the aircraft is operating in an air mass in which the movement of the air mass is moving the aircraft relative to the surface with an increase in ground speed, or a loss in ground speed if the air mass is deterring the progress of the aircraft relative to the ground. The air mass movement is a factor in flight preplanning, to plan the course of flight along the most desirable route.

When possible, flight is planned along a route which is not subject to air mass convergence zones. It is in these areas that turbulence occurs. The severity of turbulence is relative to the intensity of the air mass convergence, which is caused by the differences in temperature, and air mass directional movement.

The "frontal" conditions are defined with references to air masses, either colder or warmer. The frontal conditions are defined as Cold Front, Warm Front, or Occluded Front.

Altitudes of 18,000' and above are referred to as the High Altitude, or Jet Level Altitudes. The High Altitude En route Charts are used for navigation at these flight levels, on these routes.

The high velocity air mass movement in the high altitudes is referred to as the "Jet Stream." In reality it is not a jet, and it is not a stream. The definition is: the area is a high velocity air mass which is much higher in velocity than the air mass it is displacing or moving through. This occurs in what is termed as the tropopause. It usually exists at altitudes in the 30,000' category. The altitude at which this condition exists can be at altitudes lower than the 30,000' range, particularly in the winter period. The high velocity air mass movement has dimension. It has depth as well as breadth. It exists both vertically and horizontally. This high velocity air mass movement has been found to exist as low as 18,000'.

The high velocity air mass movement defined as: the jet stream, which constantly circumvents the earth is a result of the laws of motion. These cold dense air masses were set in motion. There is not any force of equal or greater motion to deter or change the motion, and consequently these air masses continue to move. The change in the pattern is caused by the changes in temperature in the areas.

Years of operation at jet levels revealed the lowest air temperature encountered at altitudes up to 41,000 feet, was -73 degrees C temperature. The Boeing 707 experimental fight, called the "pole cat," was flown on courses encircling the earth over both north and south poles. The coldest temperature encountered was -73 degrees C.

It is interesting to note flights of the U-2 at altitudes above 70,000 feet indicate existing temperatures well above -73 degrees C in some areas. This data indicates the standard temperature lapse rate does not exist at higher altitudes above the atmosphere.

When topography is involved in the route of flight, or is a factor in the proximity of the airport in use, air mass movement is the primary factor in flight operations. There are many airport locations situated on plateaus, extended land areas into bodies of water or bays. All of these locations often present operational situations under certain air mass movements. An airport situated on a protrusion into a body of water, or on an elevation, often has an elevation considerably higher than the water or ground surrounding it. When an air mass of considerable velocity moves over the airport, the elevation becomes a factor in the change of the air mass effect. As the air mass moves, compression takes place at the lower levels of the air mass as it moves over the higher elevation of the airport. The velocity increases with an increase in turbulence. On the approach end of the airport the air mass, after spilling over the increased elevation, causes an area of turbulence, and down forces in the flight path of landing aircraft. The weight of the air mass again attempts to regain its former layer at the lee side of the elevation. It is at this point the "rotators" develop. The resultant air mass convergence at this point causes turbulence directly proportionate to the velocity of the air mass movement.

In automated flight, by autopilot, the computer calculates what it determines as "wind." These calculations are applied to the operation of the autopilot in whatever mode is selected. This calculation is in a singular dimension. The aircraft is operating in a three-dimensional air mass. Therefore, the calculations are not adequate for all situations as the aircraft is, at all times, operating in a three-dimensional air mass. The problems are increased when the autopilot "mode" is in takeoff, or approach and landing. The application of the "Land Mode" is often limited in the amount of cross wind component, or air mass component, which exists.

The all-dimensional existence of air mass movement has an operational effect on flight operation, be it under visual flight, instrument flight, or automated flight.

It would be desirable to eliminate the word "wind" from use in aircraft operation. Perhaps this is an overly optimistic assumption. The consideration at this time would be to evaluate: when we encounter the word "wind," think "AIR MASS MOVEMENT," AMM or AMV, "AIR MASS VELOCITY." Either would be applicable and acceptable. Perhaps for all concerned AMV would be more acceptable. To clarify; wind does not technically or realistically define the movement of the air mass. This definition will at some time prove to be an advantage. To summarize: the air mass weight at sea level, at 59 degrees Fahrenheit, is 14.69 psi in all directions. It is this weight of this air mass which is moving at the existing velocity. To apply the law of motion: F=MxA in the application of air mass movement, the equation is F=MxV, where A, acceleration becomes V, velocity. F=MxV, or F=M (14.69 psi x V) or 14.69 psi corrected for altitude and temperature.

The computation of density altitude is much easier understood if the concept of air mass is applied. The correction for airport altitude and temperature is more easily comprehended when thinking in the term air mass. It is the density altitude correction in the existing air mass, for the airport of operation.

The term wind is used in all communications. Think Air Mass Velocity, "AMV," for the proper understanding of the actual occurrence.

It is air mass when you fly. If you are, "just going to flatulate around," it is wind. The problem is: you may bust your flatulator.

Water: Second only to air in the area covering the surface of the earth, is also subject to the Laws of Motion. Water, denser than air, has weight, is subject to change in volume with change in temperature. The change in the movement of bodies of water is caused by the change in temperature.

The existing "ocean currents," e.g. the Gulf Stream, are a result of the Laws of Motion. The mass water, once set in motion will remain in motion until reacted upon by a mass of equal or greater force. This law of motion has made ocean currents maintain the same relative course over centuries. The air mass movement relative to the body of water, over which it moves, has a definite effect on the air mass. The effect or reaction is the change of existing weather conditions, or in the long term climate.

The temperature of the water mass also has an effect upon the air mass movement over the water. Violent destructive storms are high velocity air masses. The world over has a different name: tornados, hurricanes, cyclones, typhoons, chubascos; terms given by the associated areas.

These violent moving air masses are so created by the result of air mass movement and the application of the laws of motion.

Sir Isaac Newton's study which evolved the laws of motion were a result of his desire to resolve the long standing question as to what forces were retaining the planets in their orbit around the sun. The solution to Sir Isaac Newton's great contribution gave the world a basic law of physics which had not been in existence prior. The constant orbits of our world and the other planets have been in their respective obits since what has been determined to be the "big bang." The precise orbit has been an assumption. A very minute divergence or change of orbit would be a possibility when considering the astronomical amount of mass of each planet to include the earth. Gravity and the laws of motion keep the planets in their orbits around the sun. The slight change in orbit of the earth would result in a variable distance of the earth from the sun. The increase or decrease in the distance from the sun would cause a decrease or increase in temperature of the planet earth. The result would account for the changes in the climate on earth which do occur.

Weather is an occurrence of a short time, usually the current existing weather. Climate is the average of weather conditions over a longer period of time. The change of climate, either warmer or cooler, could be caused by a slight change of the orbit of the earth.

Copyright '96

Lyle D. Bobzin
Captain, Trans World Airlines
International Division (Retired)
ATP CFII
DOUGLAS DC-3, DC-4, DOUGLAS B-26, MARTIN 202, MARTIN 404, LOCKHEED-I8, LOCKHEED-049, LOCKHEED-1049, LOCKHEED-1649, BOEING-707, BOEING-720, BOEING-747